CORPORATE POWER AND
SOCIAL POLICY I
ECONOMY

British welfare under t

Kevin Farnsworth

The POLICY PRESS

First published in Great Britain in January 2004 by

The Policy Press
University of Bristol
Fourth Floor
Beacon House
Queen's Road
Bristol BS8 1QU
UK

Tel +44 (0)117 331 4054
Fax +44 (0)117 331 4093
e-mail tpp-info@bristol.ac.uk
www.policypress.org.uk

British Library Cataloguing in Publication Data
A catalogue record for this book is available from the British Library

Library of Congress Cataloging-in-Publication Data
A catalog record for this book has been requested

ISBN 1 86134 473 2 paperback

A hardcover version of this book is also available

Kevin Farnsworth is Senior Lecturer in Social Policy at London South Bank University.

Cover design by Qube Design Associates, Bristol
Front cover: original illustration supplied by kind permission of Steve Bell, and adapted
Printed and bound in Great Britain by Bell & Bain Ltd, Glasgow

Contents

List of tables and figures

Tables

Figures

Acknowledgements

In writing the book, I owe the biggest debt to two people. First, to Ian Gough for his inspiration and guidance over the past few years. I am especially indebted to him for his help in formulating and moulding some of the key arguments of the book. Second, to Lata Narayanaswamy, who offered insightful comments on earlier drafts and gave me more encouragement and patience than I deserved during the most 'difficult' stages, and it is to her that I dedicate the book. Thanks also go to Frank Longstreth, Gary Fooks, Peter Taylor-Gooby and Dexter Whitfield who offered insightful comments on earlier drafts of the book.

Lastly, I would like to thank Helen Bolton, Karen Bowler, Laura Greaves, Rowena Mayhew and Dawn Rushen at The Policy Press for their assistance, hard work and patience.

List of abbreviations

BAE	British Aerospace
BCCI	Bristol Chambers of Commerce and Initiative
BEC	British Employers Confederation
BIA	business interest association
BIAC	Business and Industry Advisory Committee
BITC	Business in the Community
BP	British Petroleum
CBI	Confederation of British Industry
CCT	compulsory competitive tendering
CSR	corporate social responsibility
CTC	city technology college
DfEE	Department for Education and Employment
EAZ	Education Action Zone
EBP	Education–Business Partnership
EC	European Commission
EEF	Engineering Employers Federation
EETC	Employment, Education and Training Committee
ERA	Education Reform Act
ERT	European Round Table
FDI	Foreign Direct Investment
FE	further education
EU	European Union
FEB	Federation of Enterprises in Belgium
GATS	General Agreement on Trade and Services
GNVQ	General National Vocational Qualification
GP	general practitioner
GPF	Greater Bristol Foundation
HA	housing association
HAZ	Health Action Zone
HEFCE	Higher Education Funding Council for England
HEROBC	Higher Education Reach Out to Business and the Community
HHG	Housing the Homeless Group
ICC	International Chambers of Commerce
IGO	international governmental organisation
IMF	International Monetary Fund
IOD	Institute of Directors
LEA	local education authority
LSC	Learning and Skills Council
MAI	Multilateral Agreement on Investment
MNC	multinational corporation
NCEO	National Confederation of Employers' Organisations

NCVQ	National Council for Vocational Qualifications
NEBPN	National Education and Business Partnership Network
NGO	non-governmental organisation
NI	National Insurance
NVQ	National Vocational Qualification
OECD	Organisation for Economic Co-operation and Development
PFI	Private Finance Initiative
PMI	private medical insurance
PSDS	Private Sector Development Strategy
QCA	Qualifications and Curriculum Authority
SCAA	School Curriculum and Assessment Authority
SEA	Single European Act
SEF	Shipbuilders Employers Federation
SERPS	state earnings related pension scheme
TABD	Transatlantic Business Dialogue
TBI	The Bristol Initiative
TEC	Training and Enterprise Council
TUC	Trades Union Congress
TVEI	Technical and Vocational Education Initiative
UBI	Understanding British Industry
UBR	Uniform Business Rate
UEAPME	European Association of Craft, Small and Medium-Sized Enterprises
UN	United Nations
UNCTAD	United Nations Conference on Trade and Development
UNICE	Union of Industrial Employers' Confederations of Europe
UWE	University of the West of England
WEF	World Economic Forum
WESTEC	Western Training and Enterprise Council
WTO	World Trade Organization

ONE

Introduction: globalisation, corporate power and social policies

Interest in the power and influence of business is probably higher today than at any time in the past. Academics, journalists and political activists warn of the grave dangers posed to nations and their citizens by large corporations; governments regularly remind their citizens of the policy pressures they face from business under conditions of global competitiveness; and transnational corporations use, with increasing regularity, the threat of taking their investments elsewhere should national policies contravene their interests. The gap between the public and private sectors, meanwhile, has become so narrow that few public policy decisions and public infrastructure investments are undertaken without the inputs of business. Despite the challenges these developments present for social policy, however, their implications for social policy have been under-researched. While questions regarding the opinions and influences of business have been raised with increasing frequency, few studies have investigated these issues in any detail, let alone attempted to provide convincing answers to the questions they raise. This book represents one of the first real attempts to investigate business views and influence on social policy outcomes.

Business influence on social policy

Explanations documenting the development of social policies have been wide ranging in every way bar one: the interests and institutions of business have generally been overlooked. Explanations have included:

- the moral conscience of the middle classes and of government (Fraser, 1984, pp 134-7);
- the breakdown of former welfare institutions (Flora and Alber, 1981);
- the reliance of competitive markets on a healthy, well-educated workforce (Peden, 1985, pp 11-13);
- the extension of citizenship rights and the empowerment of individuals (Marshall, 1950);
- the dynamic of state bureaucracies (Niskanen, 1971);
- and the political mobilisation – as well as the fear of the political mobilisation – of labour (Navarro, 1978, 1989; Korpi, 1983; Castles, 1986, 1989).

Those theorists who have discussed the role of business in welfare development have tended to draw on taken-for-granted assumptions about the position of capital in relation to social policy. Waged labour has been portrayed largely as pro-welfare, capital as anti-welfare (see, for example, Navarro, 1989, pp 388-93). Social policies are said to develop out of these conflicting interests, reflecting the winners or losers on either side of the class divide. The interests of capital as a whole have been grouped together in a united mass, and the many fractional interests neglected. The situation was summarised by Hay in 1977 (pp 435-9):

> In Britain ... the attitudes of the business community to social welfare legislation have not been seriously examined.... [There has] been no systematic study of the attitude of employers to welfare legislation, or of their influence on the evolution of social policy. The reason for this neglect may be the underlying assumption of most liberal historians that welfare legislation primarily benefits the working class and is thus largely to be explained by the pressure of the latter for legislation or by concessions by the political elite to such actual or potential pressure.

Neither has the situation improved greatly since the 1970s. Writing in 1991, Rodgers (1991, p 315) echoed Hay's earlier remarks:

> ... though employers were visible, and even conspicuous in the debates over the economy, unemployment and the treatment of the unemployed (during the inter-war years), few historians have devoted serious attention to their activities and proposals.

The issue of business influence on social policy has not been totally absent from the literature, however. The globalisation literature has raised real concerns over the growing power of corporations and their impact on the sustainability of welfare states. Research has also examined employer attitudes to social policies (George et al, 1995; George, 1996; Taylor-Gooby, 1996), the increasing opportunities for private sector involvement in key welfare services (Balanya et al, 2000; Pollock et al, 2001) and the growing impact of the private sector on social policy more generally in the US and the UK (Mares, 2001; Whitfield, 2001a; Swenson, 2002). Yet huge gaps remain concerning the approach, involvement, power and changing influence of business on contemporary social policy.

Defining the variables and scope of this book

Social policy is viewed here in its broadest terms, to incorporate public and occupational provision in the main areas that make up the welfare state: education and training, healthcare, social security and housing. The time period on which it focuses is 1979 to 2002 – spanning the complete period of office of the Conservative government and the complete first term of the Labour government. This period witnessed dramatic transformations that impacted heavily on British social policy, including a clouding of the boundaries between public and private services, changing business–government relations (not to mention business–labour relations), fluctuating economic fortunes and economic restructuring. Business, this book argues, is essential to an understanding of many of these social policy developments for several interconnected and mutually inclusive reasons:

1. Many of the changes in social policy introduced since the 1970s have been in response to business demands or government perceptions of the needs of business.
2. Globalisation has increased the power of business over nation states, and while this has not inevitably led to welfare retrenchment in all states, it has certainly led to transformations in British social and fiscal policies.
3. Successive governments keen to control expenditure and introduce private sector values and business methods into services have increasingly incorporated business into the management of many areas of the welfare state. Most parts of the public sector have been forced to consult with the private sector when determining the shape and delivery of services.
4. Business has become increasingly interested in the ways in which occupational and community-wide social provision may help to improve competitiveness, recruitment, productivity and corporate image.
5. Welfare services, from hospitals to schools, have been increasingly opened up to private markets.

This book examines the role that business has played in the development of these policies and how it has reacted to these new opportunities for involvement in the welfare state.

Before proceeding, however, it is important to clarify what is meant by the term 'business'. Reference has already been made to the views and influence of business as if referring to one clearly defined and distinguishable entity where, in reality, business consists of individuals (business people), groups (the business class) and institutions (business associations and firms). Business views may be shared widely, or may represent the specific voice or voices of key individuals, sectors or firms of a certain size trading within certain locations. It is important to bear all this in mind whenever generalisations about business are made. This book examines various business engagements with social policy, although practical constraints limit the main focus to the largest and most important business organisations.

Confusion also arises over the use of the term 'capital', which is often used interchangeably with 'business'. Political and social science traditions dictate that Marxists utilise the terms 'capital' and 'capitalist' where pluralists and other non-Marxists deliberately do not, favouring instead more technically precise and politically unloaded terms such as 'firm', 'corporation', 'director' and 'business person'. In addition, both the terms 'business' and 'capital' are used within the literature to refer to economic entities (corporations and associated financial holdings) and the social class that owns and controls them. This book generally utilises non-Marxist terminology, more through a desire to avoid ambiguity than to indicate any particular ideological bent.

Theoretical framework

By focusing on business interests, this study situates itself alongside the work of those who suggest that, as a political and economic force, business is a special case: it has the ability to initiate, steer and constrain government policies in ways not open to other groups. Such a position came to dominate much socio-political analysis in the 1970s, but has declined in importance in recent years. The 'privileged interest' thesis has tended to suffer from the charge that it is too rigid and overly deterministic to be useful as a theory of power and influence in contemporary society. My response to this, drawing on the work of Vogel (1989, 1996) and Hacker and Pierson (2002), is to stress that, while business is a privileged interest, its power and influence vary over time and between policy areas; its dominance is neither constant nor unassailable.

The theoretical position of the book draws on the work of institutionalists. Despite the well-documented problems with institutionalist theory, relating in particular to the definition of institutions (Pontusson, 1995), it does offer a flexible and nuanced approach to the study of power and politics. While institutions are difficult to conceptualise and define, North's work is useful in defining institutions as simply constituting "the rules of the game in a society or ... the humanly devised constraints that shape human interaction" (1990, p 3). Thelen and Steinmo (1992) are also helpful here. They argue that the definition of institutions

> includes both formal organizations and informal rules and procedures that structure conduct.... Thus, clearly included in the definition are such features of the institutional context as the rules of electoral competition, the structure of party systems, the relations among various branches of government, and the structure and organization of economic actors. (Thelen and Steinmo, 1992, p 2)

Of particular interest to this study are policy and decision-making institutions, welfare institutions, and business institutions as economic actors, including business interest associations (BIAs) and enterprises.

Institutionalism also emphasises the importance of policy settings to an understanding of the motivations and perceptions of business actors within the policy process (Pierson, 1995). Political struggles are, as Thelen and Steinmo put it, "mediated by the institutional setting in which they take place" (1992, p 2). They go on to state that:

> On the one hand, the organisation of policy making affects the degree of power that any one set of actors has over the policy outcomes.... On the other hand, organisational position also influences an actor's definition of

his own interests, by establishing his institutional responsibilities and relationship to other actors. In this way, organisational factors affect both the degree of pressure an actor can bring to bear on policy and the likely direction of that pressure. (Thelen and Steinmo, 1992, p 5)

Hence, institutions help shape the interests of agents and help agents make sense of, and become aware of, their available options in policy arenas. Business influence will be shaped to some extent by state actors and available openings to state institutions. Moreover, as we have seen already, how business defines its own interests in relation to social policy, or indeed whether it is interested in social policy at all, will also depend on the institutional setting, including the actions of non-business actors, as well as the size, status and type of the business in question.

For institutionalists, structures "define the parameters of policy-making at the broadest level" (Thelen and Steinmo, 1992, p 10). Unlike institutions, which are often highly changeable, structures are deeply embedded in societies. They consist of taken-for-granted relations that define the workings of a given society. They constrain the choices or activities of agents. Where institutions are the rules of the game, structures help to tighten those rules and constrain the players. Given this, it is necessary, according to Thelen and Steinmo (1992, p 11), to "explore the effects of overarching structures on political outcomes" but at the same time avoid "the structural determinism that often characterises broader and more abstract" theoretical approaches.

Structures therefore reduce and constrain the choices available to policy makers. They are not, however, inevitably determining. States themselves may respond to structural pressures in different ways according to a range of other factors, although while their response is often predictable, it is by no means inevitable. The actions of business, meanwhile, have to be contextualised. Business' interest in, view of, and influence over, social policy is likely to vary according to a range of variables: the structural context, the actions of rival interests, the anticipated consequences of acting or not acting, and who or what is acting (whether a large or small firm, a financial or industrial corporation, an individual business person, enterprise or a BIA). Business agents will consider a range of factors when deciding on appropriate actions, although it is important to stress that, for institutionalists, actors are not all-knowing maximisers (Thelen and Steinmo, 1992, p 8). Actors can behave with some rationality, but the consequences of their actions are not always predictable, and they do not necessarily follow a consistent and logical path. Actors will also often seek to deliberately shift the goalposts during political negotiations by making demands that they know are unrealistic and unrealisable (Pierson, 1995, p 11). Business voice and actions, therefore, depend on a complex range of factors. Whether business is interested in social policy, whether it formulates an opinion or viewpoint, whether it chooses to act, and whether it ultimately influences policy making are all influenced by complex decisions that are taken by individual actors operating within institutions that exist within wider structures.

Investigating business power and influence on social policy

The distinction between structure and agency that institutional theory draws our attention to is a useful one in trying to make sense of the various ways in which business exercises power and influence over the policy process. Agency power is exercised by individual business people, firms or business associations and may take several forms:

- *lobbying* (either individual policy makers or ministries/groups/committees, and either as individual lobbyists or on behalf of a particular group or sector);
- *institutional participation* in government committees or in the management of social service providers;
- *sponsorship and funding* of political parties, think tanks and welfare institutions;
- *direct corporate social provision*, where enterprises are able to determine the overall shape and extent of welfare receipts among employees and other citizens.

This book investigates all four alongside structural power – that is, the power to influence without taking direct action. Structural power is derived from the ownership and control of capital. It is manifested through various channels: control over investment, control over labour and through state revenue dependence, all of which impact on employment, state spending and the employment conditions of labour. Together, structure and agency confer onto business significant power and influence over policy outcomes.

Measuring the extent of business influence, however, is an extremely complex matter. Business is not able to (nor does it have the desire to) influence all forms of policy making all the time. Where it acts, and how it acts, depends on the policy area and prevailing political context. A simple model of business engagement in the policy process is outlined in Figure 1.1.

Figure 1.1: A simple model of business influence on social policy

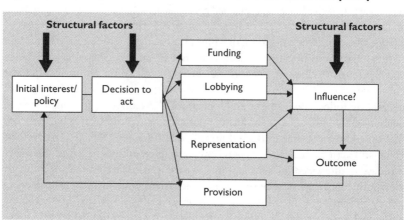

For business to influence through agency, its interest needs to be stimulated. Whether or not business chooses to act, however, depends on the policy of the particular business interest, available resources, and the likely result should it not act. Should action follow, business may influence policy outcomes, but in the case of lobbying, whether business gets its way will depend on many other factors, including the relative strength of its campaign, support or opposition from other groups including trade unions and civil society and the preferences of policy makers themselves. Business successes and even their engagement in the policy process at all, will also depend on the structural context. If business is confident that its interests will be defended by politicians without it having to act, it is unlikely to do so. In other words, the degree of structural power also shapes the policy context within which action is taken, and is therefore an important determinant in whether or not business will choose to act, and whether or not it needs to act, in order to defend its interests. Chapter Two of this book outlines the relationship between structure and agency in more detail.

As well as helping us to understand the relationship between business and policy making, this model of power and influence also highlights business' involvement in direct provision in the workplace, the wider community and in state welfare institutions. In both cases, initial interest in provision is important, as are subsequent decisions to act.

Structural power and social policy

Although corporate structural power is today less and less discussed in the social policy and politics literature, it remains crucial to an understanding of social policy development. Whenever governments introduce or shape social policies in order to meet the needs of business, as they often must, policy makers can be said to be responding to structural power. Accounts of welfare reform which highlight the role of social policies in meeting specific business needs, and the more general needs of industrial capitalism, are often termed 'functional explanations' and have been most highly developed by those working within a neo-Marxist framework (see, for example, O'Connor, 1973; Gough, 1979; Offe, 1984). According to such accounts, the needs of business are the most important determinants of welfare outcomes. Due to the importance of business, governments introduce social reforms only when due consideration has been given to their likely positive and negative impacts on productivity, profitability and competitiveness within the private sector. It is further argued that welfare states actually help to facilitate profitability through investing in human capital, and help to increase social harmony by providing important social services. On the one hand, state investment in education, training and healthcare, for example, has helped to increase productivity through fostering skills and cutting absenteeism through sickness, while measures designed to support the family, such as income maintenance, child benefits and education, have reduced the costs of raising the next generation of workers. On the other hand, welfare provision has helped to make living within capitalism more palatable for workers, which in turn has reduced the threat of political challenges to business. Without state provision, workers would more likely have pushed for employers to bear more of a responsibility for familial costs, either through occupational provision (as in the US) or through higher wages[1].

The structural mechanism operates to persuade politicians of the need to foster business-friendly policy environments. This is even more important in a globalising world, as Chapter Three illustrates. As a result of globalisation, firms have an increasing range of possible investment locations to choose from, and governments have to pay more attention to the relative attractiveness of their own states to mobile capital. Business investment helps to determine future government revenues, job opportunities and income levels. However, while governments always have to keep an eye on the ways in which policies impact on business, they still have available to them a wide range of policy options – hence the existence of different welfare states and different social policies over time. Chapter Three outlines and offers measures of changing structural power under globalisation.

Corporate agency and social policy: business opinion, business action and business influence

Just as structural power is variable, so business opinion on social policy, and agency power more generally, are variable. As we have seen already, business opinions and lobbying activities are both shaped by overriding structures. If structural power is strong, and if governments are already acting in the general interests of business, so business will not need to act. Conversely, if it is weak, business is more likely to try to steer policy towards its own agenda through political activities. However, what exactly constitutes the business agenda and business perspective in relation to social policy is not straightforward. This book illustrates that not all social policies, and not all forms of social provision, elicit the same response from business; some undermine and some better serve employers' interests than others. The type of welfare provision in question (education, social security, health, and so on), the way it is funded (or more specifically, the relative tax burden falling on business) and delivered (whether by the state or by employers), will affect how business perceives and responds to it.

The potential impact of welfare on firms also depends on the nature of the firm itself. Although industrial capital may benefit from a more highly skilled and amenable workforce, for example, some firms will face higher costs should welfare be funded from taxation on labour (in higher wage demands) and lower domestic sales (as more revenue is taken and controlled by the state). Financial capital, on the other hand, with generally smaller workforces, will benefit less directly from social investments, while spending on public programmes may both fuel inflation and reduce savings (Pfaller et al, 1991), not to mention impact negatively on private insurance sales. As a result, industrial capital more readily accepted the need to implement the 1942 Beveridge proposals than finance capital, which was generally more reticent (Melling, 1991, p 233).

Firm size is also an important determinant of business views. Larger firms and business associations tend to be more long term in outlook and, as a result, have tended to accept the case for welfare expansion more readily than smaller companies. Larger industrial firms were eager to find replacements for their own, increasingly expensive occupational schemes that many companies provided at the beginning of the 20th century. Larger companies and business collectively have also benefited from longer-term investments, most markedly in education and training, which have improved the quality of the labour they employ. Social security provision has also helped the larger and more heavily unionised employers to shed unproductive labour. Since larger firms have been able to absorb any additional costs associated with welfare expansion with greater ease, they have also gained a competitive advantage over smaller firms faced with similar welfare costs.

Despite this range of factors that militate against the formation of a coherent business approach to social policy, clear business opinions on social policy are nevertheless emerging at various levels. Chapter Four provides evidence that an international business view and approach to social policy has emerged in recent years. Globalisation has increased business' capacity for organising on the international stage, and is now far more active in engaging with social policy concerns than it has been in the past. Not surprisingly, the key concerns of international business centre round the free movement of capital and the maximisation of profits. Business requires a suitably educated and trained workforce that is productive but relatively inexpensive. It also requires access to markets. To this end, international business has pushed for general reductions in the 'unproductive' state, including taxation and spending on social protection and healthcare, and an expansion in the 'productive' state, most clearly education and training services. Thus, only minimalist welfare states, designed to provide temporary or basic protection when markets fail and where the private sector cannot provide assistance, are considered by international business to be compatible with global capitalism. These views are, in fact, very close to those promoted by international governmental organisations (IGOs) today, from the European Union (EU) to the World Bank.

The emphasis on productive welfare has also occurred at the level of the nation state. This has certainly been the case in the UK since the 1970s and under both Conservative and Labour governments. Each steered social policy towards productive provision designed to improve competitiveness and productivity. For its part, business has also played an increasingly important role in the formation of social policy discourse and has become more active in a range of welfare services since the late 1970s. These developments are discussed in Chapter Five. The key predictor of business interest in social policy, this chapter illustrates, is the extent to which social policies have an immediate and direct impact on labour costs, and the supply and qualifications of workers.

On the national level, business has defended services that directly benefit business (such as infrastructure spending and education and training) and has attacked spending on services that are unproductive. The British welfare state today fits business preferences extremely well.

Conservative and Labour governments have also been persuaded of the need to incorporate business directly into welfare services, partly to steer welfare services towards business needs, and partly to inject into them the values of the private sector. However, Chapter Six again reveals variable interest and involvement on the part of local businesses. While business generally has become more interested in the merits of closer community involvement, and while private sector sponsorship of some welfare services has become more important, there is little evidence to suggest that companies have been eager to take up these new opportunities on the scale desired, or where they have become involved, that they have brought to the public sector the benefits that governments had hoped for. Various sections of this book attest to this fact. However, the increasing opportunities for engagement in welfare services does have one unexpected outcome in that it appears to facilitate the development of local business-dominated elite networks.

Firms have also responded to this greater emphasis on business engagement in social policy by adjusting their own occupational welfare and community involvement. While Chapter Seven does not find that firms have stepped in to fill the breach left by the withdrawal of state benefits, it shows that they do continue to make sizeable contributions to overall levels of social provision, and they have adjusted their own community involvement in response to changing demands and opportunities in local social provision. Again, however, business provision is variable. Only those forms of occupational welfare that increase the availability of key workers, such as childcare and training provision, and those forms of local corporate engagement that stand to bring obvious benefits to corporations have been expanded. Unconditional corporate philanthropy appears no longer to exist, if it ever did.

Together, these chapters not only investigate business power and influence on social provision, but also the levels and determinants of business interest in social policy as well as the extent of coherence in business views and responses to social policy. Chapter Eight draws the evidence together to return to the key question of the book: what are the views of business towards social policy, and how influential is it in determining levels and types of social provision?

Note

[1] Rein (1996) illustrates that occupational welfare programmes are highly developed in countries with less comprehensive state provision, such as the US.

TWO

Business and social policy

Business is a privileged interest in capitalist societies. Its power dwarfs that of any other interest and it has greater influence on the policy process and policy outcomes than any other single distinguishable group. Yet, business does not always get its own way, and governments do not always act in its interests. Too often accounts of business power fail to adequately take account of this. What is required is a theory of business influence which clearly maps out corporate power and influence without straying into determinism – that is, the argument that government and state actions are determined by capitalist structures and the capitalist class. The argument put forward here is that business power and influence are variable over time and between policy areas. Before being able to develop this argument further, however, it is necessary to rehearse the key theoretical accounts of corporate power. To do this, a distinction is made between agency (influence *through* action) and structure (influence *without* action). Both forms of power are, in practice, interrelated, but making the conceptual distinction between them helps us to grasp better the ways in which business is able to exert influence. Following a discussion and critique of the two, they are brought together to frame the key theoretical arguments of the book.

Influence through action

Both Marxists and elite theorists have argued that the direct participation of business in the institutions of the state is important to the realisation of corporate power. Miliband (1969) provides the most familiar Marxist account. According to him, it is the ability of business to dominate the institutions of the state that is the key to business power and influence, although he also acknowledged that business people usually constitute no more than a small minority of state personnel (Miliband, 1969, p 55). More important to Miliband is the fact that key positions within the state are occupied by the natural allies of business – the middle and upper classes from which the leaders of business, the media and the state are drawn (Miliband, 1969, pp 23, 61).

Elite theorists put forward a similar argument. Domhoff (1967, 1978, 1987), for example, has provided a great deal of evidence to demonstrate that business and other elite interests have dominated the state in the US. Similarly, evidence from the UK reveals business and upper class dominance of both the Labour and Conservative governments (Scott and Griff, 1984; Scott, 1991b). In work reminiscent of Miliband's, Scott argues that political and economic elites help to preserve certain ideas that reinforce class privilege and, most importantly, quell opposition to business and free markets. Such elites are united by a "similarity of outlook and behaviour" which is underpinned by social ties and educational and family background (Scott, 1991b, p 137). Elite networks connect these major players and are an important avenue through which business is able to 'reach' and influence MPs and ministers.

Whether we are focusing on business' occupation of key positions or its links with other state players, its access to vast financial resources is one of its most important assets when it comes to political influence. To begin with, corporations and business people can make financial donations in order to steer the policies of political parties or gain access to ministers (Fisher, 1994). Until relatively recently, business funding in the UK has been directed predominantly towards the Conservative Party and this goes some way to accounting for its political success in the 1980s and 1990s (Fisher, 1994, p 699), had prevented the election of a Labour government. The fact that the Labour Party, under Tony Blair, now obtains a large amount of corporate backing (Osler, 2002; Red-Star Research, 2003) is testimony to how comfortable business is with New Labour, and is a clear illustration of how business donations are used to reward political parties and nurture closer ties with parties in power.

Business funding of other important bodies, such as think-tanks and research institutes, is an alternative way of influencing the direction of political debate. The Institute of Economic Affairs and the Centre for Policy Studies, for example, were both important in the development and fostering of neoliberal ideas during the 1980s (Desai, 1994, pp 28-9) and both were heavily funded by business. Also important, according to Leys (1989), were donations to 'union breaking' organisations such as the Economic League, Common Cause and United British Industrialists, which specialised in infiltrating and destabilising unions over the 1980s[1]. For New Labour, the Institute of Public Policy Research has been one of the most important think-tanks, aided undoubtedly by its success in attracting business support and advancing new ways of incorporating business interests into public policy areas.

In addition to these mechanisms, business is able to use the lobbying system to influence policy makers. Individual firms or business associations may make representations to policy makers or, alternatively, employ one of a growing number of professional lobby organisations to do this on their behalf (see Jordan, 1991). The important position that business holds in capitalist societies means that it is unlikely that large companies or business associations would be denied access to ministers and state officials (Offe and Wiesenthal, 1980; Bonnett, 1985, p 9). Nor does business need to try very hard to influence government; merely expressing an opinion or informing politicians of low levels of confidence within the business community is enough to influence a change in government direction (Lindblom, 1977, p 185; Block, 1990, pp 300-5; Mintz and Schwartz, 1990). Such opinions may be communicated through press releases, conferences or other media channels and, in many cases, may be directed as much towards the general public as politicians in the hope of gaining wider public support.

Agency is clearly an important mechanism through which business can influence social policy, but it is not the only mechanism. As the next section illustrates, business can also influence government decisions without acting at all.

Influence through structure

Structural power is derived, not from the actions of business agents, but from the monopolisation of capital: financial holdings, industrial plants and machinery. And since business monopolises capital, it does not need to act to ensure that the state promotes its interests. Rather, according to theories of structural power, various mechanisms restrict the policies of the capitalist state to those that are compatible with the basic needs (although not necessarily the wants) of business. Four such mechanisms can be identified from the literature: control over investment, state revenue dependence, power over labour and ideological control. These are discussed in turn below.

Control over investment

The ability of business to make free investment decisions within capitalist economies is the most important of its mechanisms of structural power. Business has an 'institutionalised right of capital withdrawal', this often being expressed more starkly as the weapon of the 'investment strike' – the power of 'exit' rather than voice, to borrow Hirschman's (1970) terminology. The source of power here is the many free and individual investment decisions taken daily by businesses. Collectively, these decisions impact on the actions, decisions and policies of governments as well as the overall welfare of other groups. Przeworski and Wallerstein (1988, p 12) have summarised this complex picture most clearly and concisely:

> Investment decisions have public and long-lasting consequences: they determine the future possibilities of production, employment and consumption for all. Yet they are private decisions. Since every individual and group must consider its future, since future consumption possibilities depend on present investment, and since investment decisions are private, all social groups are constrained in the pursuit of their material interests by the effect of their actions on the willingness of owners of capital to invest, which in turn depends on the profitability of investment.

Since both government and labour are dependent on the collective investments of business, the pursuit of personal or 'national' interest must take account of the impact that such pursuits have on future investment decisions. Given that business investment is a key determinant of future production, employment and consumption levels, low levels of investment by the business sector may also translate into electoral failure for ruling parties (Lindblom, 1977; Gill and

Law, 1989, p 481; Winters, 1996, pp 28-36). For labour, or to put it another way, the majority of the electorate, low levels of investment could result in higher levels of unemployment, reductions in wages and reductions in living standards. The fact that businesses cannot be forced to invest, however, means that governments must, as far as possible, induce them to do so. Typical inducements may include tax breaks and subsidies, as well as investments in those infrastructure services that increase accumulation and profit-making opportunities, such as investments in roads and transport and, particularly important here, certain forms of social provision, especially in the areas of education and training. Generally speaking, businesses will invest when they have confidence in their ability to make profits in the future; thus governments need to consider the impact that current policies or future legislation are having, or will have, on levels of business confidence (Block, 1990, pp 300-5). A lack of confidence may require policy changes, even if business had lived with those policies in the past. According to Mintz and Schwartz (1990, p 222), levels of business confidence and investment act as signalling devices to governments: a low level of either sends a signal to governments that current legislation may have to change, or new legislation is required.

State revenue dependence

Whether taxation is levied on incomes (profits or wages), expenditures or invested capital, the capability of the state to fund its social and political programmes depends on the production, investment and accumulation of the private sector. While the production that creates taxable resources is viewed as being essentially beyond the state's control, the state must do all it can to create the right conditions to maximise private accumulation since it is itself dependent for its revenues on this process. As Offe and Ronge (1982) argue, the state is structurally dependent on the capitalist sector for its revenue. Therefore, whatever the complexion and programme of the government in power, it cannot pursue policies which undermine capital accumulation. To do so would be to endanger the revenues of the state and thus the self-interest of state bureaucrats and policy makers. As Offe and Ronge (1982, pp 137-47) put it:

> Since the state depends on a process of accumulation which is beyond its power to organize, every occupant of state power is interested in promoting those conditions most conducive to accumulation. This interest does not result from alliance of a particular government with particular classes ... nor does it result from any political power of the capitalist class which 'puts pressure' on the incumbents of state power to pursue its class interest. Rather, it does result from an *institutional self-interest* of the state which is conditioned by the fact that the state is denied the power to control the flow of those resources which are indispensable for the use of state power. (emphasis in original)

Offe and Ronge (1982) also reveal an interesting paradox in this process. Although the state is constrained by its reliance on capital in raising resources for its programmes, many of those programmes are themselves a response to the dynamics of contemporary capitalism, including concerted drives toward greater profitability, efficiency and competitiveness. Put another way, the state must induce the private sector to invest so that it might adequately provide for those citizens who suffer the inevitable problems associated with modern capitalism: unemployment, inequality and alienation, for example. The problem with this intervention, however, is that it may undermine the accumulation process and so deny the private sector of an important source of investment revenue, not to mention the risk this carries of encouraging corporations to invest elsewhere. Given all this, the state is only able to act in the interests of labour (or its own interests) when such action does not undermine the accumulation process itself (Offe and Ronge, 1982; see also O'Connor, 1973; Gough, 1979).

Power over labour

The fact that business occupies a monopoly position over private investments, and that workers have no other means of subsistence apart from paid employment, places labour in a position of relative dependence and business in a position of power and control. Workers depend on employers for their livelihood, and they cannot realistically 'exit' from production in the same way that capital can; that is, without undermining their own financial positions. For its part, labour is undermined by the contradictory nature of the pursuit of its interests. On the one hand, labour and capital's interests collide, resulting in frequent struggles over wages and work conditions. On the other, labour must safeguard the dominant and competitive position of the firm since its own interests are synonymous with continued profitability and the accumulation of capital which can often necessitate exploitation, long working hours, redundancies and increased productivity. When labour seeks to defend its interests it may, as a result, undermine the profitability of the firm, and hence, destabilise its own future. Capital, on the other hand, can defend its own interests safe in the knowledge that what it does can be defended in the name of future competitiveness and prosperity (Offe and Wiesenthal, 1980, p 180).

Ideological control

The final structural power resource lies in the ideological domain. A group may exercise ideological hegemony if its interests can be legitimised as the 'national interest'. As a result of the foregoing arguments, this is precisely the position that capital is in. The dependence of society and the state on capital profitability and accumulation acts as a gravitational tug on the 'volitions' of the population, according to both Lindblom (1977) and the dominant ideology thesis within Marxist theory. Ideological reproduction reinforces the notion that business is the unit on which most social and economic activities depend. The state, for those reasons outlined above, plays a central role in reinforcing a pro-capitalist or pro-business ideology, which serves to further increase the power of business by preventing or neutralising opposition to it (Miliband, 1969, p 165; Poulantzas, 1973, pp 303-5). Thus, business power translates into ideological power, and this helps to shape values and interests within capitalist societies including those of labour and the state. According to Lindblom (1977, p 202),

> businessmen achieve indoctrination of citizens so that citizens' volitions serve not their own interests but the interests of businessmen. Citizens then become allies of businessmen.

It is important, then, to view the reproduction of ideas as part of the political struggle between capital and labour. The production of these ideas, and the process through which these ideas come to dominate, operates through both structural and agency forms. On the one hand, business is able to contribute to the development of ideas directly through agency (as outlined above). On the other, the manifestation of structural power in the form of ideological power can make certain policy choices appear normal while preventing others – those which undermine business interests – from ever being realistically considered (Block, 1990, p 306). Organised labour is also less likely to pursue what are considered to be unrealistic aims given the dominant ideological and political context at any one time, while business is less likely to be required to make use of its own resources in an attempt to steer policy in a given direction through agency should the dominant ideas of the time be favourable already.

To summarise, the structural power of capital rests on four related but distinguishable foundations:

- its control over investment;
- the dependency of the state on economic success for its revenue;
- its asymmetrical power over labour;
- and its hegemonic power.

The following section examines the factors which increase or decrease agency and forms of structural power.

The variability of corporate power

According to Pierson (1995, p 9):

> The assertion of business' 'privileged position' has appeared to be ill-suited for *comparative* investigations of policy development.... [M]arket systems are compatible with widely divergent relations between business and the state.

Patterns of government intervention vary greatly across countries and over
time within particular countries. (emphasis added)

This critique was aimed in particular at the work of elite pluralists such as
Lindblom, but it could equally apply to the writings of many Marxists and
some theorists of globalisation (as Chapter Three of this book illustrates). Each
could be accused of putting forward inflexible and deterministic theories that
underestimate the political autonomy of governments and overstate the ability
and willingness of governments to act in the interests of business. To reject
outright these arguments, however, is to risk underplaying and ignoring business
power. Instead, what is needed is a reassessment of the sources of corporate
power with the acknowledgement that such power is a variable rather than
constant force in politics (Vogel, 1989; Pierson, 1995; Hacker and Pierson,
2002). Several factors impact on the degree of power and influence of business.
First, business power, especially agency power, is dependent to some extent on
the organisation, unity and cooperation that exist within the business community.
Second, the nature and operation of the state is important. Of relevance here
is the age of the democracy in question, the historical dominance of particular
classes or interests, the political complexion of dominant parties, the openness
of the institutions of the state and the number of layers and access points
within it. In this case, business' ability to gain access to well-positioned decision
makers is paramount. Third, the activities and relative power of rival interests,
particularly the labour movement, are clearly important. A fourth important
factor is the actual, as opposed to theoretical, ability of capitalists to make free
investment decisions. The following sections discuss the most important of
these factors in greater detail.

Capitalist unity

The most common objection levelled against the 'business as privileged interest'
thesis is that there is no one clear, coherent and unified business view (Dahl,
1961). At least three cleavages exist: between sectors (notably between
manufacturing and finance); between groups of different sizes, for example
large versus small business; and between business interests from different nation
states (Mann, 1993). Also important, of course, is the fact that most firms, even
cartels, compete with each other on some level. A lack of coherence and unity
within the business community both reduces its capacity to act with one voice
and reduces the ability of the state, or any other institution, to act in the
interests of the capitalist class as a whole. Agency power may be reduced as a
result of disunity within the capitalist class; structural power may be reduced if
the state is not able to act in the collective interests of business.

It may indeed be the case that divisions within the capitalist class prevent it
from either acting together on all issues, or responding to the same stimuli in
the same way, but there will inevitably be points on which the capitalist class is
united. For Miliband (1969, pp 139-48), such divisions tend to centre on

smaller and less significant issues, which quickly heal when matters of substance are raised. Coates (1984, p 59) supports this thesis, arguing that capital is able to demonstrate remarkable unity if

> a general threat to the social privileges of capital and of the class that possesses it is perceived, particularly if the threat comes from the labour movement and other exploited classes on whose perpetual subordination capital depends for its very existence.

The growth of inter-corporate ties associated with globalisation also increases unity within the business sector (Useem, 1990; Clawson et al, 1986; Sklair, 2001). The most important networks develop where the connections between firms are formalised through common ownership or interlocking directorships, where directors sit on the boards of several different companies (Scott and Griff, 1984; Scott, 1985, pp 44-6; Useem, 1990, pp 268-9). Moreover, where production and ownership are concentrated in relatively few hands, greater cooperation, coordination and dependence between firms tends to be the result (Useem, 1990). International cooperation between firms, made easier by the spread of technology, is also becoming increasingly possible in the global economy (Holton, 1998, pp 62-6).

Business interest associations (BIAs) are also important in developing closer links between different sections of business and in formulating common business perspectives. This is especially true in the case of peak-level BIAs, which encompass all the main sectors and often foster close links with other associations at the regional and international level. Globalisation has also forced business issues onto the international stage, a factor that has helped to promote the development of new international BIAs, as well as strengthen existing ones. Increasingly, close international ties between national business interests are helping to establish clearer global business perspectives on a range of issues.

Despite these countervailing forces, however, it remains the case that the capitalist class inevitably holds a range of divergent perspectives and interests on policy matters, especially when we go beyond core business concerns. While there may be widespread agreement among companies to reduce business costs, for example, such agreement may not exist in relation to a range of other policies, including the extent and scope of social provision. Such perspectives are likely to depend on the size and resources of the firm, the relative costs of new or existing legislation, the sector in which the firm produces, and the nature and pattern of its markets. Also important is the fact that different fractions of capital operate to different time horizons – larger firms are more likely to consider the longer term, while smaller firms tend to be short term in outlook. This has important implications for social policy, which often requires careful planning for the future. Changes to educational provision, for example, take years for their full impact to be felt.

The autonomy of the state

Many commentators have sought to emphasise the power and autonomy of the state against what they view as the determinism of certain Marxist theorists or, more recently, the fatalism of some globalisation theorists. Institutionalist theories suggest that it is wrong to reduce the state to economic or other class interests. Rather, it is important to consider the particular interests and goals that state actors themselves formulate and pursue as well as the constraints that stem from the institutions within which they act (Skocpol, 1985, p 28). While neo-Marxists stress the fact that states ultimately have to act in the interests of capital, despite being relatively autonomous from them, for institutionalists like Skocpol (1979), the state is 'potentially autonomous', capable of acting independently of business interests. Moreover, according to Skocpol (1979), state officials are themselves innovators of social and public policies, and are able to expand, cut or alter service provision (Martin, 1989, p 194). The institutional context is also important here. The organisation of the state, the level of existing provision and the rules governing it, and other considerations such as the level of political consensus around an issue, will all help influence policy outcomes. For institutionalists, therefore, the extent of business influence on policy makers depends, to a large extent, on the ideas and outlook of the key policy makers involved, mediated by the practical constraints and political opposition they face in carrying out their duties.

The labour movement

The fact that business is generally in a more politically advantageous position than labour does not alter the fact that the labour movement itself is capable of exerting non-institutionalised and institutionalised class power to rival this. Non-institutionalised struggle, through strike action, demonstrations and riots, has been used effectively in the past to win important concessions on a range of issues. Indeed, according to Piven and Cloward (1979) and Jenkins and Brents (1989, p 896), direct struggle has often proven to be more important than parliamentary representation in winning policy battles.

However, institutionalised struggle, primarily though parliamentary representation, has also been important. The gradual extension of the franchise and the widening of the social make-up and class interests of MPs over the 19th and 20th century, both representing victories for non-institutionalised struggle, were crucial to the establishment of union and labour representation in Parliament as well as to subsequent social reforms. The extension of voting rights in particular ensured that political parties had to consider the views of workers alongside middle-class and business interests were they to gain and hold power. As a result, workers have been able to extract favourable policy outcomes from the capitalist state by exercising voting rights and having their preferences mediated through social democratic parties (Esping-Andersen et al, 1976; Korpi, 1983; Esping-Andersen, 1990, p 16).

Capital mobility, globalisation and the changing capacities of states

Should the most important form of business' structural power be control over investment, it follows that the extent of this power will relate directly to its mobility and possibilities for exit. Put another way, the extent to which capital is able to apply pressure on the state is largely dependent on how genuinely mobile capital is. When capital is immobile, then the threat of exit is reduced or even removed. A number of factors can affect the mobility of capital. First, it is far easier for capital to shift investment within rather than between states. Second, larger firms may find it easier to shift investment than smaller ones. Third, it is not possible for firms to move investment freely where production and/or trade are relatively or firmly fixed to a particular area. Mineral exploration is firmly fixed, manufacturing is relatively fixed, but call centres and financial trading are highly mobile (although the mobility of the latter does depend on the nature of its investments and the regulations governing investments, and whether we are discussing the administration of the business or its portfolio investments). It should be noted here that relocation or switched investments do not have to be wholesale, and may consist only of a small or minor part of the total level of investment.

Growing evidence suggests that, from the mid-1980s onwards, there has been a rapid growth in internationally mobile financial and industrial capital (Held et al, 1999, p 210). Parts of financial and industrial capital have become increasingly mobile in the wake of a general relaxation in capital controls since the 1970s. In a comprehensive review of the evidence relating to the process of internationalisation and globalisation, Held et al (1999, p 234) concluded in relation to financial capital that:

> Since the 1970s there has been an exponential growth in global finance such that the extensity, intensity, velocity and impact on contemporary global financial flows and networks are largely unprecedented.

The result has been greater pressure on nation states to pursue tight domestic monetary policy, primarily to retain and invoke confidence in financial markets (Held et al, 1999, p 229). International finance markets, according to C. Pierson (1996, p 180), function as a "permanent referendum upon governments' capacity to pursue a 'sound economic policy'". International finance markets, according to C. Pierson (1996, p 180), function as a "permanent referendum upon governments' capacity to pursue a 'sound economic policy'". There has been some debate regarding the extent to which financial and industrial capital are truly global as opposed to regional – restricted primarily to Europe, North America and East Asia (Hirst and Thompson, 1996, pp 2-3) – but this does not reduce the potential impact of mobility within those regions. Following their review of the evidence, Held et al (1999, p 281) concluded:

Among OECD states in particular, the magnitude and economic significance
of [Foreign Direct Investment] and MNCs in relation to national economic
activity are such that the needs of multinational capital cannot be ignored.

Marshall (1996, p 208) sums up the main reason why they cannot be ignored:
technological development has increased competition between different
countries as well as the lengths to which countries, particularly less developed
countries, must go in order to make themselves more and more attractive to
investment. Moreover, according to Gill and Law (1989, p 417), states
increasingly need to create investment opportunities within attractive investment
environments in order to strengthen their own economies. In an environment
(and in sectors) where mobility is high, and where the necessity to attract new
capital is high, the resulting pressures on governments are, according to Winters
(1996, pp 19-20), more intense than the participation of capital in decision
making. An assessment of these arguments and of structural power and
globalisation more generally is the subject of Chapter Three of this book.

These, then, are the four main factors which determine the extent and
variability of business power within capitalist societies. Subsequent chapters
assess their importance to this study more fully.

Integrating agency and structure and arriving at a useful model of business influence

While it is useful to an understanding of business influence to report how both
action and structures can operate to constrain or influence policy outcomes, it
is also important not to oversimplify the exclusivity of either form in the
policy process. Although we may conceptually differentiate between structure
and agency, it is important to recognise that, in practice, both are interdependent.
This is the basic argument of two important works on the subject, that of
Lukes (1977) and Giddens (1979). Beginning with Lukes, he argues that the
ability of agents to act actually takes place within an existing structural
framework, with the effect that an analysis of action does not make sense
without reference to structures. Structures actually determine an agent's varying
abilities and opportunities to act (Lukes, 1977). Action, in the meantime, plays
a part in creating and determining the form of structures. This would appear
to be a circular argument, and to some extent it is meant to be, although it
becomes more persuasive as we again consider the fact that the impact of
business actions and of structural power vary according to time, and according
to the policy in question. The extent to which business will take action in
order to attempt to influence governments, and the form this action takes, will
depend on current structural influences, and the extent to which business feels
that it could benefit from taking action. In turn, this action could help to
reinforce structural power. To be clear, the context in which capital is structurally
powerful helps to determine the social and political context in which business
acts. Moreover, the extent to which business is able to rely on structural power

will determine whether or not it needs to take action, and, were it to take action, how well placed (in terms of its relative power) it will be to influence policy outcomes.

According to Giddens (1979), it is not useful to separate structure and agency since they are so closely bound. He coined the term 'structuration' to emphasise the interdependency and interrelationship between the two. According to Giddens, structures define the boundaries of action, and they are themselves the consequences of some form of human action. Structures are the result of agency. It is not necessary here to engage in the level of debate necessary to support or refute structuration as a concept, although it is useful to draw from it the basic contention that structure and agency are, in many ways, interconnected and interdependent. While they are interconnected, however, the conceptual distinction between the two remains important to a proper understanding of corporate power and influence. As already indicated, business is able to influence policy outcomes through both mechanisms of power independently and, according to Marsh and Locksley (1983a), it is uniquely placed to do this.

Business power is variable, however. Thus, the extent to which corporate structural or agency power impact on policy outcomes is also variable. When corporate structural power is high (that is, when the politico-economic structure favours business), then it is unlikely to act or feel like it needs to act since policy makers will, in this case, promote business interests anyway. When it is low, business will have to exercise agency in order to ensure that its interests are noted by policy makers. This model of power is a multidimensional one, where structures define how influential actions will be; where actions and non-actions can reinforce or change structural powers; and where the actions of the state (and individual state actors) play a part in determining how influential structural or agency pressures will be on policy. Moreover, this approach allows us to accommodate theoretically the situation where capital makes explicit threats to withdraw investment – the 'threat' is exercised through agency, even though it is structural power that underpins the threat (Ward, 1987, p 597).

The theoretical point at which we have arrived, after considering these different mechanisms of variable business power, is essentially institutionalist. Structural power is an important factor in determining the context within which institutions exist and agents act, although it is not determining. States themselves have a key role to play in determining the significance and impact of structural power. While their response is often predictable, it is by no means inevitable. The actions of business, meanwhile, take place within the wider institutional context. Whether or not business actors choose to act, how they determine their own interests, and how other actors, such as labour or state actors, respond (even how they are likely to respond) will also be influenced by a range of institutional factors – for example, the 'rules' of the game, likely successes, past experiences, the likely result from not acting, the number and range of political access points, resources, the relative power of rival groups, business unity and the perceived importance of the policy in question (a more detailed discussion can be found in Thelen and Steinmo, 1992, chapter one). In short, it is important to recognise that, at different historical points and in different policy areas, both agency and structure vary in their relative importance to policy outcomes. Business power, too, varies according to the wider context. In order to understand business power and influence, therefore, we need to adopt a more flexible approach to business power.

Models of welfare state development

Although the most common explanations of welfare state development have failed to adequately take account of business power and influence, it is useful to briefly outline the most important elements of those which hold some relevance for this study. The most pertinent can be categorised into three distinct models: those that stress the functional role of welfare states to industrial societies; those that focus on the activities of the state and the actors within it; and those that focus on political mobilisation as the engine to social change. Each is discussed in turn.

Functionalist accounts

Functionalist accounts of welfare growth link social, economic and political transformations associated with capitalist development with social policy reforms. Two variants are discussed here: the first links welfare growth to economic development, the second to the needs of capital.

Economic development

Wilensky (1975) posits that the most important determinant of a welfare state is economic development and accompanying political and bureaucratic development. Under capitalism, former political and economic settlements break down, and previous institutions of care and welfare collapse. These changes can be chronicled as follows. Historically, the development of new forms of production created dislocated and increasingly mobile labour which was forced into the cities. The inevitable problems that arose from this required state solutions, particularly with regard to poverty, disease and cyclical unemployment. Later, state involvement was required to create a better disciplined, more healthy and educated workforce. Second, since industrialisation undermined those institutions that would previously have made provision for those in need (such as the family, guilds and friendly societies and the church), the state was increasingly required to step in to resolve social, political and economic problems. As state institutions developed, so did their capacity to respond to social problems and to obtain greater resources. The assumption here is that economic development has positive effects on social and political rights, although the role of class action and agitation and of different political parties and ideologies are played down (Vaisanen, 1992, p 310). Since these developments apply to every industrialised and industrialising country, welfare states should, accordingly, converge and social policy should develop in tandem with economic development.

Needs of capital

Those working within a neo-Marxist framework provide a variant of this theory. According to O'Connor (1973), Gough (1979) and Offe (1984), state expenditure fulfils different but necessary functions. For O'Connor, social capital expenditure increases labour productivity and lowers reproduction costs, while social expenses are used to maintain harmony. The former increases business profitability and capital accumulation, the latter risks undermining it (O'Connor, 1973, pp 5-10). For Gough (1979), different types of spending and production fulfil different functions which serve the interests of capital and labour in different ways: some contributing to productivity, others to the reproduction of labour power and to the maintenance of social harmony. According to Gough, business is more likely to be supportive of spending on social and capital investments (spending that increases profitability and productivity) and spending on social consumption (that which helps to lower the reproduction costs of labour, for example education, housing and health provision). It is least likely to be supportive of social expenses spending – that which adds only to social harmony and fulfils only a legitimisation function, such as social services, advice centres, or the administration of state welfare (Gough, 1979).

The ongoing challenge for the state is to strike the right balance between promoting accumulation and satisfying the basic needs of labour. However, this task is made increasingly difficult by the contradictory demands made on the state. According to O'Connor (1973), monopoly capitalism creates surplus production that, in turn, leads to surplus labour (unemployment), which the state itself is increasingly relied on to support (1973, p 161). The state responds by putting in place services to protect labour, but this means raising taxes on business and potentially undermining the accumulation process. During economic downturns, however, the state also faces pressures to reduce spending on social provision, but in such circumstances this will risk stoking social unrest and political instability.

State-centred theory

For state-centred theory, the initiative for social policy development comes from state actors. According to de Swaan (1988, p 9), the impetus behind welfare reforms is provided mainly by "reformist politicians and administrators in charge of state bureaucracies".

This is not to imply that capital, or working or middle classes for that matter, are unable to influence state policy. Where particular interests battle for changes in the levels of social provision, state actors intervene and attempt to 'manage' the situation. Their success in doing this, indeed their desire to do this, will be determined, according to Huber et al (1993, pp 714-15), by the constitutional and policy context in which the crisis and the intervention occurs. Past resolutions, successes and failures set the context within which new solutions will be offered. In this respect, therefore, state actors will generate solutions according to their own perceptions of the problems they encounter, their knowledge and experiences. However, most importantly, state officials are portrayed as innovators of social and public policies rather than merely being responsive to external forces (Skocpol, 1979). In addition, once state services are set up by statute, bureaucrats are often able to expand them without new legislation (Alber, 1982, cited in Huber et al, 1993, p 722). The fact that bureaucrats are to some extent sheltered from public scrutiny does provide some capacity for policy development based on the goals and interests of key individuals (Martin, 1989, p 194) which, according to at least one school of thought, do not include efficiency (Niskanen, 1971).

Power resources

The class struggle thesis posits that social policy outcomes are determined by class conflict and compromise played out within institutionalised and/or non-institutionalised contexts (Griffin et al, 1983, p 384). Of particular importance to welfare outcomes are the relative power resources of capital and labour (Korpi, 1983; Shalev, 1983). According to Korpi (1983), power resources stem from:

• control over the means of production; and
• the organisation of wage-earners into unions and political parties.

Since the capitalist class controls the means of production under capitalism, the extent of working-class power is determined by its ability to organise itself collectively and to compete for electoral power. The most important determinant of working-class power, therefore, is the extent to which it is organised. The history of its success in collective organisation affects not only the final distribution of resources and levels of inequality within societies, but the extent of welfare services (Korpi, 1983, p 187). Korpi does not ignore the fact that this is only part of the equation. Economic growth, historical context (the past successes or failures of the labour movement) and the composition of the population are also important, as is the organisation and unity of business and the Right more generally (Castles, 1986, p 672; 1989, pp 432-3). A fragmented Right will be unable to oppose the emergence of a strong Left which, in turn, will tend to lead to a more generous welfare system. Conversely, a strong and unified Right will challenge the development of a strong Left and so impede welfare state growth. The only exception here is education. In the area of education spending there is a strong correlation, according to Castles (1989, p

---

432), between the political dominance of parties of the Right and generosity of expenditure.

Once universal suffrage was established, institutionalised struggle became an extremely powerful weapon for workers to extract favourable policy reforms from the ruling classes, including business (Korpi, 1989; Esping-Andersen, 1990, p 16). Labour parties were important to winning welfare concessions (Korpi, 1983, 1989; Castles, 1986; Hicks et al, 1989; Hicks, 1991; Vaisanen, 1992) and each victory that passed added to working class strength and unity, not least because they increased income security and reduced debilitating poverty (Esping-Andersen, 1990, p 16).

It is doubtful, however, that any real progress in social policy would have been made without non-institutionalised struggle. Piven and Cloward (1971, p 7) offer one of the clearest accounts of the significance of non-institutionalised struggle to social policy development:

> [M]ass unemployment that persists for any length of time diminishes the capacity of other institutions to bind and constrain people.... The result is usually civil disorder – crime, mass protests, riots – a disorder that may even threaten to overturn existing social and economic arrangements. It is then that relief programs are initiated and expanded.

According to this argument, the more the working class is organised and prepared to agitate, the more comprehensive the system of welfare provision is likely to be. However, such concessions are often short-lived.

According to Piven and Cloward (1979), welfare reforms are often a result of both institutionalised and non-institutionalised forms. First, events such as economic depressions lead to working-class frustration and grievances. Second, because of this, workers change voting allegiances and seek to air their grievances through more institutional channels, for example through trade unions, the media, elected representatives, and so on. Third, as previous efforts prove fruitless, and as economic and political crisis increases, so workers turn to more collective action in order to defend their interests. Fourth, social unrest then occurs and political action takes non-institutionalised forms. Depending on the frequency, ferocity and length of such action, business, other elites and policy makers may either ignore or respond to it. This will then often trigger the development of welfare policies, although the nature of these policies will vary. It is important to note, however, that once social unrest has subsided, past concessions are often reversed (Piven and Cloward, 1971, p 45).

Although class rivalry is important to welfare outcomes, so too are class coalitions. Two such coalitions are identified by Esping-Andersen (1990) as being particularly important. The alliance between farmers and workers in Sweden is argued to have been decisive in the development of expansive Swedish welfare, although an alliance between rural workers and conservative interests in Austria is argued to have hindered the development of social policies (Esping-Andersen, 1990, p 18). Also important, especially in post-Second World War history, have been working- and middle-class coalitions. Since the major demands of the working class – full employment and income equality – have been peripheral concerns for the middle classes, welfare state development has often been dependent on the extent to which middle classes could be incorporated within them and encouraged to support and defend them (Esping-Andersen, 1990, pp 29-32). Indeed, according to Baldwin (1990, p 111), the resilience of welfare states has depended largely on the extent to which they have successfully integrated middle-class support with working-class support.

These, then, are the three key models of welfare state development. While each one touches on the influence of business, discussion tends to be rather general and ill-suited to a detailed examination and understanding of the role and importance of business to welfare state outcomes. Missing from each one is an adequate analysis of how business agency and structural factors combine to influence social policy. Nonetheless, they do provide important indications of the complex range of influences that shape welfare state outcomes.

Business and social policy

This final section attempts to piece together various accounts of welfare state reforms in an attempt to build a more complete picture of business views and influences on British social policy. Although no study has yet examined this issue adequately, some important indications of business influence are nonetheless present in some of the more detailed literature on welfare state histories.

Looking at the history of welfare state reforms since the early 20th century reveals a murky picture as far as the views and influence of business are concerned. However, it is clear that business did play an important role from the outset. To begin with, employers dominated the key modes of social protection for most of the period leading up to the liberal reforms at the beginning of the 20th century through their dominance of the administrative structures of the Poor Law and through their own occupational welfare schemes (Hay, 1977, 1978b; Melling, 1991; Russell, 1991). However, transformations in the political and economic landscape since then have brought changing political fortunes for business and employers were forced to engage in debates concerning a whole range of social reforms. In some cases employers promoted reforms, in other instances they opposed them. In many others, business was split. Generally, business has been able to agree on the bigger questions relating to reforms, but has been divided on the minutiae. As political and economic environments change, so too does the extent to which business stands to benefit from social policy. Of course, different sectors of business and different sized firms will also stand to benefit or lose from social reforms to varying degrees. The nature of political institutions also plays an important role in framing social policy debates and determining the capacity of business to shape or veto proposed legislation. The importance and relevance of these issues increase with the variability of the political and economic landscape under review.

Generally and historically business has been either hostile or lukewarm to welfare reforms and has favoured private welfare over state provision (Hay, 1978, p 115). However, business has also been adept at responding to pressures from labour and the state in order to push welfare reforms to those least harmful to its interests. The evolving BIAs that began to play a more active role in politics from the beginning of the 20th century, including the Chambers of Commerce and the British Employers Federation, the precursor to the Confederation of British Industry, were important to the formulation of common business positions, to countering an increasingly powerful and well-organised trades union movement, and to lobbying an increasingly centralised state. And since they were better placed to consider the long-term interests of employers, BIAs were also able to see merit in limited welfare reforms, and, according to Melling (1991), they succeeded in winning over some sceptical employers to these arguments. Hay (1977) also suggests that some chambers actively supported social security provision as a strategy to control worker militancy during the early 20th century and, in a similar vein, pushed for reforms that would fit with the interests of employers (for example, pushing for the retention of the distinction between the deserving and undeserving poor). The key for employers, then as now, was to ensure that social provision did not undermine control over workers or the competitiveness of firms (Melling, 1991). For example, in 1925 the National Confederation of Employers' Organisations (NCEO) argued that:

> There is a definite limit to the amount of money which any country can afford to spend in the providing of Social Services. The purpose of the Statement is to show that the cost of these Services is more than the industry of this country can continue to bear and immeasurably greater than that which the industry of any other country is called upon to bear; that the existing cost of the Health Insurance Service is out of perspective in relation to the cost of the other Social Services; that the existing system of Health insurance is over-financed, and that an immediate and substantial reduction in the present rate of ... contributions can be effected. (Submitted to the Royal Commission on Health Insurance, 1925, cited in Rodgers, 1991, p 332)

Familiar arguments are being put here: public spending has ill effects on employers; the taxation of corporations in the UK should be commensurate with the burdens imposed on their competitors in other countries by other governments; and cuts are necessary in spending and contributions. According to Rodgers (1991), the Federation of British Industry, on the other hand, was more sanguine in its assessment of social provision, acknowledging its importance to post-First World War economic reconstruction, job security and the adequate maintenance of the growing numbers of the unemployed.

Such divisions as these were replicated in other areas of social reform. The NCEO, for example, opposed the 1930 Education Bill, which sought to raise the school leaving age and widen access to secondary education. According to

Rodgers (1991), the NCEO managed to persuade the government that raising the school leaving age beyond 14 would interfere with the supply of juvenile labour, increasing the costs on manufacturing industry and, therefore, leading to higher unemployment (Rodgers, 1991, p 336). In general, however, business has been supportive of increased educational provision (Hay, 1977, p 442).

Business is also reported to have been generally more positive about Beveridge's proposed reforms in the 1940s than they were about social legislation leading up to the Second World War. The war itself created conditions ripe for the expansion of social policy, and one of the important contributing factors was the reduction in corporate power. Most importantly, the Second World War meant the exertion of greater levels of state control over industrial production as well as the virtual halting of capital mobility. In addition to this, opposition to social reforms by major industrial interests paled in significance when compared with the need to maintain the morale and support of labour during this period. The immediate popularity of the Beveridge proposals among the general population persuaded the coalition government to ignore the demands of both the NCEO and the BEC that more time be given to a consideration of the reforms (Hay, 1978b, p 50; Harris, 1997, p 408). In all other ways, employers were remarkably sanguine in their approach to the Beveridge proposals, at least in their public pronouncements. The NCEO, for example, gave the Beveridge plans qualified support providing that the state – and not the unions – ran the schemes and that attention continued to be paid to overriding industrial performance (Hay, 1978b, p 48). More surprisingly, in 1942, prior to the publication of the Beveridge Report (1948), 120 industrialists formulated proposals for a range of social reforms to be implemented following the end of the war. These included:

- a minimum wage;
- sickness and disability allowances;
- paid holidays;
- family allowances;
- state pensions;
- affordable housing;
- an extended school leaving age (Hay, 1978a, pp 51-2; Timmins, 1996, p 40).

For Timmins (1996), this represented a common underlying move towards more active welfare policies, although it should be noted that these proposals also asked for generous government subsidies to industry.

While business' public responses to Beveridge were relatively positive, in private they were more reticent. The BEC and the Shipbuilders Employers Federation (SEF), for example, stated respectively that

> I want to say here – it will go on the shorthand note, but I do not know that I want to say it publicly – we did not start this war with Germany in order to improve our social services; the war was forced upon us by Germany and

we entered it to preserve our freedom. (Sir John Forbes Watson, Director of the BEC, speaking in response to the Beveridge Report, cited in Addison, 1977, p 214)

I am saying something I would not like printed – there may have been excellent reasons in the last war for talking about homes fit for heroes and there may be excellent reasons today for talking about improving the social services, but at the same time any of us who are trying to think at all do realize and do appreciate the problems after the war are not problems that the man in the street concerns himself about, and you may be causing a much greater degree of danger by telling him something which in fact even the most optimistic of us may fear will be impossible after the war. (J.S. Boyd, vice-president of the SEF in response to the Beveridge Report, cited in Addison, 1977, p 214)

The key to understanding business responses to Beveridge is to understand the impact reforms would have on them. For example, the insurance companies were said to initially favour the extension of unemployment insurance provided they could carry on selling their own policies or that they were allowed to manage the scheme (Harris, 1997, p 407). Their support waned, however, when the number of private insurance policies began to fall as a result of the state scheme (Harris, 1997, p 418). To be clear, support for social reforms was determined by the relative size of the burden businesses would have to face comapared with their competitors and the extent to which they could pass on the costs of state welfare to workers and consumers.

This brief review of British business opinion reveals a number of important findings:

- divisions within the business community based particularly on size and sector;
- changing business perspectives over time according to costs and the actions of labour and the state;
- the importance of the economy to the acceptance of reform by business;
- some evidence of initial opposition from business towards social reforms followed by grudging acceptance once it had been introduced.

Since business views and approaches to social policy are shaped by prevailing structures and institutional opportunities, we would expect to find variable approaches and varying degrees of influence over time. However, on the bigger questions of welfare state reforms it is nonetheless possible to extract reasonably constant business approaches over time. Here the work of Therborn (1984, 1986) and George (1998) are important. Dealing first with Therborn, his work documented the competing positions of business and labour on social policy and welfare reforms and, through this, formulated ideal-type welfare outcomes of these competing interests.

In order to gauge labour's position, Therborn looked at a number of programmes and resolutions of the First, Second and Third Internationals[2]. This, Therborn argued, revealed the perspectives of the labour movement on social reforms before it was shaped by parliamentary experiences. For the business perspective, Therborn looked at the responses of bourgeois parties to early welfare reforms together with more recent responses produced by the OECD Business and Industry Advisory Committee in 1981 (Therborn, 1986, pp 155-6). The results are summarised in Table 2.1.

Generally speaking, organised labour pushes for rights-based, universal and nationally based welfare systems, underpinned by full employment, income and wealth redistribution, and controlled by labour. Capital, on the other hand, tends to push for welfare that assists accumulation and profits, primarily by helping businesses to acquire a sufficiently skilled, loyal and flexible workforce. It also tends to push for income protection programmes that are selective, based on insurance and contributory principles, and controlled by employers (Therborn, 1986, pp 155-7).

Vic George's (1998) paper is based on a cross-national and collaborative study that investigated elite opinion (drawn from various groups across Europe including business associations, trades unions and political parties) on various social policies. Interview data revealed that the class divide between business and labour organisations was persistent and wider than party political differences.

Table 2.1: Ideal welfare types

Labour	Capital
Assertion of workers' rights above principles of insurance and charity and the requirements of capital accumulation, competitiveness and work incentives.	Welfare arrangements should be adapted to the requirements of capital accumulation, competitiveness and work incentives.
Priority task is for workers' protection (safety at work, leisure from work and union rights). Second top priority is the right to work, and employment under non-punitive conditions.	Priority task is to secure an adequately skilled, able and loyal workforce.
Administrative control of income maintenance schemes and welfare services to be in hands of unions. Bipartite or tripartite control is a second-best solution.	Administrative control should be in the hands of the employers or specialised private enterprise or associations. Bipartite or tripartite control is a second-best solution. Exclusive union or state control should be resisted.
Schemes should have wide coverage and uniform organisation of social institutions. Financing through redistribution – through progressive taxation or employers' contributions.	Coverage and organisation of schemes should not be universal and uniform. Financing of schemes should be based on insurance and contributory principles.

Source: compiled from Therborn (1986, pp 155-6)

Not surprisingly, the views of business and the political Right were broadly in line, as were those of the Left and trade unions. As far as social policy is concerned, business overwhelmingly supports private provision, means testing and deregulation. In each of these cases, trade unions hold the opposite views.

Conclusion

This discussion has highlighted and distinguished two forms of power: agency and structure. It has argued that each form is important today and both are interrelated. Most importantly, agency is exercised within a wider structural context. Their significance varies over time and between states. These conclusions are important for the rest of the book. The model of influence that was developed in the introduction suggested that, in order to influence through agency, business first needed to be interested in an area of social policy and then needed to follow this through. What this chapter has demonstrated is the sheer complexity of this process. Since structural power can determine policy outcomes, it is often not necessary for business to resort to agency. Should it do so, it has a number of means of direct and indirect influence. Business also holds real advantages here (such as privileged access to policy makers, access to networks and greater resources) over other groups. However, as I have mentioned already, business power and influence is variable over time. Business is split on many levels, and many forces and factors may impact on its power.

To be clear, then, both agency and structural power vary in relative importance over time. It also follows from this that both these forms of power may be variable between policy areas. The lessons this holds are that in trying to establish potential influence over social policy, it is necessary to consider each of the following:

- both agency and structural factors;
- how both structural and agency influences have changed over time;
- the variability of agency and structural influences between policy areas;
- varying business views over time and between policy areas;
- how and why different parts of business may try to influence social policy.

Notes

[1] One estimate (Leys, 1989, p 137) put the finances of these organisations above the combined funds of the Conservative and Labour parties during a typical election year.

[2] The various Internationals were successive attempts by the organised Left to unite and struggle for the socialist transformation of industrial societies. The First International was established in 1864, the Second in 1889, and the Third in 1919.

THREE

Globalisation, corporate structural power and social policy

Much has been written on globalisation and its impact on the politics and economies of nation states. Politicians and the media regularly highlight its dangers and opportunities, while academics from most disciplines debate its significance and implications for their own fields of study. Today it is almost impossible to discuss contemporary social and political problems without reference to the impact of globalisation. Such has been the speed with which the notion of globalisation has come to dominate contemporary thinking that, to repeat Hay and Watson's (1999, p 418) tongue-in-cheek assertion,

> To have no opinion on globalisation is effectively to disqualify oneself from having anything to say about the way our world looks as we reach the millennium.

So, what is globalisation, and why is it important? For a term that has so caught the imagination, there is considerable disagreement surrounding its meaning and impact. As Yeates (1999, p 373) points out, globalisation is

> a highly contested term whose frequent usage has obscured a lack of consensus with regard to what it entails, explanations of how it operates and the direction in which it is heading [and] is often used inconsistently, at times to describe trends, at other times to explain them.

At its simplest, globalisation refers to the dramatic increase in the flow of goods, services, economic stocks and information between people, firms and states, over increasingly large distances, since the 1970s. Political globalisation – the extension of political power and political activity across the boundaries of the nation state (Held et al, 1999, p 49) – is of growing importance as international and supranational governmental organisations such as the EU, the World Bank, the International Monetary Fund (IMF) and the World Trade Organisation (WTO) have increasing influence on governments. Although these organisations hold some relevance to structural power, however, their biggest impact is on corporate agency power (which is the focus of the next chapter). This chapter looks specifically at economic globalisation – the international growth of trade in goods and services and the increased movement of capital across borders – and its impact on corporate structural power which, in turn, has implications for social policy. The argument here is that globalisation impacts on the balance of power within capitalist states in favour of capital, and that this can have a negative impact on social policy, although this is neither inevitable nor uniform in its occurrence between states and over time. The task in this chapter is to gauge the extent to which economic globalisation impacts on corporate structural power and assess the possible implications of this for social provision.

Economic globalisation and the welfare state

According to Martin and Schumann (1997, p 7), economic globalisation acts as a 'pincer movement' that

> is turning whole countries and social orders upside down. On one front, it threatens to pull out altogether according to the circumstances of the hour, thus forcing massive tax reductions as well as subsidies running into billions ... or the provision of cost-free infrastructure.... If that doesn't work, tax-planning in the grand style can often help out: profits are revealed only in countries where the rate of taxation is really low.... On the other front, those who manage the global flows of capital are driving down the wage-levels of their tax-paying employees. Wages as a share of national wealth are declining world-wide; no single nation is capable of resisting the pressure.

Under such conditions, according to Deacon (1997, pp 195-6), welfare states are set "in competition with each other" with the result that social policies are subsequently eroded. According to Mishra (1998, p 485),

> Late twentieth-century globalization is dissolving the nexus between the economic and the social as it ... exalts the economic and downgrades the 'social', seeking to relegate it to the private sphere.

The main danger, predicted by some, is social dumping which is the result of increasing competition between states to attract inward investment through cutting taxation and social protection. According to Stryker (1998, p 13),

> Welfare retrenchment becomes part of the competition to attract foreign investment and to retain domestic capital since it enables what business groups desire – lower corporate taxes, lower wages and greater labor market flexibility.

The prognosis for democracy and social inclusion under such conditions appears bleak, with state actors unable to respond to the needs and demands of the electorate. Few tell this depressing story as well as Susan Strange (1996, pp 3-4):

> Today it seems that the heads of governments may be the last to recognise that they and their ministers have lost the authority over national societies

and economies that they used to have.... [I]mpersonal forces of world markets ... are now more powerful than the states to whom ultimate political authority over society and economy is supposed to belong. Where states were once the masters of markets, now it is the markets which, on many crucial issues, are the masters over the governments of states.

As if to prove that he himself does not suffer the delusion that governments have retained the authority they used to have, and to highlight the restrictions on his own government, Tony Blair explained in 1995 and 1999 respectively that:

> The determining context of economic policy is the new global market. That imposes huge limitations of a practical nature ... on macroeconomic policies. (Interview in *Financial Times*, 22 May 1995)

> If the markets don't like your policies they will punish you. (Speech to the Economic Club, Chicago, 23 April 1999)

Business, for its part, has also wasted few opportunities to remind governments of the gravity of the situation. Digby Jones, Director General of the Confederation of British Industry (CBI), used the occasion of the run-up to the 2001 general election to point out the dangers:

> Nobody can afford to ignore the shift towards a more globally competitive world in which investors and companies are extremely mobile. Any government must create an environment that not only attracts business but also encourages companies to stay. (CBI, 2000a)

Such pressures are, according to some important sources (Strange, 1988, 1996; George and Taylor-Gooby, 1996; Mishra, 1998, 1999; Alber and Standing, 2000), impacting on domestic policies in clear and predictable ways. Taxation systems are being undermined and becoming less progressive; states are finding it increasingly difficult to tax capital; and government subsidies are being redirected away from labour and towards capital (Whitfield, 2001a, pp 142-64). As a result, the welfare state is being undermined, with social protection systems being transformed into more selective and more minimalist business-oriented social policy regimes.

Globalisation threatens the future of the welfare state: this much is clear. Or is it? In actual fact, the evidence is much less clear-cut. Recent history has not necessarily followed the predictions of what Yeates (2001) refers to as the 'strong' globalisation theorists and Held et al (1999) refer to as the 'hypoglobalists'. Two key countervailing arguments have been formulated.

The first questions the accuracy of the term 'globalisation' as a description of recent trends in financial and information flows. Hirst and Thompson (1996) argue, for example, that financial flows and foreign trade have actually increased

35

very little as a proportion of world GDP since the early part of the 20th century. In fact, they argue, the world was as globalised at the beginning of the 20th century as it was at the end. Hirst and Thompson also point out that, rather than being global, increased trade and investment flows since the 1970s are, for the most part, restricted to the triad of North America, Japan and Europe. It is certainly the case, as Chapter Two of this book argued, that corporations are in reality less mobile than is sometimes believed. Most transnationals have identifiable national-bases and many expand into other regions as much for access to new markets as to take advantage of cheap labour or low taxation (Yeates, 1999, pp 48-55). Once companies have branches elsewhere the possibilities for switching production between various branches of the company increase. A decision by a firm to shift investment elsewhere does not necessarily entail the complete closure of plant in one country and the opening up of new factories in another. Rather, it is more likely to mean a decision to expand production in other parts of the company based in other jurisdictions. The ability of corporations to switch production in this way will essentially depend on the costs of rebuilding plant elsewhere, or for some industries their dependence on raw materials within particular localities.

The issue of capital mobility is, of course, central to structural power. But the extent of structural power is not necessarily related to the degree of capital's global reach. In fact, regionalisation can amplify structural power to a greater extent than would be the case were capital truly global. This is especially true within the EU, where mobility is high but political institutions are weak, although moves towards common regulations on labour, such as the Social Charter, have mitigated against structural pressures to some extent. Thus, 'Europeanisation' is as important to growing structural power as globalisation. The influx of capital into Europe from North America and East Asia has also clearly encouraged nation states to actively compete with each other for new investment, although some states, most notably the UK, have been more eager to play this competitive game than others. The most recent countries to do so were those due to join the EU in 2004. In June 2003 alone, both Slovakia and Poland announced their plans to reduce their corporate tax rates to 19% from 25% and 27% respectively, and the Czech Republic announced plans to cut its rate from 31% to 24% by 2006 (Testault, 2003). This point will be expounded later.

When reviewing the actual mobility of capital, it also has to be borne in mind that mobile industrial capital is only one aspect of economic globalisation. More highly mobile financial capital is also extremely important to the exercise of structural power (Singh, 1999, Ch 1). Strange (1988, p 30) argued in the late 1980s that this facet of structural power had risen faster since the 1960s than any other. Since new investment within countries is often dependent on international company mergers and the availability of foreign credit, financial capital is increasingly important to the structural constraints faced by national governments (Swank, 1992).

The second counter to the globalisation thesis maintains that the impact of globalisation on states has more to do with politicians than transformations in contemporary capitalism. According to Gordon (cited in Wilding, 1997, p 414), globalisation has become "a spreading political fatalism in the advanced countries" where politicians have become convinced that competitive economies are incompatible with welfare provision and regulations on business. Hay (1999) similarly seeks to demonstrate that the imagined consequences of globalisation on welfare states are far greater than the reality and that politicians have overreacted to it with negative consequences for welfare. The suggestion is that the political fatalism that accompanies globalisation owes more to the spread and dominance of free market ideas, propagated by business, than to the intrinsic qualities of globalisation per se.

Such arguments are important reminders that governments, and other interests within nation states, retain a great deal of power, influence and autonomy under globalisation, yet it is important not to play down the lengths to which some states must go in order to maintain or increase levels of investment within a country *regardless of the preferences of politicians*. This is not to argue that states do not have any freedom to act – but their freedom is often circumscribed, not least by the legacies of previous policy decisions (Pierson, 1994, pp 39-50). Regardless of the theoretical choices they may have, many states have felt compelled to adjust domestic policies in order to attract new investment through reducing corporate taxation, relaxing controls over labour and cutting levels of social provision. Any reversal of these policies – or attempts to buck current policy trends by increasing corporate taxation, labour regulations and social provision – could put at risk existing and future investments. The level of this risk will depend on how a country has been 'sold' to investors in the past, and how quickly the economy is able to adjust to different ways of securing investments in future. However, within the prevailing global climate, it is far more difficult to expand welfare and taxation than to reduce them. In this respect, even if it is the case that globalisation has given birth to political fatalism, this fatalism has increased capital's structural power over the state and labour, although, as this chapter will later illustrate, this exertion of power has frequently been uneven between states. Moreover, if the threat of capital flight has been exaggerated in the minds of policy makers, international and national business interests have been complicit in generating such scares. The net result has been the promotion of corporate power. The aim of the rest of this chapter is to investigate more fully how, and to what extent, globalisation impacts on corporate structural power before outlining the possible implications of this for social policy in future.

Assessing the impact of globalisation on corporate structural power

The following sections of this chapter present some simple measures of changing corporate structural power as outlined in Chapter Two: control over investment, state revenue dependence, and power over labour. The analysis traces some factors that may increase or decrease these forms of power within nation states.

Control over investment, capital mobility and opportunities for exit

Capital's first source of structural power is its control over investment. Since this is a key source of business power over society and the state, the share of such investment in total investment should provide a critical measure of its variability. The higher the share of investment undertaken by the private sector, the greater the dependence of the state and labour on the investment decisions of capital. Table 3.1 shows the shares of total fixed capital formation undertaken by the public and the private sector (the remainder is by the household sector). Since the mid-1970s, public investment has fallen sharply in Germany, the US and the UK which experienced the biggest fall, from over 25% to just over 12%. Meanwhile, the share of private corporate investment has risen in most countries.

A more important determinant and indicator of structural power is the extent of capital mobility. Increased capital mobility between states is, of course, one of the key arguments behind growing corporate power under globalisation. To measure the extent of mobility, indicators are needed of both the constraints over capital mobility between political jurisdictions and of the extent of capital flows in practice. An indication of the expanding importance of foreign investment is provided in Table 3.1. The extent of capital mobility can be illustrated with reference to levels of foreign direct investment flows across borders. This increased sharply in all countries apart from Japan.

Table 3.2 illustrates the growing significance of inward and outward investment flows as a percentage of home country GDP. Increased dependence on foreign investments, as opposed to domestic investments, will generally place states in a more vulnerable position, since policy has to be geared towards the needs of relatively footloose and disloyal forms of capital. This is especially the case in the UK, which has the highest level of inward Foreign Direct Investment (FDI) as a percentage of GDP when compared with other G7 countries, and receives almost 25% of the total inward investment into Western Europe (Held, 1999, p 249). At the same time, the UK also has the highest level of outward FDI, which in 2000 was almost double the equivalent rate of the next highest country, Canada. This, together with the fact that the UK has historically had relatively low levels of domestic business investment (Gamble, 1990; Bond and Jenkinson, 1996), creates disproportionate dependency on mobile capital.

The figures presented so far confirm that most economies have become more open under globalisation. Further confirmation of this is provided by Quinn and Inclan (1997) who provide an index of 'openness' for six countries (US, UK, Germany, France, Japan and Italy) based on the extent to which these economies are 'open' to internationally mobile capital. According to this measure, all of these countries became more open since the 1950s, with the UK, US and

Table 3.1: Composition of gross fixed capital formation (% of total gross fixed capital formation)

	1975	1980	1985	1990	1995
France					
Government	15.8	12.7	16.3	15.1	17.2
Domestic capital	44.7	43.0	48.8	50.3	49.9
Foreign capital			2.2	6.0	7.4
Germany (West Germany before 1995)					
Government	19.5	14.5	11.5	10.4	11.2
Domestic capital	83.2	82.0	88.2	85.9	85.3
Foreign capital			0.4	1.5	0.7
Italy					
Government		11.8	16.6	15.6	12.5
Domestic capital		29.4	30.8	42.0	36.7
Foreign capital			1.1	1.7	1.8
Japan					
Government			16.9	15.6	22.5
Domestic capital			55.4	58.7	53.4
Foreign capital			0.2	0.1	0.0
UK					
Government	25.4	14.5	11.2	12.0	12.3
Domestic capital	62.1	68.0	61.8	63.7	58.3
Foreign capital			7.6	15.2	10.6
US					
Government	12.5	9.3	8.1	10.8	10.1
Domestic capital	53.3	54.0	49.4	49.7	55.2
Foreign capital			2.5	5.0	5.4

Source: OECD Statistical Compendium (National Accounts) (1997, table 1); OECD International Direct Investment Statistics (1996)

Germany revealed as the most open economies. The ability of states to control financial capital has therefore been reduced and the structural power of capital has increased accordingly (for a discussion see Farnsworth and Gough, 2000). The ability of most countries to control financial capital has become extremely weakened under these conditions. The exposure of most countries to multinationals has also increased rapidly in recent years (see Table 3.3). In Canada, the UK and France, foreign manufacturers now account for more than 30% of total production. The biggest growth in the significance of foreign firms in production between 1981 and 1995 has been experienced by the US and the UK, although less than 16% of manufacturing, almost half the UK figure, is accounted for by foreign firms in the US.

Table 3.2: Inward and outward FDI stocks as a percentage of home country GDP

	1980	1985	1990	1995	2000
Canada					
Inward	20.4	18.4	19.6	21.1	28.8
Outward	8.9	12.3	14.7	20.3	32.4
France					
Inward	8.2	12.6	8.2	12.3	19.9
Outward	3.6	7.1	9.9	13.2	33.4
Italy					
Inward	2.0	4.5	5.3	5.8	10.5
Outward	1.6	3.9	5.2	8.8	16.8
Germany					
Inward	3.9	5.1	7.1	7.8	24.1
Outward	4.6	8.4	8.8	10.5	25.2
Japan					
Inward	0.3	0.3	0.3	0.6	1.1
Outward	1.8	3.2	6.6	4.5	5.8
UK					
Inward	11.8	14.1	20.6	17.6	30.5
Outward	15.0	22.0	23.2	26.9	63.2
US					
Inward	3.0	4.4	6.9	7.3	12.4
Outward	7.8	5.7	7.5	9.5	13.2

Source: UNCTAD (2002, table B.6)

Table 3.3: Share of foreign affiliates in manufacturing production (%)

	1981	1988	1995
Canada		27.3	31.2
France	29.4	28.4	31.0
Germany	16.7	13.1	12.8
Japan	4.7	2.4	2.5
Italy	16.9	21.3	24.6
UK	19.3	20.2	30.5
US	7.0	10.6	15.7

Source: Coppel and Durand (1999, table 6)

State revenue dependence

A frequent, although increasingly challenged, argument within the international relations and globalisation literature is that there is an inverse relationship between the share of taxation levied on business and corporate structural power. This argument was summed up in an influential report published by the OECD entitled *Beyond 2000: The new social policy agenda* (OECD, 1997a), which stated that:

The growing integration of capital markets world-wide has reduced governments' ability to tax mobile capital. The result is that social protection expenditure is predominantly financed by taxes on labour. (OECD, 1997, p 10)

Ian Gough and I (Farnsworth and Gough, 2000) have also previously argued that increased corporate structural power should be reflected in the changing relative share of taxation levied on capital. Under increasing structural power, taxation levied on businesses, through employers' social security contributions and taxation on profits, would be expected to decline while labour's contribution would be expected to increase. The problem then, as now, is that corporate taxation is extremely difficult to gauge and interpret for the reasons outlined below.

Focusing on headline rates provides the simplest method. Looking at Figure 3.1, there is a clear trend towards reductions in headline rates. The UK actually had the second highest rate in 1979, but by 1999 had the lowest of its major competitors. Some convergence also occurred. Seventeen percentage points separated the lowest and highest rates in 1979, but by 1999 this had narrowed to ten percentage points.

These headline rates of taxation act as highly visible 'signs' of business-friendliness within a nation state, and they are openly paraded by governments on the international stage in order to attract inward investment (discussed later in this chapter). What they do not reveal, however, is the total taxation levied on corporations or the relative tax burden imposed on businesses. However, such measures of corporate taxation introduce more complexities and problems.

Figure 3.1: Headline corporate taxation rates

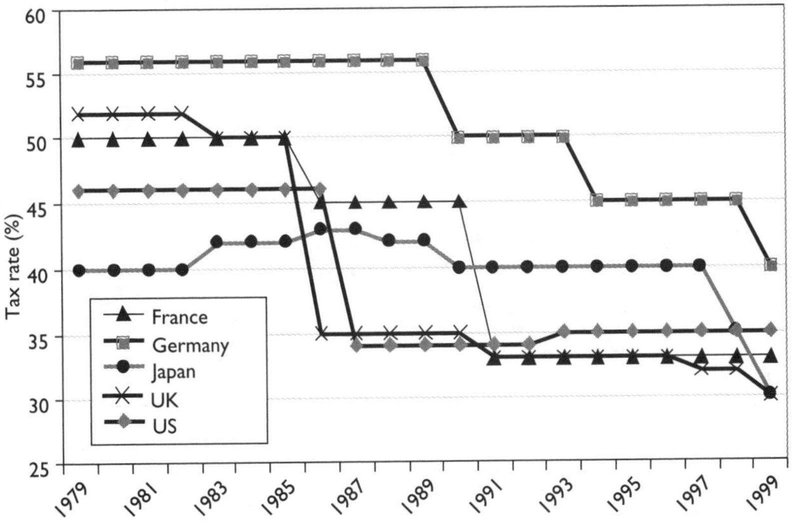

Source: Bond and Chennells (2000)

To begin with, individual companies (especially large transnationals) may make counter-claims on state finances in the form of government subsidies or tax-exemption schemes that are not properly accounted for in the figures. Second, the volume of corporate tax paid will naturally vary with profitability and with policies to broaden the tax base. Thus, taxation paid by corporations remained relatively high in the 1980s, despite sharp reductions in headline rates. Third, the ability of corporations to transfer capital and distribution centres to lower tax regimes and declare intra-company sales and profits in such regimes, also complicates matters[1]. Clearly, we cannot simply take the amount of corporate taxation paid as a solid indicator of corporate power. Increases in corporate tax revenues due to higher company profits or increased capital flows to lower tax countries would hardly suggest declining corporate power, nor would the ability of transnational corporations to win more generous direct and indirect financial support.

Given these complications, it is not surprising to find that the share of overall taxes levied on corporations is mixed and uneven across countries (Table 3.4). This share fluctuates cyclically in all countries, and in the case of the UK, increased between 1965 and 1985 before falling and stabilising in the 1990s. The other G7 countries followed similar patterns, with some convergence occurring at the end of the 1990s from very different starting points. This is more clearly illustrated in Figure 3.2. Twenty-three percentage points divided the highest and lowest shares of taxation in 1975, but by 1995 this had been reduced to 13. From this relatively small sample, two clusters are revealed: the US, UK and Canada clustering around a corporate tax share of around 20%; Italy, France and Japan around 30%.

Figure 3.2: Corporate taxation as a percentage of total taxation (1965-97)

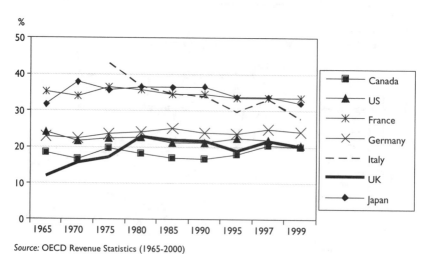

Source: OECD Revenue Statistics (1965-2000)

Table 3.4: Corporate taxation as a percentage of total taxation (1965-99) (selected countries)

	1965	1970	1975	1980	1985	1990	1995	1997	1999
Canada									
Taxes on income	14.9	11.3	13.6	11.6	8.2	7.0	7.1	10.3	9.8
Employers' social security contributions	3.5	5.3	6.1	6.6	8.6	7.5	8.6	8.1	8.0
Payroll taxes	–	–	–	–	–	2.2	2.3	2.1	2.1
Total	**18.4**	**16.6**	**19.7**	**18.2**	**16.8**	**16.7**	**18.0**	**20.5**	**19.9**
France									
Taxes on income	5.3	6.3	5.2	5.1	4.5	5.3	4.8	5.8	6.4
Employers' social security contributions	25.3	26.6	29.3	28.4	28.0	27.2	26.2	25.2	25.0
Payroll taxes	4.6	1.2	1.9	2.2	2.1	1.9	2.5	2.5	2.1
Total	**35.2**	**34.1**	**36.4**	**35.7**	**34.6**	**34.4**	**33.5**	**33.5**	**33.5**
Germany									
Taxes on income	7.8	5.7	4.4	5.5	6.1	4.8	3.8	4.0	4.8
Employers' social security contributions	14.4	16.1	18.3	18.4	18.9	19.1	19.9	20.9	19.3
Payroll taxes	0.6	0.6	0.8	0.2	–	–	–	–	–
Total	**22.8**	**22.4**	**23.5**	**24.1**	**25.0**	**23.9**	**23.7**	**24.9**	**24.1**
Italy									
Taxes on income	6.9	6.5	6.3	7.8	9.2	10.0	8.7	9.5	7.7
Employers' social security contributions	–	–	36.8	28.4	24.8	23.6	20.7	23.5	20.0
Payroll taxes	–	–	–	0.6	0.6	0.3	0.3	0.1	0.0
Total	**6.9**	**6.5**	**43.1**	**36.8**	**34.6**	**33.9**	**29.7**	**33.1**	**27.7**
Japan									
Taxes on income	22.2	26.3	20.6	21.8	21.0	21.6	15.3	15.0	12.9
Employers' social security contributions	9.5	11.6	15.1	14.8	15.4	15.0	18.5	18.8	19.1
Payroll taxes	–	–	–	–	–	–	–	–	–
Total	**31.7**	**37.9**	**35.7**	**36.6**	**36.4**	**36.6**	**33.8**	**33.8**	**32.0**
UK									
Taxes on income	4.4	8.7	6.2	8.4	12.6	11.6	9.4	12.1	10.4
Employers' social security contributions	7.6	7.1	10.9	10.1	9.2	10.0	9.6	9.6	9.7
Payroll taxes	–	–	–	–	–	–	–	–	–
Total	**12.0**	**15.8**	**17.1**	**18.5**	**21.8**	**21.6**	**19.0**	**21.7**	**20.1**
US									
Taxes on income	16.4	13.2	11.4	10.8	7.5	7.7	9.4	9.4	8.3
Employers' social security contributions	7.6	8.5	10.9	11.9	13.7	13.4	13.0	12.5	12.2
Payroll taxes	–	–	–	–	–	–	–	–	–
Total	**24.0**	**21.7**	**22.3**	**22.7**	**21.2**	**21.1**	**22.4**	**21.9**	**20.5**

Source: OECD (2001, tables 13, 19 and 21)

While it would be incorrect to argue, from this small sample, that corporate taxation has been cut in all countries as a result of globalisation, it would appear to be the case that higher tax regimes have cut corporate taxation faster than lower tax regimes. All states, apart from Canada, which began with the lowest corporate tax-take, have either cut or stabilised corporate taxation since the early 1980s. This may indicate that tax competition has occurred, where countries are prepared to see corporate taxation increase, provided it does not creep higher than its major competitors.

Such a conclusion would not, however, meet with universal support. Debates over the impact of increased capital mobility have become especially heated in recent years. Quinn and Shapiro (1991), Garrett (1998) and Swank (2002), for example, find little evidence to suggest a link between globalisation and taxation on business. Bretschger and Hettich (2000, pp 25-6), on the other hand, challenge the basis on which most empirical research is carried out and, after making appropriate adjustments, concluded that, for 14 OECD countries between 1967 and 1996, "globalisation has indeed a negative and significant impact on corporate taxes". Devereux et al (2001, 2002) find strong evidence to suggest that countries compete over statutory rates and effective marginal rates of corporate taxation. After reviewing the empirical evidence, Swank and Steinmo (2002, p 651) conclude that: "From the early 1980s to the mid-1990s, governments across the developed democracies have systematically lowered statutory rates on corporate and personal income", but they conclude that this coincides with stability in the incidence of tax burdens between capital and labour. Finally, Genschel (2002) argues that although the thesis that globalisation places pressure on states to reduce corporate taxation is both empirically and theoretically correct, this has not led to a race to the bottom because globalisation has also created countervailing pressures on governments to maintain spending. What globalisation has done is prevent governments from responding to these pressures in the 'usual' way – through increases in spending. All states have had to try to deal with the dilemmas this presents, and most, as a result, have suffered significant fiscal pressures and failings (Genschel, 2002, p 266).

This evidence would suggest that the extent of the impact of globalisation on nation states depends on a range of economic, political and institutional factors. The impact of capital mobility on taxation rates is likely to vary. The reactions of states to structural pressures also play a key role here. Putting the empirical evidence to one side, it is important to note that some countries have openly engaged in tax competition with other states and have themselves publicly advertised their low tax regimes in order to lure new company investment (as detailed later in this chapter). In such environments, the true impact of globalisation on corporate taxes will depend on the nature of the economy in question – its relative dependence on inward investments and its willingness to compete on the basis of low taxation. I will return to this point later.

Power over labour

The relative power of capital vis-à-vis labour can be assessed using a variety of indices. First, a surplus of potential workers over jobs will undermine labour and empower capital; the rate of unemployment is a basic, if crude, index of capital's power relative to labour. Second, the lower the cost of job loss, the greater will be labour's ability to stand up to employers over wages and/or conditions of work. This will be affected by the existence of alternatives to wages, notably the generosity, coverage and access to public welfare benefits in cash and in kind. Esping-Andersen's (1990) concept of decommodification is directly relevant here. Third, the ease with which capital can control, hire and fire labour is not only crucial in affecting profitability; it is also another determinant of the relative distribution of power. Labour has two countervailing powers to set against capitalist control over the labour process. One consists of state regulation, and is discussed later; the other comprises trade unions. Extensive trades union membership and cohesive union organisation not only enhance the relative agency power of labour but can also be interpreted as a constraint on both the structural and agency power of capital.

Beginning with unemployment, high levels of unemployment undermine the bargaining position of labour for higher wages and, at the same time, reduce the chances of labour finding new employment opportunities if investment falls. On this measure, Table 3.5 suggests that the relative power of capital continued to rise with each of the time periods since the 1960s. The US and the UK are the exceptions to this, with unemployment in the US falling since the mid-1980s and in the UK since the mid-1990s. For all countries, apart from the US, unemployment for all periods since the 1970s is higher than it was during the postwar period up until the 1960s. In the US, unemployment has generally been higher until the mid-1980s. On this simple measure, the structural power of capital has been strengthened overall since the 1960s.

The second measure, a low concentration of trades union membership, will, all other things being equal, weaken the bargaining position of labour, and make it less likely that unions will engage in the lengthy battles necessary in order to win concessions from employers. Under such condiitons, employees will be less likely, and less able, to challenge the hegemonic position of capital.

Table 3.5: Unemployment rates (1963-2000)

	1963-73	1974-85	1986-96	1996-2000
UK	2.2	6.7	8.5	6.5
France	2.3	6.4	10.6	11.0
Germany (West Germany until 1996)	0.9	4.9	7.3	8.9
Italy	4.0	6.1	10.3	11.3
Japan	1.3	2.2	2.6	4.0
US	4.7	7.5	6.2	4.6

Sources: OECD (*Employment outlook*, July 1997, table 3.2); OECD (*Employment outlook*, 2002, statistical annex, table A)

Table 3.6: Trade union density (trade union membership as a percentage of those in work)

	1980	1990	1994	2000
UK	50	39	34	29
France	18	10	9	9
Germany	36	33	29	30[a]
Italy	49	39	39	35.4[a]
Japan	31	25	24	21.5
US	22	16	16	13.5

[a] 1998 figures – more recent data was not available at the time.

Sources: OECD (*Employment outlook*, July 1997, table 3.3); Carley (2001, table 2)

Table 3.6 illustrates clearly the sharp fall in trades union density since the 1980s.

Third, the opportunity costs to labour of unemployment have also to be taken into account. These will be primarily affected by the extent to which the welfare state enables workers and their families to sustain a socially acceptable standard of living regardless of their ability to participate in the labour market. Should social citizenship rights supplant wages in part, the structural dependence of labour on capital is then reduced. This is what Esping-Andersen (1990) attempted to gauge in his measure of 'decommodification'. The extent to which unemployment benefits decommodify labour in his study is based on unemployment benefit replacement rates, the duration of benefits, the proportion of workers covered by the various schemes and measures of benefit eligibility. Table 3.7 presents his overall decommodification score for the unemployed in 1980 together with an imitation score calculated for 1992 by Fawcett and Papadopoulos (1997). The higher the score, the more decommodified the economy and, therefore, the less dependent labour is on business. Together these scores show that for Germany and France the decommodification of labour increased over the period. However, the UK, together with Italy, moved

Table 3.7: The decommodification potential of unemployment insurance (1980 and 1992) and the strictness of employment protection regulation (1989)

	The decommodification potential of unemployment insurance, Esping-Andersen index		Strictness of employment protection regulation[c]	
	1980[a]	1992[b]	Late 1980s	Late 1990s
UK	7.2	6.8	0.5	0.5
France	6.3	11.3	2.7	3.0
Germany	7.9	11.6	3.2	2.5
Italy	5.1	3.0	4.1	3.3
Japan				2.4
US			0.2	0.2

Sources: [a] Esping-Andersen (1990); [b] Fawcett and Papadopoulos (1997); [c] OECD (*Employment outlook*, 1999)

in the opposite direction – labour was partially re-commodified in the 1980s. On this basis, the structural power of capital over labour was reinforced in the UK.

Table 3.7 also presents an index of the strictness of employment protection regulation calculated by the OECD and Table 3.8 ranks selected OECD countries according to labour market flexibility scores compiled from survey data collected by the World Economic Forum and presented in its Global Competitiveness Report for 2001-02. Each clearly illustrates relatively low labour controls and relatively high labour market flexibility in the UK and the US.

The 1980s and 1990s, then, witnessed a general resurgence in the structural power of capital over labour based on these various measures. Business power has expanded most in the UK. Its economy is lightly regulated and flexible in relation to some of its major competitors.

Facilitating corporate structural power? The role of international institutions

The introductory sections of this chapter highlighted the growing influence of international governmental organisations (IGOs) such as the EU, World Bank, the IMF and the WTO on governments. The following section considers the increasingly important role IGOs play in enhancing and reinforcing corporate structural power.

It is worth pointing out from the outset that supranational and international governmental organisations are not subject to structural power in the same way that governments are. The key structural mechanisms relating to the unequal dependency of governments and labour on capital do not impact in the same way on international or even supranational bodies, such as the institutions of the EU. The most important tool of corporate structural power, the investment

Table 3.8: Rank of labour market flexibility in selected countries

1997	2001
UK	US
US	UK
Ireland	Luxembourg
Netherlands	Ireland
Portugal	Spain
Luxembourg	Finland
Spain	Austria
Austria	Netherlands
France	Italy
Germany	Portugal
Belgium	Belgium
Finland	Germany
Italy	France

Source: World Economic Forum (2002, table 4)

strike, is clearly meaningless at the international level, and even at the level of the governing institutions of the EU. European Union policy makers would not necessarily worry were corporations to relocate to other EU countries and know that the benefits to business of relocating outside EU markets are limited. Free and unhindered access to European markets is far too great for many companies to contemplate wholesale relocation. As a result, corporations have to rely much more heavily on agency in order to influence policy decisions at the international and supranational level, as Chapter Four makes clear. Although structural power does not impact directly on IGOs, however, international politics can play a significant role in reinforcing and amplifying structural power within nation states. As Deacon (1997, p 10) put it,

> The social policy of a country or locality is no longer wholly shaped ... by the politics of the national government. It is increasingly shaped ... by the implicit and explicit social policies of numerous supranational agencies, ranging from global institutions like the World Bank and the International Monetary Fund, through supranational bodies such as the OECD and the European Commission....

These IGOs play an increasingly important role in advising and even determining the policies of nation states (Strange, 1988, pp 112-14; Deacon, 1997). The problem is that, until recently, these organisations have tended to push very narrow ideas, influenced by US politics and neoliberal economics. The effect has been to push welfare states towards unregulated and flexible labour markets as well as deregulated and open industrial and financial markets (Cerny, 1997, p 259; Martin and Schumann, 1997, p 7; Crouch and Streeck, 1997; Mishra, 1999; George and Wilding, 2002). The neoliberal 'Washington Consensus' that has dominated international politics since the early 1980s has promoted, according to Stiglitz (2002, p 51), "fiscal austerity, privatisation and market liberalisation". Within the IMF and the World Bank this has been translated into neoliberal conditionality rules that require trade liberalisation and public spending cuts as a precondition to loans or other funds. The IMF, World Bank and OECD have promoted neoliberal solutions which, according to Mishra (1999, p 124), have required

> governments to reduce national debts and deficits mainly through slashing social expenditure and privatizing social welfare [in what amounts to a] supranational steering of social policy in a neoliberal direction.

This supranational steering of social policy is, according to Stiglitz (2002, p 81), prescriptive and narrow in terms of the policies that are generally considered:

> Stabilization is on the agenda; job creation is off. Taxation, as its adverse effects, are on the agenda; land reform is off. There is money to bail out banks but not to pay for improved education and health services, let alone

to bail out workers who are thrown out of their jobs as a result of the IMF's macroeconomic mismanagement.

This circumscribed policy arena is partly the outcome of institutional domination of IGOs by the US. As Wade (2002) points out with respect to the World Bank,

> The US in effect chooses the president of the Bank, and the president has always been a US citizen. It has by far the largest share of votes (17 percent as compared to number two Japan's 6 percent and number 3 Germany's 4.7 ...). On some issues it can exercise a veto, the only member state able to do so on its own.

The extent to which neoliberalism is embedded into social policy making can be illustrated with reference to the OECD's (1994) Jobs Study. This influential report recommended that governments tackle inflation, increase wage and employee flexibility, eliminate "impediments to the creation and expansion of enterprises", relax regulations on employment, increase employee skills and reform social protection systems to ensure they do not impinge on labour markets (OECD, 1994, p 2).

Despite the recent dominance of neoliberal ideas, however, several authors have pointed to policy differences between IGOs. Deacon (1997, pp 70-1), for example, argues that, in contrast to the IMF and World Bank, the OECD has historically tended to take a more positive view towards social policy. Deacon (2000) also detects a change at the international level towards a more "socially responsible globalisation" within the World Bank and the IMF. He draws particular attention to the changing rhetoric of IGOs on social policy, typified by the OECD's 1998 Social Policy Ministerial Meeting entitled 'The New Social Policy Agenda for a Caring World' and the subsequent report, published in 1999, entitled *A caring world: A new social policy agenda*. Both acknowledged the positive role that good social policy can play in competitive states. The latter also went on to acknowledge that social policy may be made more necessary, rather than less, under the conditions of globalisation.

While Deacon may be right in discerning a rhetorical move against neoliberalism and towards a more socially responsible globalisation, this does not detract from the continuing impact of neoliberal ideas on economic and social policies at the international level in practice. Nor, on balance, does it yet pose any significant challenge to the corporate agenda. The key policy solutions offered in *A caring world* still tend towards basic and targeted welfare provision, complimented by private provision. It also continues to stress the importance of supply-side labour market solutions such as welfare to work, lifelong learning and work flexibility for carers. These solutions are, in fact, remarkably close to international business opinion, as the next chapter illustrates. Its less hostile views towards social policy make no mention of 'classic' solutions to inequality, such as redistribution through the taxation system, but instead tend to promote similar proposals for productive welfare as those advocated by business.

More importantly, there are reasons to question the extent to which this more socially responsible globalisation is presenting any real challenge to structural power. Wade (2002), for example, points to the gap between the aspirations and beliefs of political and social reformers and the policy prescriptions of economic reformers within IGOs such as the World Bank. On the one hand, as a political organisation, the World Bank reflects and affirms the beliefs of its constituents and other interested parties as increasing expectations and demands are placed on it to tackle poverty and social exclusion. As a result of the strength of international political opposition typified by the anti-capitalist/anti-globalisation movement and general declining legitimacy (Farnsworth, 2003), the World Bank must try to deliver in these areas (Wade, 2002, pp 218-19). On the other hand, such endeavours are constantly challenged and undermined by the more powerful finance arm of the bank, which remains firmly committed to core neoliberal solutions to economic and social problems (Wade, 2002, p 219). Although Wade acknowledges that the finance lobby has conceded some ground in recent years, so there is now some agreement on the importance of limited state intervention in education and healthcare, this has served to further strengthen its commitment to certain core values, including privatisation and greater trade liberalisation (Wade, 2002, p 21). Allowing the Bank to develop in this way is convenient for the Right since it legitimates its activities while, at the same time, the institutional weakness of the 'alternative' social project prevents it from seriously challenging neoliberal policies.

The World Bank's Private Sector Development Strategy (PSDS), launched in 2001, is a good illustration of this. Although the PSDS was presented by the Bank as a mechanism for facilitating growth and tackling poverty, this initiative is primarily designed to promote competitiveness and privatisation (Bayliss and Hall, 2001, 2002). Under the PSDS, greater emphasis will be placed on targeting subsidies to NGOs and loans to help develop private markets through the direct funding of private services rather than providing monies for government purchases. The fear is that this will place even greater pressure, through a different set of mechanisms, on states to privatise services.

Lending by the World Bank and IMF is also often conditional on changes in public policy, imposed through structural adjustment policies which demand privatisation, social spending cuts, lower levels of taxation, expansion of exports of natural resources, and the removal of restrictions on foreign investments and trade barriers (Stiglitz, 2002).

The WTO has also operated to strengthen neoliberalism. Established in 1995, the WTO's main function has been to ensure trade liberalism and, in carrying out this task, it has tended to add to the structural power of international business. Within current WTO rules, any member state can challenge the laws of any other member country should it believe that they present unreasonable barriers to trade (Retallack, 1997). Once an accusation of unfair trading practices has been made against a country, the onus is on the 'accused' to defend itself to the WTO's satisfaction. Should it fail to do so, it could face fines and trade sanctions until it makes the necessary changes to its laws and practices. According to Retallack (1997) and Korten (1995, p 175), the WTO tends to rule in favour of large corporations. Under WTO rules, states cannot impose trade barriers on the basis of health or environmental concerns unless scientific proof can be put forward in defence of the decision. It was on this basis that the EU's ban on US hormone-treated beef was ruled illegal in 1999 (Monbiot, 1999; Derber, 2002, p 122).

The WTO and OECD-sponsored Multilateral Agreement on Investment (MAI) would also have allowed corporations to seek financial redress from states which hindered their investments within another state (Davis and Bishop, 1998-99). The MAI raised a number of concerns among NGOs, activists and some governments that it would further empower corporations and undermine national sovereignty, transferring power to an unelected IGO (in this case the WTO). Although the MAI negotiations failed in the face of widespread political opposition in 1998, a more recent development, the WTO's General Agreement on Trade in Services (GATS), was more successful.

The GATS was signed by many governments, including the UK, in 2002. Its primary aim is to open up services to international trade through reducing state provision and lifting barriers to trade. More worryingly, this agreement could place pressure on states to open up a range of state services, including social policies, to the private sector. The problem is that the definition of services within the agreement is so wide as to include social policies such as education, care services and health provision (Price et al, 1999; Cohen, 2002; Ellis-Jones and Hardstaff, 2002). Subsidies designed exclusively for the voluntary or public sectors could be challenged, therefore, on the grounds that they create barriers to competition by companies keen to access multibillion-pound 'markets'. The WTO (2003) has sought to reassure its critics that the agreement excludes those services that are "supplied neither on a commercial basis nor in competition with other suppliers". The problem, as Cohen (2002) points out, is that welfare services are becoming increasingly difficult to define as strictly public and non-profit making. State schools that are managed by the private sector and public health systems that treat private patients are two such cases that cross the public–private divide. The GATS agreement also commits governments to launch "successive rounds of services negotiations with a view to achieving a progressively higher level of liberalization" (WTO, 2003). Whether or not GATS will indeed impact on public services in the ways feared by its critics remains to be seen.

International governmental organisations thus amplify corporate structural power in a number of ways. States do voluntarily adjust policies in order to attract foreign investments, but IGOs play an increasing role in either encouraging or forcing states to open up their economies to foreign capital and to adopt free-market solutions.

As already noted, closer political union provides the EU member states with greater capacity to resist structural power. By establishing more uniformity in fiscal and social policy, the EU is well placed to prevent nation states from driving down social costs in order to attract mobile capital. However, the pace of economic union has far outstripped political union with the result that business has been given far more mobility within Europe without having to face commensurate controls over the rates of taxation levied on corporations or regulations over the employment of labour. Rather, states have faced incentives to reduce corporate taxation and labour regulations in order to compete for investment flowing into Europe.

It is also important to note here the role of government in increasing corporate power. International negotiations on trade and other regulations are undertaken by national governments, often acting in the interest of their own corporations. Due to the importance of exports, national governments are directed by self-interest (or structural pressures) to promote sales abroad, while at the same time protecting their own markets. Moreover, it is governments rather than corporations that bring charges of unfair trading practices against other states. Of course, the relative power and importance of different nations will play a part in determining how successful they are in influencing the agendas of the international community; the power and dominance of the US within international politics, for example, has been important to the propagation of the international neo-liberal Washington consensus.

While it is clear that IGOs can be important in helping to shape international social policy discourse, and that they can help to reinforce structural power within states, IGOs themselves are also better placed, at least theoretically, than individual states to regulate capital. This is because IGOs are not themselves subject to structural power in the same way that states are. Unlike states, IGOs are not exposed to any of the mechanisms of corporate structural power outlined in this chapter, apart from hegemonic power. What they do face, however, is greater agency mobilisation on the part of business (as Chapter Four illustrates).

Globalisation, changing corporate structural power and its implications for British social policy

Based on the above variables and indices, globalisation has helped to increase corporate structural power during the 1980s and 1990s. Capital mobility and the volume of cross-national financial flows have increased as national and international regulation of capital mobility has been cut back, along with employment regulations. Corporate taxation has also tended to decline or converge between countries. In addition, IGOs have helped to promote structural power by preventing states from controlling capital flows or, in relation to welfare provision, pushing social policies towards more productive and competitive models. The impact of all this has been especially felt in the UK.

In the UK, weak levels of domestic investment have been accompanied by high inflows and outflows of capital which have the effect of increasing its dependence on mobile capital. Over the past 30 years, the UK economy has been transformed to one that is more highly dependent on mobile capital than any of its major competitors. This has both been influenced by, and been the influence of, policies to compete for investment on the basis of costs to (especially multinational) business. It has also had huge implications for social policy. The UK has tended to sell itself as a country with low labour regulations, low taxation, low wage costs and low social costs, facilitated by a significant weakening of trade unions. The 1982 Green Paper, *Corporation tax*, stated that

> The UK system of company taxation must be capable of application to multinational concerns, overseas shareholders and so on. It must also command a degree of acceptance from the international community.... Any major change in the level or incidence of tax on company profits would affect the balance of advantage between the United Kingdom and other countries. (HMSO, 1982, p 5)

Later, in 1993, the British government placed an advertisement in the German business press which encouraged firms to take advantage of

> lower wage costs in Great Britain [where] wages and social charges are significantly lower . [T]he labour costs index for Britain is 100 compared to 178 for Germany. (cited in IDS, 1993, p 8)

The following speech by Tim Eggar, Minister for Energy and Industry in 1994, reiterated the message:

> Today, the United Kingdom attracts more FDI than any other country in Europe.... Our European partners are becoming more competitive ... we are competing for new investments in an ever tougher market.... We have a pro-business environment that is unequalled in Europe. Commitment to deregulation has played a major role in securing the level of inward investment.... We have no foreign exchange controls, nor restrictions on spending profits abroad. We have a transport infrastructure that provides fast and easy access to the rest of Europe ... the English language [and] the best available combination of a skilled and flexible workforce, with lower production costs than our neighbours. By coming to Britain, inward investors get access to the single European market *without the costs of the Social Chapter*.... UK non-wage labour costs are below those of nearly all other European Union countries. It was Jacques Delors who remarked that the Social Chapter opt-out 'makes Britain a paradise for foreign investment' – a most helpful endorsement of the [former Conservative] government's policies. Inward investors also know that they can negotiate single and non-union agreements with an adaptable workforce that is ready to learn new skills and willing to work flexible hours.... The UK strike rate has been below the EU average for each of the last nine years. (Eggar, debate on inward investment, House of Commons, 29 October 1994; emphasis added)

Despite the fact that the Labour government has subsequently signed up for the Social Chapter, introduced a national minimum wage and made the joining of trade unions easier, these proposals have not seriously altered the general sales 'pitch' used to sell the UK to foreign investors. The Labour government has tried to assure business that, taken together, its labour market, taxation and social policies have made the UK a better place to invest. The Labour's Party's 2001 Business Manifesto spelled out the government's thinking on the central role that tax competition continues to play in UK strategies to attract inward investment:

> The taxation system is one aspect of a country's environment of relevance to inward investors and others. We have created a tax framework which encourages investment and enterprise by reducing the rate of corporation tax, making capital gains tax more pro-enterprise, introducing incentives for R&D and making permanent the capital allowances available to small firms. Taken overall, UK business taxation levels, including employers' social security contributions and corporation tax, are competitive with the rest of the European Union. This is a situation we intend to maintain. In Europe, we successfully opposed a withholding tax for savings income. We will continue to make the case for fair tax competition, not tax harmonisation. (*The best place to do business*, Labour Party 2001 Business Manifesto)

The 2002 statement on the *Invest in Britain Bureau*'s web pages also explained that Britain had a "skilled and adaptable" workforce coupled with "high standards of education with a strong emphasis on vocational education and training". It went on to state that:

> Labour market regulations in the UK, including working hours, are the most flexible in Europe, and staffing costs are highly competitive.... Plus, the UK has the lowest main corporation tax rate of any major industrialised country, and there are no additional local taxes on profits. (www.invest.uk.com/investing/benefits_of_the_uk.cfm, November 2002)

Thus, successive British governments have lowered corporate taxation and sought to deregulate labour as deliberate strategies to compete for inward investment during the 1980s and 1990s. The figures already presented on UK investment levels would suggest that this strategy met with some success.

Although growing corporate structural power may well persuade governments to compete in this way, statements from equivalent departments in France and Germany tend to stress different advantages for employers wishing to invest there, such as employee skills, infrastructure and geographic location. This reveals that, despite facing similar increases in structural power, states can choose to compete in different ways to encourage investment. The fact that the UK chooses to stress its low cost advantage may have something to do with ideology, history or a more powerful capitalist class – but whatever the explanation, it would be extremely difficult for future British governments to change this strategy in the short or medium term. As Rhodes (2000, p 21) puts it,

> Low corporation taxes and social charges are vital, not just for sustaining Britain's FDI dependent manufacturing sector, but also for meeting the demands of the large low-wage, low-skill, low-productivity sector of the economy....

At the same time, competing in this way amplifies structural power as dependence on those forms of capital that are attracted by low-cost, flexible labour and low taxation increases and as governments are forced to constantly review their fiscal and regulatory competitiveness. For example, KPMG, in its 2003 survey of corporate taxation (KPMG, 2003), stated that:

> While the figures show that the UK's corporate tax rate is at a respectable 30, this is only just below the EU and OECD average rate. And with increasing competition from countries such as the Netherlands, Belgium and Ireland ... there is no room for complacency.

In 2003, Ireland reduced its rate of corporate tax from 16% to 12.5%, and Belgium reduced its rate from 40% to 34%.

These reductions in corporate taxation do not benefit all businesses, of course, and some may suffer as a result of such policies, especially indigenous firms who may face tax increases in other forms in order to make up for lost revenue from taxes on profits. Other firms may benefit from more extensive social provision. Some commentators (Yeates, 1999) have suggested that this fact weakens the argument that states act in the interests of business under the conditions of globalisation. The reality, of course, is that governments can and do react to structural and agency pressures under globalisation; but they do so in different ways at different times. Moreover, the ways in which they act and react to corporate power will impact on subsequent levels of corporate power. Responding positively to structural pressures will often serve to reinforce and amplify structural power in future. To be clear, the more that states give in to structural power – willingly or otherwise – the more they will be likely to feel the impact of structural power in the future. As Cerny (1997) points out, those states that deregulate their economies in response to global pressures will find it very difficult to re-regulate them. This becomes more true as competitor states relax regulations on global corporations. This is something that is often forgotten by those who stress the freedom and autonomy of states to resist globalisation and corporate power. In the British case, given the UK's high level of dependence on foreign investment, and given this strategy to try to attract and retain mobile capital, it is clear that it would feel far greater structural pressure from any future attempts to regulate labour or increase taxation on employers than Germany or even France. While many commentators stress the fact that states still have choices under globalisation, it is probably more accurate to say that some states have more flexibility and more choices than others.

Under these conditions we would expect to see expansion in those parts of the welfare state that contribute most to profitability and competitiveness, along with the simultaneous withdrawal of those services which undermine, or at least do not promote, private markets. Rather than forcing spending cuts, therefore, increased structural power tends to steer social spending towards provision that promotes the interests of business by increasing skill levels, productivity, flexibility, work incentives and discipline among employees. These changes are not inevitable: the greater the dependence of a state on mobile capital, the more likely it will be forced to compete for mobile capital by introducing these types of reforms. However, the extent to which a state is dependent on mobile capital is also an outcome of past decisions and power struggles played out between labour, state agents and organised business.

What *is* clear is that this is the direction UK social policy has proceeded. It is also clear that structural power has played a key role in this. As has been outlined here already, previous governments have gone out of their way to persuade foreign firms to invest in the UK to take advantage of its low regulations, low taxation and low labour costs. This has hardly changed under the present Labour government; indeed, the Blair administration has acknowledged the loss of power that accompanies globalisation, as the early sections of this chapter illustrated. The guiding principles behind the Labour government's Third Way approach, which claim to steer a path between neoliberalism and socialism, are themselves shaped by the need to find a way of offering social protection to individuals while at the same time preserving and furthering the basic interests of business. With almost every policy turn, consideration of the potential impact on business has been a primary concern. The private sector is much more integrated into welfare provision and decision making; the distance between work and welfare has been narrowed so that far greater emphasis is placed on in-work subsidies than out-of-work benefit payments; and progressivity as an objective for taxation policy has been all but abandoned. All this is against a backdrop of Conservative policy which has transformed the UK's political institutions and reconfigured the welfare state so that it was compatible with a very different economic trajectory (Rhodes, 2000, p 57).

Should a future government want to try to resist corporate structural power and reverse these trends, therefore, it would first have to transform the British economy into one which is not so dependent on mobile capital, low labour costs and regulation. Companies attracted to the UK on account of low-cost labour would be likely to reduce investments were the government to try to impose greater regulations or social costs. Radical short-term changes would therefore take a huge amount of political determination, although governments could be aided in this by countervailing forces opposed to business, such as a strong trade union movement or a well-organised Left. The present Labour government, however, appears to be going in the opposite direction – reinforcing rather than challenging corporate structural power. It has to be borne in mind, however, that as well as responding to structural pressures, the UK is, like other nations, responding to the demands and preferences of an increasingly well-organised business lobby. The nature of these demands and how they are played out takes us away from structural power to agency, and leads us to consider the position and strength of organised business on various levels. The following chapter focuses on the agency power of international business.

Note

[1] The OECD has attempted to minimise such practices through 'arm's length' agreements, where the price for goods flowing between branches of a multinational located in other states should be agreed as if the companies were independent. However, this depends on cooperation between tax authorities and multinationals which is often difficult to achieve. For a more detailed discussion and analysis, see Neighbour (2002).

FOUR

Globalisation, Europeanisation, corporate agency power and social policy

The previous chapter examined the impact of economic globalisation on structural power and its subsequent implications for social policy. This chapter shifts the focus to political globalisation – the extension of political power and political activity across the boundaries of the nation state (Held et al, 1999, p 49) – and investigates its impact on corporate agency power before examining, in more detail, the social policy agenda of international business. This is important, since international business opinion helps to shape social policy discourse and welfare outcomes at various levels of governance.

Globalisation, Europeanisation and corporate agency power

Should globalisation have had the effect of increasing structural power, as the previous chapter has argued, we might conclude that under these altered conditions, business is less likely to resort to agency in order to influence national governments. However, such a conclusion would not accurately reflect the political activities of business at the supranational and international levels during the 1980s and 1990s. Capitalists are today better organised and have stronger voices at these levels than ever before. Several factors have been at work here. First of all, supranational and international governmental organisations, the most important of which are the EU, the North American Free Trade Agreement (NAFTA), the IMF, the World Bank and the WTO, have played an increasingly important role within the globalising world as a result of what Stiglitz (2002, p 42) refers to as "mission creep", where organisations have become responsible for a growing number of policy areas that go beyond their 'core' areas of competency. This is true of the World Bank and IMF in particular, which have increasingly widened their focus beyond macroeconomic policy to include, within their remit, public policy and privatisation, pensions and labour markets (Stiglitz, 2002, pp 42-3). Even more importantly, Europeanisation has meant closer economic and political union where member states have forfeited sovereignty and their ability to veto policy proposals in many areas. In such contexts, national lobbying alone has proved increasingly ineffective; business has had to coordinate its efforts at the international level in order to avoid the risk of unfavourable policy outcomes and in order to steer policy making towards its own agenda.

Second, structural power is weak at the international level. This is an obvious but nonetheless important point. Corporations cannot wield the same threat of withdrawing investment over EU decision makers as they can national governments – decision makers are well aware that corporations are much more likely to shift investment within the EU than take investments outside. Business has therefore had to rely more heavily on agency in order to increase its influence at the regional and international levels, involving increased coordination and cooperation between firms and business interest organisations (BIAs) to maximise influence (Coen, 1997; Sklair, 2001). Business lobbying at the EU level has expanded greatly; by the 1990s, over 200 large corporations and around 500 corporate lobby groups had established bases in Brussels (Coen, 1998, p 78; Balanya, 2000, p 3).

The third factor behind the increased voice of business under globalisation is due to the formulation of common ideological and class positions between governments, IGOs and international capital. According to Sklair (2001), globalisation has spawned the development of a transnational capitalist class made up of business leaders and sympathetic government elites. Where unity between capitalist interests has been the problem in the past, this new transnational class, Sklair (2001) maintains, is ideologically united. It dominates emerging global political institutions and acts as the main force behind the development of globalisation itself. Whether it is accurate to talk about such a class, it is certainly the case that shared ideological positions, based primarily on neoliberalism, have played key roles in globalisation processes (as argued in Chapter Three). The representation of business ideas at the international level is about more than international ideology, however; it is also partly to do with the institutional mechanisms of decision making. International trade agreements, for example, are made by country representatives who are more likely to defend the interests of capital above others. As Stiglitz (2002, p 19) puts it,

> ... problems also arise from who *speaks* for the country. At the IMF, it is the finance ministers and the central bank governors. At the WTO, it is the trade ministers. Each of these ministers is closely aligned with particular constituencies *within* their countries. The trade ministers reflect the concerns of the business community.... (emphases in original)

A related problem is that, since the 1970s, the posts within the dominant economic institutions, including the World Bank, IMF, WTO, and the European Central Bank, have been dominated by neoliberal ideas espoused by neoliberal economists. In the past, those who have challenged neoliberal orthodoxy have been vilified, as Stiglitz found during his period as senior economist at the World Bank. Stiglitz's view was that IMF and World Bank strategies were based on "market fundamentalism" that often made economic situations worse rather than better (see Stiglitz, 2002, pp 34-8).

Fourth, at the same time as structural power (and capital mobility) has grown, so decision makers have been increasingly eager to find out, through regular exchanges with corporate 'representatives' of mobile capital in particular, the preferences and needs of business. In contrast to the familiar portrayal of corporations struggling to make their demands known to policy makers, governmental organisations frequently seek to establish closer links with business in order to facilitate the exchange of information and to learn how they might create more attractive investment environments or how they might smooth the introduction of new policies. Even for IGOs, getting the backing of powerful business interests can be crucial to winning the support of member states. Business leaders who are supportive of proposals put forward by international governmental bodies are also useful exponents of ideas and arguments. This is clear from the following extract, written by Keith Richardson, secretary general of the European Round Table (ERT) between 1988 and 1998, which illustrates the importance of business to the work of the European Commission leading up to and following the introduction of the 1987 Single European Act (SEA) during the mid-1980s:

> For the Commission it was uphill all the way, and there can be no doubt that [they] were grateful for the support they received. They needed the encouragement that ERT leaders gave them, they needed to be told how much industry wanted the single market, and they needed to know that industrialists were also presenting their arguments direct to heads of government. (Richardson, 2000, p 25)

Recent evidence has also emerged that suggests that corporations have been consulted by governments even when negotiations were supposed to be in secret. According to official documents leaked to the BBC and Corporate Watch in 2001, UK government officials openly briefed the leaders of some of the UK's and US's largest companies on their negotiating position at the 2001 GATS meetings (Palast, 2001a, 2001b). As Chapter Three made clear, GATS facilitates the opening of domestic markets in service provision to international competition, and as such has consequences for state social provision.

The fifth factor that has increased the voice of business at the international level is due to the institutionalising of exchanges and linkages between national and international business organisations and IGOs such as the WTO, IMF, World Bank, UN and institutions of the EU. The move towards more 'open-door policies' within IGOs has played a part here, aided by the endeavours by key actors within these institutions to help establish new routes of exchange and influence for business. The best illustration of this is Leon Brittan's attempts, as UK commissioner to the EU between 1989 and 1999, to help establish the Transatlantic Business Dialogue (TABD). Brittan viewed large corporations as having an important political as well as economic role to play within societies, and he, along with colleagues from the Commission and the US Department for Commerce, accordingly set about trying to find ways of increasing the involvement of the heads of the largest European multinationals in the political decision-making process. The result was the establishment of the TABD in the mid-1990s (Balanya et al, 2000, p 103). Brittan summarised the development of the TABD in 1995 and its subsequent success thus:

> We and the American government had asked businessmen from both sides of the Atlantic to get together and see if they could reach agreement on what needed to be done next. If they could, government would be hard put to explain why it couldn't be done. The result was dramatic. European and American business leaders united in demanding more and faster trade liberalization. And that had an immediate impact.... (cited in Balanya et al, 2000, p 104)

This quote not only demonstrates the perceived importance with which business is viewed by policy makers, but also the instrumental role played by key individuals in helping to strengthen its voice so that politicians have little choice but to listen to corporate interests.

International business also enjoys good access to the IMF, World Bank, WTO and the UN. Organised business and large corporations play key roles, as lobbyists and participants in the IMF, World Bank, UN and, especially, the WTO, where organised business helped to establish the GATS agreement (discussed later in this chapter) (Mishra, 1999; Woods and Narliker, 2001; Yeates, 2001; Stiglitz, 2002). Stiglitz (2002) provides evidence of the central role played by business in the formation of IMF and World Bank policy from an 'insider's' viewpoint. As already pointed out above, the position of business is further enhanced within the governing committees of both institutions through country representatives, who tend to be finance ministers and central bankers with obvious links to their business communities (Stiglitz, 2002). Moreover, their senior management also tends to be drawn from major companies:

> Robert Rubin, the [US] treasury secretary ... came from the largest investment bank, Goldman Sachs, and returned to the firm, Citigroup that controlled the largest commercial bank, Citibank. The number-two person at the IMF during this period, Staf Fischer, went straight from the IMF to Citigroup. These individuals naturally see the world through the eyes of the financial community. (Stiglitz, 2002, p 21)

While the UN has been viewed as an important bulwark against corporate power in the past, it has also come under mounting criticism in recent years for its increasingly close relationship with business (Korten, 1997; Madely, 1999; Monbiot, 2000b; CEO, 2001). The UN Conference on Trade and Development (UNCTAD) has, since the 1960s, maintained a careful watch over the activities of transnational corporations, although Madely (1999, pp 162-3) has accused the organisation of becoming "tame" and of turning into a "corporate poodle" in recent years in the face of growing criticism from western governments. Since the early 1990s, the UN has also developed ever-closer links and exchanges with international business. The most important business link has been forged with the International Chambers of Commerce (ICC), which has played, since 1997, an increasingly important advisory role to the UN (Korten, 1997; Monbiot, 2000b; Tesner, 2000). The ICC, along with other business organisations, has also been increasingly involved in UN meetings on a range of issues, from poverty reduction to health provision (Ollila, 2003, p 36). In 1997, the newly elected secretary-general of the UN, Kofi Annan, explained to the business audience of the 1997 World Economic Forum, that:

> Strengthening the partnership between the United Nations and the private sector will be one of the priorities of my term as Secretary-General. (Annan, 1997)

The establishment of the UN's 'global compact' with business in 1999 (discussed later in this chapter) further cemented its closer working relationship with big business. Political globalisation has meant that business and government leaders increasingly meet and collaborate in such forums on the international stage. The 2002 European Business Summit, to take one example, was sponsored by the Union of Industrial Employers' Confederations of Europe (UNICE), the Federation of Enterprises in Belgium (FEB) and the European Commission. It brought together senior business people from some of the world's largest corporations, including Unilever and Microsoft, senior politicians, nine members of the EC including one of its director generals, two members of the European Council and the president of UNICE. Such forums provide valuable opportunities for business to inform governmental organisations of its policy preferences, and their importance today is increasing.

Various business-coordinated meetings, the largest of which is the annual World Economic Forum (WEF) meeting at DAVOS, Switzerland, are also important to the spread of business influence. Established primarily by business, the meetings of the WEF attract senior officials from governments and IGOs to discuss issues of importance to the organisation's members – the leaders of some of the largest transnational corporations (Hutton, 1998; Derber, 2002, p 163). As already mentioned, Kofi Annan announced his intention to strengthen UN-private sector partnerships at the 1997 WEF meeting.

Through these various routes, international business gains important access to the international policy arena. It also helps to shape policy discourse and influence the policy prescriptions of international institutions. The rest of this chapter investigates, in more detail, the views and policies of key business organisations at the supranational and international levels.

Key international and European business organisations

A cross-section of international and EU-based business organisations, representing large as well as small- to medium-sized enterprises, is investigated here, including the Business and Industry Advisory Committee (BIAC) to the OECD, the ICC, and ERT, UNICE, and UEAPME, the representative body for small- and medium-sized enterprises in Europe. Table 4.1 provides some important background information on each of these organisations.

Together, these organisations represent some of the most important business players at the international and European levels. Their influence and importance stem from the strategic positions they occupy, both as partners within decision-making bodies and as the representatives of the most important corporations internationally and within Europe. The importance of their members alone is enough to guarantee that they have good access to policy makers at various levels. Together they provide a valuable indication of business approaches to social policy.

Globalisation, business agency and social policies

The bottom line on social provision for international business is that it is defensible only when it contributes directly to economic growth, and is affordable only when underpinned by profitable and successful corporations. As UNICE (1999a, p 4) put it:

> ... social challenges cannot be tackled except through economic growth, creation of new wealth and expansion of employment. These, in turn, cannot be achieved except through the competitiveness of European enterprises.... [A]ny attempt to extend social measures without serious regard for the requirement to live within our means is ultimately counterproductive, damages the prospects for growth, and undermines the capacity of society to support social measures....

According to Richardson (2000, p 12), the ERT also devotes much of its time to putting these kinds of arguments to politicians:

> ... the central task for the ERT was to explain that competitiveness and job creation went together ... [and] the ERT was there to spell out what European business needed in order to do its job of wealth creation effectively, but it had to say more, it had to convince politicians that these measures were in the interests of their voters too.

Thus, international business has devoted a great deal of time and resources trying to persuade policy makers that markets rather than social provision are the best way to resolve social problems and guarantee well-being. It was acknowledged that social provision could contribute to productivity, but a great deal of effort has been made by business to focus the minds of politicians on the harm it can do to corporate interests and capitalist economies. The priority for UNICE was to ensure that social policy remained "a productive factor" (UNICE, 2000b) and it has lobbied hard against those forms of social provision which were perceived to be undermining economic growth and, ultimately, "the capacity of society to ensure well being" (UNICE, 1999a, p 4).

Table 4.1: International business interest associations

	Membership	Organisation
BIAC	Membership is made up of the largest business organisations of the member states of the OECD. The CBI is a member, as is UNICE.	BIAC, along with the International Labour Organisation, is consulted on major OECD policies. Its main role is to put business arguments to OECD committees and member states.
ICC	Membership is made up of various trade associations and companies representing all sectors from over 130 countries throughout the world. Although it draws part of its membership from chambers of commerce from around the world, it is not primarily a vehicle for these organisations.	According to its own literature, the ICC is the "world business organisation, the only representative body that speaks with authority on behalf of enterprises from all sectors in every part of the world". Has direct access to the most important political and economic institutions, including the OECD, World Bank, IMF and UN where it promotes "open international trade and investment ... and the market economy" (ICC, 1998). Tends to focus on bigger questions concerning trade and investment, but not so much on social policy.
ERT	Represents around 45 of the chief executives of leading EU companies. Membership is by invitation, and only the most powerful and largest corporations are allowed to join. As a result, this commands a huge amount of attention from Europe's decision makers.	The ERT views itself as a "strategic organisation" (Green Cowles, 1995). Its purpose is to develop and promote ideas on bigger issues of substance rather than to merely respond to EU legislation. Often coordinates its lobbying efforts with UNICE.
UNICE	Membership consists of 33 employers' federations from 25 European countries, not just the 15 member states of the EU.	Has been the official voice of industry in the EU since 1958 and is presently an official partner in the EU's Social Dialogue, alongside the European Trade Union Confederation. Its strategy of influence is to access decision makers at the EU level, and to combine this with parallel lobbying by the national employers' federations within the EU member states. Often coordinates its efforts with the ERT.
UEAPME	Represents the interests of SMEs within the EU. Has a relatively small membership which is drawn from SMEs' trade associations from each of the EU member states.	Lobbies on a range of issues that directly impact on SMEs within the EU. Sits alongside UNICE within the EU's Social Dialogue.

SME = small- and medium-sized enterprise

The solution, for UNICE, was to steer the social policy debate towards productive provision. Outside of education and training, the priority was to reduce taxation and expenditure and to use existing provision as a stick rather than as a carrot in order to reduce disincentives to work, reduce the propensity towards early retirement, and increase productivity.

Given the general concerns about the negative impact of globalisation on workers, business feared that IGOs would respond by establishing minimum and universal social policy standards at the regional or international levels. While the international business community pushed for international agreements on trade liberalisation and the opening up of national economies to the multinationals – even against the wishes of nation states if necessary – it viewed as inappropriate the international imposition of minimal social policy standards. This included the EU Social Charter, which was fiercely opposed. For UNICE and the ERT, global competitiveness could only be achieved where labour costs reflect price competition, productivity and location rather than high non-wage costs associated with generous social protection regimes (UNICE, 1999a; ERT, 2001a). Despite the widespread fears of critics that such conditions would result in social dumping, UNICE (1999a, p 6) argued that:

> ... there is no case for forced social harmonization in Europe. Proposals for European legislation that do not respect subsidiarity and proportionality will be met with strong resistance by UNICE and its member federations.

This position is not surprising given that social harmonisation at the EU level would undermine corporate structural power within nation states. A lack of strong EU social policy allows businesses within nation states to argue that unilaterally increased social costs would damage their competitiveness. National governments, meanwhile, will naturally guard against imposing higher costs on their own corporations than those faced by companies in other nation states due to the risks of damaging national competitiveness or risking reduced or relocated investments. In many respects, therefore, EU social provision could reduce the threat of the investment strike and so corporate structural power (as highlighted in Chapter Three).

Although some steady progress has been made in European social policy, the EU has tended to move closer to the position of business in recent years. Today, in common with business, it stresses competitiveness first and social provision second. The 1997 EU summit, held in Amsterdam, urged that "more attention be given to improving European competitiveness as a prerequisite for growth and employment" (cited in Balanya et al, 2000, p 64) while the more recent Lisbon Summit in 2000 promoted the goal of making Europe "the most competitive and dynamic knowledge-based economy in the world" (European Council, 2000) by 2010. The summit encouraged member states to improve investment in education and training, reduce red tape and regulations and increase work incentives through making work pay. It therefore mirrored the key demands of business and was heavily praised by UNICE, the ERT and UEAPME. According to Keith Richardson (2000, p 26), one of its most senior members at the time, the ERT helped to establish this shift by blocking

> ... unhelpful proposals for social regulation [and through using] its contacts, including the good personal relations with Jacques Delors, to launch a constructive discussion about policies conducive to job creation.

Richardson points to the success of this strategy, arguing that by 2000 EU governments had

> ... finally come to see that a higher level of employment would follow from getting other policies right, rather than pressing some magic regulatory button, and this had been a consistent ERT message. (Richardson, 2000, p 26)

As for the question of social provision more generally, BIAC (1998a, p 13) captured the sentiments of international business perfectly when it told representatives of various governments in 1998 that

> When commentators look back on the history of the twentieth century, the major trend that will stand out will be that of the engagement of the state in the economy in the first half of [the] century and its withdrawal towards the end of the second half – a development that has happened in an evolutionary manner where the private sector has been allowed to explore and experiment, and in a revolutionary manner where it was suppressed. The large forces at work will affect some social structures; governments must be prepared to recognise these movements and take the steps that will allow these forces to improve the well-being of their citizens – to delay inevitable change will only increase the disruption it will cause.

While it went further than most other business organisations in outlining its position on social policy in such stark terms, the sentiments of the BIAC were, in essence, shared by all the key business organisations investigated here.

It is possible to summarise the position of international business towards social policy as follows:

• increases in spending can only be afforded through the increased productivity, investment and profitability of business;
• public services should be opened up to more competition;
• public services should be made to emulate the private sector.

According to the BIAC, there is no real difference between investments in social policy and investments in markets; hence exposure to competition from the private sector is urged (BIAC, 1996). Contemporary global capitalism, according to international business, required radical transformations in welfare systems. International business has not only promoted globalisation, as Sklair argues (2001, p 3), but has talked up the potential dangers posed by globalisation in order to steer welfare systems towards those which benefit global corporations.

The option that had been closed by globalisation, all organisations agreed, was the imposition of higher taxation on corporations.

What emerges from this analysis is a surprisingly clear and coherent business approach towards general social policy. The approach of international business to specific policy areas is examined in the following sections, beginning with taxation and expenditure.

Taxation and the funding of social provision

Each of the business organisations under investigation here had lobbied for reductions in taxation, especially taxes on corporations. Taxation on companies, it was argued, harms competitiveness by pushing up wages and dissuades employers from taking on more workers, which then leads to higher levels of unemployment and poverty. Lower taxation on companies was proposed in order to increase investments, profitability and innovation. Cuts in general taxation were also advocated in order to increase the productivity and hard work of employees. Such cuts would also increase their consumption power, of course, while higher taxation tends to push up wage inflation. The BIAC summed up the position of business well when it argued that

> The burden imposed both on companies and employees by taxes and social security contributions must be reduced.... By increasing the overall cost of hiring workers, the growth in social transfer expenditures worsens the labour market situation, in particular for low-skilled workers. A broad reduction in non-wage labour costs is therefore essential. (BIAC, 1998b, p 2)

This call for a reduction in non-wage labour costs was put as a general one, to all states, regardless of whether they were relatively low or high taxing ones.

In general, then, there was widespread agreement between the organisations under investigation here. However, the issue of tax competition did divide the representatives of small and large businesses. Since the 1990s in particular, the international community has become increasingly concerned about harmful tax competition between states and the risk that it may lead to social dumping since it places downward pressure on corporate taxation and state spending. The OECD (1997b, 2000) has moved to combat harmful tax competition since 1997 and the EU, in 1997, adopted its own Code of Conduct designed to eliminate harmful tax competition between member states (EC, 1997). The ICC, UNICE, BIAC and the ERT have responded by defending tax competition for the very same reasons. A joint paper written by the chairperson of BIAC's taxation committee and the head of fiscal affairs at the OECD argued that tax competition should be encouraged in order to maintain downward pressure on taxation systems (Hammer and Owens, 2001, p 2). To try to stifle tax competition, according to the ICC, would reduce cross-border trade and investments, capital mobility and the spread of technological advancement (ICC, 2000). In other words, it would halt the speed of economic globalisation by reducing the extent to which states would and could compete for new corporate investment. Tax competition, the BIAC argued, held many benefits for business and would be fiercely defended:

> The multinational business community speaks with a single voice when it puts forth the view that tax competition, generally, is a healthy phenomenon.... We believe that it is not erroneous to state that it is unwarranted taxation by governments, rather than competition among them in the tax area, that is stifling to economic and business development.... Tax competition tends to keep tax burdens lower, which creates pressure for less wasteful, and, therefore, more efficient use of public funds. Lower tax burdens also translates into lower cost for multinationals operating within the territory and internationally. (BIAC, 1999, p 2)

UNICE (2000a, para 9) similarly argued that it

> ... does not believe that eliminating tax competition is the way forward. On the contrary, Europe needs to reduce the fiscal and social security charges on labour in the context of a reduction of the overall tax burden and allow sound tax competition in order to promote economic growth and employment.

In an important illustration of how business organisations can group together to strengthen their positions, UNICE also issued a joint statement with the ERT which stated that "[tax] competition is a necessary counterweight to the constant upward pressure on government spending" (UNICE, Joint statement, 17 September, 1999). The ICC and BIAC also worked closely together on the issue. Since BIAC already had the ear of the OECD, the ICC used its links with the UN to put its case to the UN's international committee on taxation, convened in 2000:

> BIAC ... has submitted a note to the OECD which points out certain shortcomings, fundamental flaws and biased and onesided opinions in the OECD's Report [into harmful tax competition]. Furthermore, it emphasizes that the thrust against low or lower tax burdens or jurisdictions is inappropriate and that the outcry against tax competition is counterproductive. ICC shares the views expressed in BIAC's Note and herewith respectfully submits the Note to the UN Ad hoc Group of Experts on International Cooperation in Tax Matters for consideration in their future work. (ICC, 2000)

It was not quite accurate to suggest, as BIAC did, that the international business community spoke with one voice on this issue. As a representative of smaller businesses within the EU, the UEAPME argued that tax competition disadvantaged indigenous and less mobile businesses since it effectively reduced the ability of states to tax multinationals and risked governments making up any shortfalls in revenue through the imposition of higher taxation on smaller businesses and employees:

> The SMEs' point of view regarding European tax issues is different from that of big companies, especially due to the fact, that SMEs cannot use loopholes in the current tax-regimes in the same way as bigger enterprises.... Tax competition forces Member States to shift tax burdens from mobile to immobile tax bases.... (UEAPME, 2002a, p 1)

For the UEAPME, the solution was not to encourage tax competition, but to reduce it by moving towards some level of tax harmonisation within the EU. This was one of the few areas to divide the international business community.

This brief review of business approaches to taxation reveals a recurring paradox. On the one hand, business views taxation negatively and as harmful to competitiveness, especially that levied on businesses. On the other hand, certain forms of state spending are viewed as crucial to securing higher productivity and competitiveness in future. Part of the explanation for this, of course, is that business supports some forms of state spending while opposing others, according to an assessment of its merits for employers. However, business' demands for higher spending on business-friendly services, if met, would not leave much room for general tax cuts. This places additional pressure on governments to redirect the tax burden away from capital and towards labour which, as Chapter Three illustrated, accurately describes the fiscal policies of many governments in recent years.

Employment markets

International business predictably calls for a reduction in labour regulations within nation states. The UNICE, UEAPME and the ICC put forward similar arguments for combating unemployment through supply-led solutions such as improving education and training provision and increasing flexibility within labour markets. Regulations of wages and the working week, on the other hand, were heavily criticised on the basis that they undermined competitiveness and increased unemployment (BIAC, 2002a). The creation of publicly funded 'artificial jobs' was also condemned as a flawed and ineffectual solution to unemployment. What was needed, according to BIAC (2000, p 3), was the creation of "productive jobs in the private sector operating under competitive conditions" together with policies designed to help the unemployed "to become competitive for these jobs" through the provision of more business-centred education and training. The assumption underpinning business approaches to employment markets appears to be that skills shortages rather than a lack of jobs is the root cause of unemployment. Generous social security is viewed as having a negative impact on unemployment, but state education and training provision is viewed as essential to creating jobs.

Education and training

Of all the different parts of the welfare state, education and training receives by far the most attention from international business. Three main objectives drive the business agenda for education:

- to increase awareness among educators and policy makers of the real needs of business;
- to increase the quality of education and training to ensure that workers possess the skills employers need;
- to increase the adaptability and flexibility of workers so that they better meet the demands of the modern workplace (BIAC, 2002a; UNICE, 2002).

According to business, these are the necessary ingredients for higher levels of employment and, ultimately, sustainable social provision. Without necessary changes in educational systems, BIAC warned governments in 2002, employers would continue to bear the burden of lost productivity, growth and profits due to failing educational systems which would prohibit expensive social provision in future (BIAC, 2002a). The ERT argued that this was the case particularly in the EU where relatively high social and labour costs demand productivity gains through higher skills and technological advancement. According to the ERT, were governments to invest more heavily in improving skill levels, the unemployed would gain work and this would make social protection, especially pensions provision, more affordable.

> Without qualifications, the risk of unemployment is high. Europe's population is ageing, as fewer young people are being born to enter the labour markets to earn the taxable income which must meet the growing pension and welfare costs. A pool of unskilled unemployable workers is a burden on the welfare state and a threat to social stability. It is unthinkable to consider a model of competitiveness for Europe based on low wages and low skills. Europe's future relies on skills and striving for ever-improved research, innovation and quality. (ERT, 1994, p 10)

A great deal of emphasis was also placed by business on the importance of lifelong learning, employee adaptability and preparedness to change outdated working practices, and the fostering of better attitudes towards work among workers. The ERT complained that current educational systems failed to encourage the basic behavioural qualities which were essential for contemporary labour markets. It stressed the importance of schools in developing "appropriate attitudes, skills and competencies to enable [employees] to be receptive to lifelong learning" and encouraging workers to "re-train and relocate to new roles" as and when required by changing demand within the labour market (ERT, 2001a).

The ERT also stated that employers required employees to have the "ability to work in a group", a "sense of responsibility and personal discipline", "civic mindedness" and "a sense of professionalism" (ERT, 1994, p 13). According to the BIAC, employers require literate and numerate employees with good analytical, organisational and communication skills. The BIAC also argued that it was important that schooling fostered an "entrepreneurial attitude" and "favourable attitudes toward seizing business opportunities and accepting risks" (BIAC, 2001). In addition, UNICE (2000c, p 7) argued that employers require workers who are not only flexible and keen to acquire new skills, but are also able to "learn how to learn to cope with changes in the work place". In short, employers require workers who are prepared to skill themselves for jobs today, but who are also ready to accept that they are likely to face unemployment and the need to retrain in future. The problem is, as various parts of this book illustrate, employers are not quite as willing to accept that such unpredictable and flexible labour markets require greater levels of social protection to assist workers who fall victims to it.

As for educational curricula, international business called for more standardisation and greater emphasis to be placed on the teaching of maths, literacy and science in schools. With regard to adult training, it was felt that there should be more investment in science and technology subjects. The ERT called for a higher status to be given to vocational qualifications which "should be the recognised start of specialisation" leading to work or to higher education (ERT, 1994, p 7).

Each of the organisations investigated here also called for higher levels of spending to be directed towards education and training provision. The ERT, for instance, encouraged EU governments to increase their educational spending so that it was more in line with the US[1]. BIAC also stressed the importance of a higher quality, publicly financed education system in addition to higher levels of public investment in training in order to facilitate greater participation in skill development in later life and to boost the economy (2002b). This was also important to reduce the burden on companies to make up for poor schooling later on (BIAC, 1998c). Concurring with this, UNICE argued that employers could only be expected to fund training that is directly job-related; hence a bigger financial contribution was needed from government and from employees themselves (UNICE, 2000c).

In order to arrive at the necessary transformations in educational systems, international business also urged a greater role for the private sector, with markets playing a more significant role in the provision and management of education and training services. According to both the BIAC (2002b) and UNICE (2000c), the private sector should undertake a bigger role in the management of schools, increasing with the age of the student. All the organisations under investigation here also called for the establishment of business–education partnerships as a way of ensuring that the needs of employers are met by state educational systems. These comments by the BIAC (2002a, p 1) were typical:

> To better adapt school programmes to the needs of the employment market, a careful analysis of the skills required for specific sectors/jobs and their broad commonalities is an essential step, which can be facilitated by close co-operation with the business community.

More concrete recommendations from the BIAC and the ERT of how schools could become more business-friendly included:

- regular exchanges between head teachers and business leaders to identify best teaching practice;
- business assistance to governments and schools to identify the information technology needs of employers and foster better skills among teachers;
- the use of guest teachers from industry in the classroom;
- workplace exchanges for teachers and pupils.

These proposals are broadly in line with those advocated by British business associations.

Both the BIAC and UNICE have also lobbied for local government, schools and adult training institutions to be given more freedom from central administrations in order to enable schools to better meet the needs of local employers. Skills gaps, the argument went, could only be gauged and responded to at the local level where local businesses can draw attention to them (UNICE, 2000c).

As far as adult education is concerned, even greater involvement by business has been advocated. The ERT envisaged a much bigger role for the private sector in developing the educational services of the future. In particular, it wanted to see an expansion of universities, run by corporations along US lines. Without these changes and the increased inputs of the private sector, educational and training services would continue to fail employers, according to the ERT (1998, p 18):

> We cannot leave all action in the hands of the public sector. The provision of education is a market opportunity and should be treated as such. Nowadays there are far more players in the higher education market. Industry also has a role to play. A large number of industrial companies are running their own programmes to degree standard and above, some in partnership with a university, others on their own.

Despite advocating a more prominent role for the private sector, however, business views the public funding of education and training as crucial to competitive economies.

At the heart of the business approach to education is the belief that its primary function is to meet the needs of employers; whether directly, through vocationally relevant training, or indirectly, through fostering behavioural traits demanded by business. The problem with this approach, however, as subsequent

73

chapters will illustrate, is that different businesses, operating in different sectors, have different needs which vary over time. Business' views of their own needs also change over time. The assumption that individual firms will have a clear view about how they feel schools should be run, or that they will enthusiastically take up the challenge to get more closely involved in business–school partnerships is also open to question. It is certainly the case, however, that current EU and British education policy mirrors closely the arguments set out by international business. These issues receive further attention and investigation later in the book.

Social protection

With regard to social protection, business attentions predictably centre on the growing cost of social security, the extent of employers' mandated benefits for employees (sickness benefits, national insurance contributions, maternity payments, and so on), and the impact of social security on work availability and incentives. High social security costs and accompanying administrative burdens are said to damage profits and discourage firms from employing new workers (BIAC, 1998b). The familiar neoliberal critique of social security – that welfare benefits undermine work incentives and create dependency – is also levelled by business. A clear distinction is also commonly drawn between the deserving and undeserving poor. The following statement made by the BIAC in 1997 is typical:

> ... there will always be people who experience difficulties in adjusting to change despite their personal willingness to adapt. These individuals ... deserve targeted programmes to facilitate re-integration to the labour market. While the precise measures may vary ... such programmes might include temporary income support combined with re-training and re-location assistance. BIAC (1997, p 5)

The problem, according to BIAC (1998b, p 2), is that:

> In many countries, a dependency culture has been created with unemployment benefits being so high that active job-seeking is discouraged.... Appropriate schemes need to be designed to ensure that people have the incentives to enter the labour market where their skills are most applicable. The difference between remuneration for work and benefits should always be high enough to stimulate increased individual motivation for active job-seeking. Likewise, compensation for sick-leave should not discourage employees from resuming work when sick-leave is no longer justified.... Particular attention should be paid to low-paid workers, who need to be offered better incentives to accept employment. An employment-oriented social policy which supports work rather than inactivity, a reform of the benefit system and increased individual responsibility are indispensable

if social protection systems are to remain viable and continue to provide assistance to those in real need.

International business therefore supports only time-limited, minimalistic and conditional benefits.

Poverty and social exclusion are, accordingly, largely ignored by international business, although the BIAC (2002b, p 8) did acknowledge that situations where "individuals are permanently stuck in poverty" undermined economic growth and support for free markets. Again, the solution was seen in the creation of strong economies which, in turn, would bring with them

> a sustained growth of income and opportunities for society broadly, and especially for lower income individuals. (BIAC, 2002b, p 8)

To avoid any ambiguity, however, BIAC went on to state that:

> This is not a statement about 'equity' or 'distribution' of income. The market economy and the characteristics of human capital accumulation [processes] usually imply that individuals' earning [capacities] vary considerably across their life span and between one another. (2002b, p 8)

The ERT was equally clear on this question, arguing that successful labour markets required disparities in income and wealth to reward entrepreneurs:

> [There needs to be a] move away from a fixed-wage-earning society to a performance-linked compensation system. Successful entrepreneurs and their staff should be allowed to earn and to keep more of their own money.... (ERT, 2002)

For those on lower incomes, the only solution to poverty and inequality, according to BIAC, was through work:

> [T]here is a need to restore the understanding that, especially at lower income levels, the ability to work is ultimately the main determinant of sustainable income growth. (BIAC, 2002b, p 8)

The only responsibility that employers have, according to this view, is to try to foster strong economies so that employment levels increase (UNICE, 1999a, 1999b; UEAPME, 2000). Social exclusion, the argument goes, can only be tackled through the fostering of more competitive business environments in order to create work opportunities and reduce the need for state assistance.

Those in work, meanwhile, are expected to make adequate provision for themselves, through savings and private insurance, in order to protect them when they are too old or sick to work. Private insurance was viewed as the main solution to pressures on state schemes. Both the BIAC and the ICC expressed concern about the projected future costs of pensions more generally, while the European-based UNICE and ERT expressed more specific concerns about pay-as-you-go schemes that dominate EU countries. The ERT feared that, were pensions to remain unchanged, companies would have to pay higher contributions to fund pension schemes and higher wages to employees to compensate for increases in national insurance schemes (ERT, 2000). None of the organisations advocated abolishing public pensions altogether, however. All agreed that states had a responsibility to provide a basic pension that could be supplemented by a second tier of occupational and private pensions and third tier of individual savings, underpinned by generous tax subsidies (ERT, 2000; UNICE, 2001a). These proposals are in line with the conclusions of the World Bank's major review of pensions, published in 1994 (for a review of World Bank pensions policy see Holzmann, 2000). They are also broadly in line with the current pensions strategy pursued by the UK Labour government.

Other reforms were also needed to guarantee the survival of even basic state pensions according to international business. The ERT (2000) and BIAC (1998b) were joined by UNICE (2001a) in arguing for an increase in the age of retirement and strongly opposing any reduction. None proposed a definitive retirement age, but instead argued for more flexibility around retirement so that employees could be encouraged to work longer when they were needed by business. The UEAPME (2002b) lobbied governments to reduce the non-wage costs of employing older workers, thereby reducing the high costs, "relative to their productivity levels and outdated skills" (UEAPME, 2002b, p 3), of employing older workers.

Both the UEAPME (2002b) and BIAC (1998b) also argued that it was important to tackle the trend towards early retirement, and urged the introduction of policies to increase female participation in employment markets in order to reduce the ratio of retirees to those in employment. The UNICE suggested that governments increase the age of retirement by extending the reference period used to calculate pensions or reducing the replacement rates of pensions altogether (both suggestions would increase the incentive to stay in work longer, although they would also result in additional hardship for many) (UNICE, 2001a).

Although international business is generally critical of social security, this area of social policy, more than any other, raises questions about business' approach to welfare. Although social security comes in for a great deal of criticism, it nonetheless remains extremely important in flexible employment markets, especially given the fact that the risks to the private sector of providing unemployment insurance deter the private sector from providing such policies. Both state social security and pensions enable employers to lay off workers when they are no longer wanted or needed. However, these are expensive forms of provision, and business, as already indicated, feels that lower taxation and private provision will both be necessary in future. The solution, advocated by business, is to maintain minimum social security systems that help to commodify workers, forcing younger and older workers to work harder at selling their labour power.

Healthcare

Healthcare receives relatively little attention from internationally organised business. Only the BIAC (1998b, p 4) discussed state health services in any detail, acknowledging that they were "an important source of jobs, education, technological developments and innovations" and were "fundamental for a stable and a coherent social climate ... sustained economic growth and innovation in other sectors". Public health systems were also criticised, however, for imposing "a heavy cost burden for tax and contribution payers, mainly employers and employees". The wider business solution was again to increase the role of the private sector, both in the wider provision of health insurance and the direct provision of healthcare; a suggestion, it maintained, was met favourably by ministers attending a business–government forum organised by the BIAC on health insurance in 1998. Following this meeting, BIAC argued that there was general agreement among the ministers present, that

> [As] long as there is a basic safeguard that people with low incomes do not go untreated – social insurance will begin to cede its quasi-monopoly position in funding access to healthcare.... (1998a, p 2)

The first important step towards this goal of increased reliance on the private sector would entail opening up the public sector to competition from private health providers. Competition was viewed as essential to achieving greater cost-efficiencies for taxpayers at the same time as allowing the market to create disincentives to the ever-greater demand for healthcare. Merely creating greater efficiency in public healthcare would, the BIAC argued, create extra problems for state services:

> [A]ll the politicians have done with this efficiency drive is make the state a stick with which to beat itself: where there is no effective restraint on demand, an improved provision of service only encourage(s) people to consume more, thereby increasing voter pressure on already strapped government resources. An organisation operating in an open market, by contrast, reacts very differently.... (BIAC, 1998a, p 3)

This is an interesting variation on the anti-public health service argument: that the market is needed not because it delivers services best, but because it more effectively deters consumers. This alone is enough to convince the BIAC that public health systems should play only a minimal role in healthcare, while the private sector should be relied upon much more heavily to provide and manage health provision:

> There is now little disagreement that the private sector must take on some
> of the risks that were formerly held to be the reserve of the state; and,
> indeed, the private sector has already evolved to take over some of the
> functions of the state – in, for example, the construction and running of
> hospitals. (BIAC, 1998a, p 2)

As in other instances, the views of international business on healthcare are
remarkably close to some of the key initiatives introduced in the UK over the
past two decades. Under New Labour, the government has moved closer still,
especially in respect to the expansion of the Private Finance Initiative (PFI)
and recent proposals to allow the private sector to treat NHS patients.

Corporate social responsibility

Corporate social responsibility (CSR) is one of the key ideas of the moment.
It has been enthusiastically endorsed by IGOs, national governments, non-
governmental organisations (NGOs) and key sections of the business community
since it offers a response to growing concerns over the negative impact that
economic globalisation can have on communities and nations. Governments
and IGOs look to CSR as offering a mechanism to mitigate against the worst
aspects of global corporate activities that can undermine social conditions and,
in the worst cases, erode basic human rights. The UN established its Global
Compact in 2000, an initiative that encourages CSR by setting out key principles
of responsible corporate behaviour which companies can sign up to voluntarily.
The Global Compact states that one of its key objectives is to

> ... advance responsible corporate citizenship so that business can be part of
> the solution to the challenges of globalisation. In this way, the private sector
> – in partnership with other social actors – can help realize the Secretary-
> General's vision: a more sustainable and inclusive global economy.
> (www.unglobalcompact.org/Portal, February 2003)

Companies, for their part, benefit from positive publicity from their association
with the UN, as well as free publicity from the Global Compact website which
lists all participating companies along with case studies
(www.unglobalcompact.org). Associating with the UN in this way is an
especially attractive prospect for companies that face allegations of poor
employment or environmental practices. The obvious risk is that unscrupulous
companies will take advantage of their links with the UN while still employing
questionable or even illegal practices. This is made more likely by the fact that
the UN is not in a position to regularly and completely monitor corporate
activities (see Utting, 2000, for a fuller discussion of these issues).

The OECD's contribution to creating more responsible corporate behaviour
has been to draw up a set of 'Guidelines for Multinationals', first established in
1976, while the European Commission (EC) has recently published a Green

Paper on CSR (EC, 2001) for corporations operating within the EU. As a result of business lobbying, however, all of these initiatives, including the Global Compact, are merely recommendations or guidelines with no legal basis.

International business has responded to the CSR debate in several ways. The ICC (2002) has sought to promote CSR in order to foster "peaceful conditions, legal certainty and good human relations" which are necessary for stability and productivity and help to engender customer loyalty. The ERT (2001b, p 5) argues that CSR helps to foster "credibility and trust among stakeholders". Companies promoting responsible behaviour can capitalise on this through increased legitimacy at the point of production and increased profits at the point of sale. Even more importantly, the promotion of CSR by international business is viewed as important to the prevention of more restrictive international codes of conduct. The international business community has come out strongly against such regulations. The ERT (2001b) and ICC (2002) have made strong representations to reassure governments that existing business commitments to responsible behaviour, kept in check by market pressures, makes the imposition of international codes of conduct unnecessary. The ERT (2001b, p 1) argued, in its response to the EC's 2001 Green Paper, *Promoting a European framework for corporate social responsibility*, that

> [C]ompanies in general have a clear understanding of their social responsibilities, which means they are prepared to invest time, money and effort in the longer-term interests of the company, its employees, customers, shareholders, and the community at large. There is no need for further regulation of corporate social responsibility as a whole within Europe. (EC, 2001a)

The ICC (2002) echoed these sentiments. In its formulation on CSR it urged governments to "reject demands to impose codes on companies", especially companies that invest "outside their home countries" (ICC, 2002), since lower controls in some countries were viewed as important to encouraging new investments. Voluntary guidelines allow companies to adjust business activities to the demands of the market rather than to universal principles such as the rights of workers or the protection of the environment. The key driving force for higher standings, in the view of the ICC, should be competition, which will force corporate executives to recognise that CSR is good for business. Indeed, the ICC (2002) argued that this was already happening in 2002.

> While all businesses have an implicit set of inherent values, the number of businesses having formally written values and principles is rapidly increasing.... Indeed, sustained profits and principles are mutually supportive and an increasing number of companies view corporate responsibility as integral to their systems of governance. This is part of the requirements for doing business in today's global economy.

The ICC (2002) also argued, however, that voluntary agreements are preferable since they allow companies to adjust their behaviour according to prevailing local conditions:

> ... self-regulation is far more easily adaptable to the vast differences in circumstances, objectives, operating methods and resources of individual companies.

Both the UNICE and the ERT concur broadly with this view. International regulations, according to UNICE, risk imposing high additional costs on companies and distracting companies from their core activities: profit making or, as UNICE puts it, "creating prosperity" (UNICE, 2001b). In any case, both the ERT and UNICE maintain that the ultimate legal framework for protecting social and environmental rights has to be provided by nation states rather than regional or international bodies. As the ERT (2001b, p 4) puts it,

> Where the framework in a given country is deemed inappropriate by the international community, the main responsibility for promoting change rests with governments.... Companies should not be held responsible for the lack of political will of certain governments to implement basic labour standards.

While it may be true to suggest that the imposition of international standards on corporate behaviour risks undermining competitiveness within a region, and while there is a danger that such regulations could be used by western governments to protect their own products against cheap imports[2], the absence of binding regulations also helps to sway the balance of power in the interests of business. Under voluntary conditions, business can rely on structural factors (primarily the investment strike) to prevent governments from imposing more regulations on corporate activities.

This places governments in a difficult position (Richter, 2001). International opinion appears to suggest that voluntary codes of conduct should be enough to regulate corporate behaviour, yet the absence of binding regulations means that individual governments inevitably find it more difficult to regulate corporate power at the national level, especially when confronted by increasingly powerful corporations.

Conclusion: globalisation, corporate agency power and social policy

Globalisation increases the scope and reasons for business organisation and lobbying at the international and regional levels. Such activity is greater now than it has been at any time previously and the range of issues that international business lobbies on inevitably includes social policy. What this analysis has revealed is a surprisingly high level of business interest in general questions relating to social policy and a relatively coherent and unified view on the future direction of welfare. In some ways, cooperation between various business groups at the international level has facilitated a greater degree of cohesion than that which often emerges at the level of the nation state. One of the reasons for this is that international business tends to deal with general social policy questions, on which there is more agreement, rather than the specifics of social policy, which is where disagreement and confusion often creeps in. In addition, the analysis here has focused on a temporarily narrow 'snapshot' of business opinion which tends to disguise differences over longer periods. What will be interesting to observe in future is how this will impact on the policies of national business interest associations.

Table 4.2 summarises the views and proposals of international business on key areas of social policy. It illustrates that business does not have one view on social policy, but has different views according to the area of social policy in question. The key concerns of international business centre round the free movement of capital and the maximisation of profits. Business requires a suitably educated and trained workforce that is productive but relatively inexpensive. It also requires access to markets. To this end, international business has pushed for general reductions in the 'unproductive' state, including taxation and spending on social protection and healthcare, and an expansion in the 'productive' state, most clearly education and training services. With regard to international regulations, business has argued, above all else, that rules should be voluntary and have regard to how they will impact on international investment flows and the competitiveness of TNCs. Thus, only productive welfare states, designed to provide temporary or basic protection when markets fail and where the private sector cannot provide assistance, are compatible with global capitalism. Questions relating to the quality of welfare services tend to be neglected, and questions of equity hardly figure at all. Business has expressed concern that highly efficient public health services would lead to insatiable consumer demand and that introducing private medicines would solve this problem, primarily by pricing many consumers out of the market. The only area where business felt that the quality of service could not be left to chance was education. Only in this case is generous public funding for education and training defended; privatisation and spending cuts continue to be advocated for other parts of the welfare state.

The role played by international business organisations has been to try to influence policy debates at the international, national and regional levels. This has been most important within the EU since it has gone furthest in introducing multilateral social policy standards within member states. International business has also campaigned heavily against regional and international agreements on minimum social standards. Agency power has been utilised at the international level to guard against the implementation of international policies business feels will undermine its interests, and this has helped to preserve structural power by allowing corporations to continue to play states off against each other. Without international standards, companies can rely on the simple threat

Table 4.2: A summary of international business opinion on social policy

	View	Proposal
Taxation	Taxation reduces competitiveness and productivity. Tax competition benefits business by placing downward pressures on company taxation. Tax competition encourages nation states to impose greater taxation on immobile capital and on employees.	Reduction in all taxation, but especially taxation on corporations and wages. Reduce taxation and spending, but only if this does not impact negatively on small and immobile businesses.
Education and training	Systems must be geared more towards the needs of business. Educational systems are the key to the creation of a skilled and flexible workforce needed by business. It is necessary for education systems to impart good attitudes towards work, in addition to basic skills.	Provision is primarily the responsibility of governments, although business should be more involved in the management of schools. The private sector should play a greater role in the provision of education and vocational skills especially in post-compulsory schooling.
Employment markets	Governments should intervene less in employment markets, and reduce regulations in order to increase competitiveness and attract investment.	
Social protection	Social protection is only affordable if the economy is healthy, but social security systems generally undermine competitiveness. State pensions are untenable in the longer term. Taxes on employers to fund systems create higher unemployment. Employee disincentives are a major problem. Unemployment is largely caused by employees being work-shy, or government policies (regulations or taxation primarily) that dissuade employers from expanding the workforce. Social protection can undermine work incentives.	Benefits should be provided to the deserving poor – for short periods and with conditions. Increase the age of retirement or introduce more flexible retirement. Introduction of multi-tiered pension system, with basic pension, supported by occupational pensions. Increases in incentives to employ (older) workers. Increased female participation in employment markets. Increased social provision is ruled out.

Table 4.2 cont.../

Table 4.2: contd.../

	View	Proposal
Healthcare	Public health systems play an important role in fostering social cohesion and economic growth, but are expensive and impose too high a cost burden on taxpayers (and businesses).	More competition with the private sector advocated. Encourage a greater role for the private sector in the provision and funding (through insurance) of healthcare.
CSR	Encouraged as a way of improving corporate image and the well-being of workers and wider communities.	Argue that CSR should be voluntary. Oppose international and national regulations. Argue that companies are already aware of their obligations.

of disinvestment should they face greater controls within nation states. The ERT and UNICE have therefore campaigned heavily to shape the social policy debate within the EU and push its member states towards a pro-business agenda, leaving national organisations to place pressure on their own governments and iron out compromises at the level of the nation state. In so doing, international business has sought to emphasise the importance of global competitiveness between states, and focus the minds of policy makers on the risks presented by globalisation in order to push policy agendas towards those which favour business. A key strategy often employed by business in order to steer policy making towards its own agenda is to regularly remind governments of the wide range of investment options now open to businesses.

The only real division in international business opinion identified here centred, not on social policy, but on the question of tax competition, although this is an important indicator of the possible divisions between large international and small nationally based capital.

Partly as a result of its lobbying activities, the gap between business views and international and regional governmental bodies has become very small indeed. As Chapter Three has already illustrated, the OECD, World Bank, WTO, UN and the EU have all played a part in opening up new markets for business and in pushing social provision towards a business agenda. The OECD has promoted business-centred approaches to employment markets and social policy; the World Bank, IMF and WTO have promoted the development of policies to reduce the restrictions on capital mobility and, in certain instances, encouraged the privatisation of welfare services. Increasingly, international organisations and international business promote similar ideas and priorities: the importance of flexibility in labour markets, increased productivity and increased mobility for business. Where they vary most is around the importance of social protection and regulations on business. While the IMF, World Bank and WTO tend to promote fewer regulations, the UN, EU and the OECD view corporate regulations and state welfare as complimentary rather than detrimental to business activities. Even so, the EU Council summit in 1997 pushed member states towards promoting global competitiveness through a "skilled and adaptable workforce responsive to economic change", and recommended "a reduction in the overall tax burden" and "training and lifelong learning in order to increase employability" (Balanya et al, 2000, p 65). The Lisbon Summit in 2000 similarly pushed member states to improving education and training provision, cutting regulations on corporations and increasing work incentives. The EU has also backed the introduction of GATS, which, as discussed earlier, risks undermining state welfare services in future (Whitfield, 2001b).

In many respects, when we consider business opinion, the current positions of the UN, EU and OECD are actually closer to international business than strict anti-public sector and anti-interventionist neoliberalism. International business does not, for example, advocate the wholesale privatisation of all welfare services, but rather takes a more pragmatic approach that tends to support some state services but with more business inputs.

The biggest concern is what this will mean for social policy in the future. Given the fact that the institutional framework of the EU already serves to increase structural power (as discussed in Chapter Three), this does give some cause for alarm. Counterveiling forces, including trade unions and governments themselves, may mean that this will not inevitably lead to cuts in social provision, but it will undoubtedly add momentum to the present shift towards competitive and productive welfare states. The UK has clearly responded more speedily to these pressures by introducing sweeping changes to its welfare system, and this has benefited British business a great deal. The opinions and role that business has played in this at the national and local levels is investigated in subsequent chapters.

Notes

[1] Education is one of the few areas of social policy where the US is a relatively high spender in international terms. Gough (1979) considers this to be a clear indication of the importance with which education is viewed by business; other welfare services that were viewed as detrimental to employers were stifled by powerful business interests and a relatively weak labour movement. Total educational spending in the US in 1999 was 5.2% of GDP, whereas in Europe it ranged from 3.6% in Greece to 8.1% in Denmark. The figure for the UK was 4.7% of GDP.

[2] Western governments are accused, by Southern hemisphere governments and NGOs, of seeking to impose tighter restrictions on labour and environmental standards as a means of protecting their own producers or their "favoured" trading partner (Kabeer, 2002).

FIVE

The national level: business and social policy in the UK

Introduction

This chapter considers the national picture, examining the role that business has played in British social policy since 1979. It focuses on the views of organised business on social policy and its influence on the policy process and institutions of the welfare state. It also considers the role played by central government in creating a more influential and prominent role for business interests, and the private sector more generally, in social policy development and delivery. The chapter looks primarily at the Confederation of British Industry (CBI), the most important of the UK's business interest associations (BIAs), although the views of other BIAs, including the Institute of Directors (IoD) and the Engineering Employers Federation (EEF), are considered where appropriate. As the UK's only peak-level BIA, the CBI incorporates a national membership of firms of different sizes, originating from a range of different sectors, as well as smaller business associations. Peak-level BIAs tend to be the most influential of business organisations since they represent a diverse range of business opinion, drawn from the largest and most important national companies (Offe and Wiesenthal, 1980).

Corporate power and national politics from 1979

The period immediately before the election of the Conservative government in 1979 was marred by economic weakness, high levels of inflation, increased government borrowing, growing unemployment and recession. Although economic crisis was not confined to the UK, relative economic decline over several decades placed Britain in a particularly vulnerable position (Gamble, 1990). High inflation, accompanied by high levels of unemployment, posed a challenge to Keynesian demand management that the Labour government felt it could not resolve. The priorities for government spending gradually shifted over the 1970s from state investment, geared towards boosting consumer spending and promoting economic equality, to investment in order to boost private sector competitiveness and productivity. So began the ascendance of neoliberal ideas.

The victory of neoliberal ideas was not firmly established, however, until after the election of the Conservative government in 1979. According to the

Conservative's brand of neoliberalism, economic growth could best be guaranteed through free market principles underpinned by private rather than public investment. Accordingly, regulations on the free movement of capital were relaxed and a concerted effort was made to ensure that the interests of the business community were placed centre-stage. Prioritising and promoting the interest of business did not mean the political incorporation of business into decision making for the Conservatives. While structural pressures continued to steer policy outcomes, the UK's largest employers' organisation, the CBI, found that they were denied the level of access to Conservative ministers that they had enjoyed under the previous Labour administration. The Thatcher government firmly opposed Labour's 1970s corporatist experiment that sought to integrate the Trades Union Congress (TUC), as the representative of employees, and the CBI, as the representative of employers, into policy decision-making bodies (Grant, 1993, pp 31-2). Rather, the early Conservative government sought to court those organisations, including right-wing think tanks and the IoD, that would engage with and promote the neoliberal experiment regardless of the short-term impact on entrenched interests, including employers. In the early 1980s, CBI opinion was considered to be far too dominated by the interests of old industries that relied on the kind of state support that was anathema to the new politics. Even so, this did not mean that the CBI lacked the ability to influence government – it still remained the largest employers' organisation; rather, that it was not as closely integrated into policy making as it had been under Labour.

For its part, the CBI was at first less than enthusiastic about, and even openly hostile towards, Thatcher's brand of Conservatism (Boswell and Peters, 1997, pp 142-6, 152-5). Its hostility did subside after 1983 which, after a highly public disagreement with the Conservative government, was a particularly low point for the organisation. The CBI began to make use of more sophisticated mechanisms for gaining influence from this point onwards, including appealing directly to public opinion, producing clearer, more ordered and coherent policy statements, and relying much more on its local branches to influence local policy making and provision (Farnsworth, 1998). This strengthened the standing of the organisation in the eyes of the general public, the media and politicians of both main parties, and by the late 1980s, the IoD had almost slipped into obscurity while the CBI had reasserted itself as the dominant voice of business. It enjoyed far greater access to the Major government during the 1990s, and under the post-1997 Labour government, the CBI enjoys better access than it has enjoyed anytime since the 1970s. The outgoing president of the CBI, Clive Thompson, told *The Financial Times* in 2000 that the working relationship between it and the Labour government is "probably closer than at any time in the last 25 years" and explained that it was certainly closer than under the Thatcher or Major governments (Brown, 2000).

Leaving to one side the mixed fortunes of the CBI, it is clear that business became increasingly important to social policy developments over the 1980s and 1990s. Many of the changes in social policy since 1979 have been introduced either in response to business pressure (agency) or in response to perceptions of the needs of business (structure). The following section examines this process in greater detail.

Central government, business and social policy since 1979

As already indicated, the principal solution to the economic and political challenges of the 1970s offered by the Thatcher government was to reduce the size, duties and costs of the state. According to *its* diagnosis, the economic and social policies that underpinned the postwar consensus in the UK had undermined the operation of labour markets. It was argued that universalism, unionisation and state interference in the workplace (in particular, wage regulation) had stifled competitiveness. Solutions were seen in the reduction of regulations and taxation imposed upon business, as well as the promotion of business-friendly public services that would foster entrepreneurialism and promote risk taking. Left to prosper, the argument went, business would bring social and economic rewards that governments were incapable of delivering. To introduce such radical and transformative change would take time, however, and the Conservatives accordingly embarked on a long and systematic period of reforms.

Cuts were easiest where spending was resource driven, or where the criteria determining spending were set directly by central government. Social security payments were devalued, as in the case of pensions and unemployment benefits, for example, or removed altogether, as in the case of benefit provision for 16- to 18-year-olds. In the case of local authority expenditure, the Conservative government used treasury rules and reductions in subsidies to control capital expenditure. In many other areas of social policy, however, it first had to wrestle control over expenditure from local authorities, welfare professionals and the trade unions. Towards this end, the Conservatives introduced a number of reforms which gradually, but purposefully, squeezed elected representatives and organised labour out of locally managed services and replaced them with business people (discussed in Chapter Six of this book). Local authorities were also transformed from being providers to enablers of services, purchasing and contracting out services from outside bodies, including corporations. Compulsory competitive tendering (CCT), first introduced in 1980 for construction and extended to other services from 1988, together with the establishment of the Private Finance Initiative (PFI) in 1992, forced local authorities to open up services still further to private contractors. This move towards an 'enabling', as opposed to 'providing', role for local authorities has been strengthened under Labour (Whitfield, 2001b). Before coming to power, the Labour Party had promised business that it would take steps to improve the competitive environment by forging more constructive partnerships with business. As promised, Tony Blair has gone out of his way to foster such relationships with business interests more generally, and with the CBI in particular. He spelled out Labour's achievements and ambitions to the CBI conference in 1997:

> Two years ago when I last addressed the CBI's national conference, I promised a new partnership between New Labour and business. Six months into office, we have laid the foundations of that partnership. There are business people bringing their experience and expertise by serving in Government, on Advisory Groups, leading task forces, all contributing to the success of Government policy. But there is also great commitment and enthusiasm, right across the Government, for forging links with the business community. That this is the approach of a Labour government is of historic importance. It demonstrates we are entering a new era in British politics. (Blair, speech to the CBI conference, 11 November 1997)

A Labour government that was keen to promote entrepreneurialism and increased productivity in the public and private sectors in order to underpin future expansion in social policy would govern this new era in politics. While this had some parallels with the Conservative project before it, the key difference was that New Labour envisaged a more positive role for social provision than the previous administration had; although this role would be clearly different from that advocated by 'old' Labour. The priority for New Labour has been the transformation of social policy from unproductive to productive welfare that more clearly contributes to competitiveness. An emphasis on partnership with business has replaced the Conservative's dogmatic privatisation programmes (Whitfield, 2001b, p 68; Grimshaw et al, 2002, p 478). While this has meant the introduction of greater social protection for some workers, the government has proceeded cautiously on all key reforms in order to ensure that they do not impact unduly on business:

> We will keep a flexible labour market. Even where you may have doubts about certain parts of policy – a minimum wage or trade union representation – remember: that we are consulting business every step of the way; and that taken altogether, the entire changes proposed would still leave us with a labour market considerably less regulated than that of the USA. (Blair, speech to the CBI conference, 14 April 1998)

Where the Conservative government attempted to retrench and roll back the welfare state, the Labour government, in partnership with business, has sought to transform it to a new 'corporate-centred' Third-Way project. The Third Way, which has defined Labour's approach to social policy, prioritises according to Giddens (1998, p 117), one of its architects:

> ... investment in human capital wherever possible, rather than the direct provision of economic maintenance.

Tougher qualifying conditions have been imposed on less productive parts of the welfare state, including social security, while productive education and training provision have been promoted as key routes through which individuals can increase their life chances and incomes. The concerns of the private sector have been put centre-stage; employers have benefited from tax cuts and new subsidies; and big business has been given new opportunities to profit from capital investment projects in most parts of the welfare state, including schools and hospitals. Business inputs into social provision have also been increased in a number of initiatives, including the health and education action zones, city academies and specialist schools. Various public–private partnerships, including CCT and the PFI, meanwhile, have narrowed still further the gap between the public and private sectors. Various parts of the public sector have also had to face up to the fact that they operate increasingly along similar lines to the private sector where

> ... schools and colleges are subjected to a system where failing to meet production targets results in the closure of plants and the sacking of both management and workers; or even the threat of compulsory privatisation. (Allen and Martin, 1999, p 14)

In short, business has been held up as a panacea to an increasingly wide-ranging set of social problems to which, governments appear to believe, the public sector alone can no longer offer credible solutions.

Business has played its role in all this, of course, by bringing to the attention of politicians the problems that it feels state welfare provision presents. It has made public its dissatisfaction with labour productivity, work incentives, the skills base of those graduating from state education and training institutions and the general cost and tax burdens of the welfare state. However, the position of business has not been as simple as merely calling for cuts in state provision or mass privatisations, as is often assumed. In fact, business' stance towards state provision has been far more variable: it has pushed for reductions in certain forms of spending but for increases in other forms; it has promoted state controls in some instances, free markets in others and has called for greater public funding for private sector provision in still others. These various business approaches to social policy are examined in detail below under the following headings: taxation and expenditure, education, training, healthcare and social security.

Taxation and expenditure

Battles over expenditure and taxation have defined business–government relations in the UK since 1979, with employers campaigning heavily and at times aggressively for reductions in government spending and cuts in taxation levied on businesses and higher earners. While this battle has at times been fierce, however, business opposition to public spending has been neither even nor constant across services and over time. On the one hand, the more Thatcherite IoD campaigned long and hard against government spending and general taxation since the 1970s. The CBI, on the other hand, was more pragmatic; while it pushed for tax and spending cuts, it did so in a more selective way. The CBI did support the Conservative government's attempts to combat inflation, but pointed to the damaging effects of the 'cure' for this: cuts to state capital investments and high interest rates. Conservative policies hurt many parts of business in that they reduced consumer and public sector demand for goods and services, increased the price of borrowing and inflated the value of sterling which, in turn, damaged the competitiveness of British goods abroad.

While the CBI pushed for state spending cuts during the early 1980s, therefore, it insisted that these cuts be made in ways that would impact less on business. This was driven by the perception that the public sector was inefficient and overstaffed and that high levels of public spending had led to inflation and the necessary imposition of increased interest rates. The CBI also felt that industry had paid a disproportionately high price for the failure of central government to keep spending under control. Its message for the public sector was unequivocal:

> ... they will have to do what the private sector has been doing for the past
> 18 months – manage with fewer people, pay them more sensibly and get
> them to work harder. (Terrence Becket, director-general of the CBI, cover
> story of *CBI News*, 27 March 1981, p 3)

The CBI accordingly urged the government in 1981 to be "ruthless in its attack on waste and overmanning in the public sector" and to "get a grip on public spending" (CBI, 1981a, p 23). This attack on spending was geared towards both central and local government. At the national level, the CBI urged the government to exert greater control over local taxation and spending. At the local level, it encouraged local branches and individual members to lobby local councils directly, and pushed business people to get involved directly in local politics, including standing for election, in order to bring "commonsense to local affairs" (*CBI News*, 30 January 1981, p 5). Such campaigns were encouraged by central government and they allowed the Conservative government to draw on business opinion and activities to justify clamping down on local spending and taxation (see also May, 1984, p 3). Chapter Six discusses some of these issues in more detail.

While the CBI has actively called for selective spending and taxation cuts at both the local and national levels, it has also defended spending in those areas that make obvious contributions to business, either by improving the skills or qualities of labour or through direct public sector purchases of goods and services from the private sector:

> The CBI has advocated reductions in government expenditure as part of an
> overall policy designed to secure a better balance in the economy between

the public and private sectors and to reduce the level of taxation.... The CBI has stressed, however, that the necessary economies in spending should be made in the internal operation of government and not by concentrating cuts solely on reducing purchases from the private sector or capital expenditure, which shifts the burden of reduced expenditure onto trade and industry. (CBI, 1980b)

The CBI has defended capital expenditure in particular, since it both boosts the demand for private building services and helps to improve the transport infrastructure on which business depends; hence, the CBI has regularly called for large increases in such spending. The following extracts are from 1986 and 1992 respectively:

> The CBI welcomed Nigel Lawson's announcement in his Autumn Statement of additions to planned capital expenditure of getting on for £1 billion in 1987/88. The CBI had put forward the case for almost £1 billion pounds of extra capital spending.... (*CBI News*, 21 November 1986, p 14)

> During the year the CBI kept up pressure on the Government to achieve restraint in the real growth of government current spending and to get the resources saved directly into capital expenditure.... The CBI pressed the Government hard to step up its expenditure on trunk roads, by-passes, sewers, and other parts of the infrastructure – especially important in view of the burden of recession which has been borne by the construction industry.... [This] would generate employment and would benefit the cost competitiveness of British industry as a whole, for example through reduced transport costs. (CBI, *Annual Report*, 1992)

While the CBI has continued to campaign for increased capital expenditure since the 1970s, it has gradually focused more positively on the potential benefits of public spending since the late 1980s. As inflation has decreased and public borrowing turned into surplus, and as respective governments since 1979 have demonstrated their resolve to keep public expenditure under control, the CBI's message has become less fixated on general questions of taxation and spending levels, and more focused on specific questions of how taxation is levied and how the money is spent. Rather than arguing for reduced spending and across-the-board tax cuts, the CBI has instead adopted an upper spending limit 'benchmark' of 40% of GDP[1] and campaigned for higher spending on services that benefit business within this limit.

The CBI of the 1990s and the 2000s has generally become more accepting of social provision and less cautious about the role that government spending and social policy could play in furthering business interests. This is not surprising given that most welfare and other state spending has been increasingly geared towards those programmes that will benefit business. The emphasis on skills development and improved work incentives at the heart of current Labour policies greatly assists business, while infrastructure spending has benefited the private sector through the extension of PFI. Even large increases in spending were deemed to have been necessary in order to make up for under-investment during the 1980s and 1990s, the very same under-funding that organisations like the CBI pushed for at the time. The CBI's 2002 submissions on the budget and spending reviews were remarkably positive about large increases in spending:

> The commitment to greater spending on the transport infrastructure was clearly needed.... Increments for education, overseas promotion and Regional Development Agencies were also applauded by business. As a result, rather than oppose the significant spending increases ... we have urged the Government to push through with them – though always bearing in mind the importance of quality of delivery, value for money, efficiency and not going over budget. (CBI, 2002a)

> Decades of under-investment have created this need. The rise in expenditure to 42% of GDP should be viewed as a catch-up following a period of under-investment, and not as a permanent feature of policy. Once the legacy of underinvestment has been tackled, the share of public spending in GDP must be brought back down. The CBI continues to believe that, over the medium term, 40% of GDP would be a realistic but necessary ceiling to allow the business tax to be set at a reasonably competitive level. In this context, it is all the more important that public expenditure is undertaken effectively and efficiently and delivers real improvement – public sector reform is vital to ensure that money is well spent. (CBI, 2002b)

Although the CBI supported significant increases in spending and investment in some public services, however, it did not signal any willingness on the part of business to pay for it. The Chancellor of the Exchequer, Gordon Brown, surprised many – and not least the CBI – when he announced plans to pay for increased investment in health by increasing employers' and employees' national insurance (NI) contributions from April 2003. Not surprisingly, the proposal was met with a great deal of opposition from business, including the CBI, which condemned it as a "tax on jobs" (Jones, 2002). The fact that this increase was to pay for extra spending on healthcare – not one of the CBI's priority areas – added to its opposition. Given the choice, the CBI would probably have favoured an increase in income tax or VAT. The CBI was also caught off guard by the increase because of Labour's previous commitments to reduce taxes on business. Only five years earlier, the government had assured the CBI that it was taking its lead on business taxation from business:

> The 2 percent cut in corporation tax to its lowest level ever, the reduction to 21 percent of small business corporation tax, and the new investment incentives for small and medium sized companies ... reflect a Government

that listened to the CBI's proposals. (Gordon Brown, speech to the CBI's National Conference, 10 November 1997, www.hm-treasury.gov.uk/ newsroom_and_speeches/press/1997/press_138_97.cfm)

Noteworthy here is the clear operation of both structural and agency influence: *structural*, because tax reductions are identified as important to future investment; *agency*, because it represents the outcome of active lobbying by the CBI. Given this, it is surprising that the government chose to increase taxation on business. However, it clearly did so with reluctance, and it attempted to spread the burden by increasing rates for employees as well as employers. The tax increase was also against a backdrop of two decades of taxation cuts for UK businesses and relatively low levels of taxation, especially in the form social security contributions, compared with their international counterparts. Given this, and the even higher risk of alienating voters by breaking a key election pledge not to raise income tax, the increase in NI contributions begins to make more sense.

The general approach of business to taxation and spending, as expressed through the policies of the CBI, is that resources should be geared towards productive welfare, after considering the scope for private sector inputs, with the costs being borne primarily by labour. The CBI has called for:

* increases in spending in certain policy areas, for example education and training;
* expenditure stabilisation in areas such as capital expenditure and private sector purchases;
* spending restraint or cuts in relation to labour costs and local services.

In this respect, increases in NI contributions aside, its priorities are broadly in line with those of the current Labour government.

Education

School education

As outlined in Chapter Four, governments have a structural interest in promoting competitiveness and business prosperity, and education and training make important contributions to achieving these objectives. The preparation of school leavers for the world of work has remained one of the key objectives of mass education systems since their inception, and the postwar British system has, historically, fulfilled this function relatively well. It produced a moderately literate and numerate working class that could carry out relatively skilled tasks, together with a more highly educated middle class for senior management posts. Changes in the economy and workplace since the 1960s, however, meant that increasing numbers of more highly skilled and educated workers were needed. Consequently, employers and politicians have pointed with increasing frequency to the failure of the education system to meet the needs of business. This even meant defending expenditure on education against a tax-cutting government. In 1996, Adair Turner, then director-general of the CBI, stated that:

> ... on some things we are clear: within the total of government expenditures, we place the very highest priority on education and training spend, and we don't want it cut to finance tax cuts. (Adair Turner, speech to the CBI's annual conference on education, 1996)

This again emphasises the importance of selected (rather than general) tax and spending cuts for business.

Beyond this, successive governments formulated two clear strategies to shift education towards the needs of business. First, they have encouraged closer linkages between schools and employers through the incorporation of business into the funding and management of schools. Second, they have promoted the development of a business-centred curriculum in schools. These two strategies are discussed in turn.

From informal school–business linkages to business-run schools: The attempt to incorporate business into the management of schools began with a number of initiatives aimed at establishing informal school–business linkages. There was recognition, beginning with the Labour government in the 1970s, that more needed to be done to establish closer links between education and business. James Callaghan, as Labour Prime Minister, stated in his famous Ruskin College speech in 1976 that poor schooling was contributing to Britain's lack of competitiveness and argued for greater emphasis to be placed on the needs of employers (Timmins, 1996, pp 234-5). Similarly, the CBI argued that competitiveness and productivity, especially within industries such as engineering and construction, were being undermined by a lack of understanding and appreciation of the needs of business within schools. In 1981 it argued that:

> There must be closer links between school and industry so that potential employers can help teachers and children to understand the nature of business and working life, the opportunities that are available and the basic skills which will be required. (CBI, 1981a, p 33)

Such concerns kick-started a number of initiatives designed to develop closer links between companies and schools. The CBI launched its own initiative, Understanding British Industry (UBI), in 1977 with the aim of increasing the voice of business within schools and improving levels of understanding among teachers and pupils of the needs of business (CBI, 1977). Towards this end, it established exchanges between teachers and industrialists, headteacher mentoring and school placements in industry for pupils.

Both Conservative and Labour governments also launched their own initiatives, each one promising to further narrow the gap between business and education, beginning with Labour's School Council Industry Project, which was launched in 1978. Subsequent initiatives launched by the Conservatives included: the Technical and Vocational Education Initiative (TVEI), launched in 1983; Education–Business Partnerships (EBPs) in the early 1980s (although these really took off from the early 1990s); Industry in Education in 1992; and, in the case of the higher education sector, the Council for Industry and Higher Education in 1995.

These relatively informal mechanisms for developing closer business–educational linkages were complimented by a number of initiatives designed to establish more formal partnerships. Under the 1980 and 1986 Education Acts, for example, schools were required first to establish governing bodies that incorporated representation from employers, and later forced to "have regard to the extent to which [parents] and the other governors are members of the local business community" (cited in Thody, 1989, p 142). The 1988 Education Reform Act (ERA) further cemented business–education linkages. By establishing the national curriculum and allowing schools to opt out of local authority control, the ERA helped to ensure that business preferences were placed centre-stage. Introducing the bill in December 1987, Kenneth Baker argued that it would

> ... create a new framework, which will raise standards, extend choice and produce a better-educated Britain [by] freeing schools and colleges to deliver the standards parents and employers want. (House of Commons, Cmnd 771/2)

The CBI welcomed the main provisions in the Act and considered it to be

> ... a milestone in education provision, likely to have a major impact on young people and the economy. It includes a number of major changes to the education system, many of which have been advocated by the CBI for a number of years. (CBI, Annual Report, 1988, p 26)

It went on to stress its own role in the development of the national curriculum, especially in pushing for skills-centred learning.

The Conservative government also responded to demands by the business community, again led by the CBI, to gear education more directly towards the need of employers. Its most ambitious initiative was the establishment of city technology colleges (CTCs) in 1986, which established formal partnerships between schools and the private sector. The CTCs were established as "centres of technological excellence" (Margrave, 1994, p 66) for 11- to 16-year-olds which would place greater emphasis on technological and vocational education. Local companies, for their part, were asked to contribute around £2 million to their set-up costs, and take an active role in their management (Margrave, 1994, p 66). Sponsors, however, were much more difficult to attract than the government and the CBI envisaged.

The post-1997 Labour government has taken an even more active role than the Conservatives in attempting to cement closer business–educational linkages. Gordon Brown took the opportunity of his 2000 speech to the CBI to make clear that Labour expected business people to take a more active role in schools than they had in the past:

> I want businessmen and women going into schools and teaching enterprise classes. So I urge all businesses throughout the country to adopt a school – whether it is by taking students on work experience and teachers on work placements, sending employees into schools to help run enterprise classes, or being business governors. By adopting a school, every business in the country will be helping to build the new enterprise culture that we all want to see. (Gordon Brown, speech to the CBI annual conference, 6 November 2000)

Labour sought to facilitate and encourage such informal involvement through the establishment in 1998 of a national coordinating body for business linkages, the National Education and Business Partnership Network (NEBPN). The Labour government also charged the new Learning and Skills Councils (LSCs), launched in 2001 to replace the former Training and Enterprise Councils (TECs), with the responsibility of overseeing and coordinating local EBPs, increasing significantly the funding available to help establish new partnerships.

As well as supporting the development of informal linkages between education and business, the Labour government, like the previous Conservative administration, has attempted to establish more formal education–business partnerships. Labour has moved closer to the CBI's demand for more business-focused schools, free from local education authority (LEA) control, by effectively extending technology colleges in its 1998 city academies and its 2001 specialist schools initiatives. Both schools have some freedom to depart from the national curriculum and are able to set wages and staff bonuses. According to the Department for Education and Employment (DfEE), sponsors of city academies will have:

> ... considerable freedom over management structures and processes, and other features such as the length of the school day, terms and year. Academies will be expected to offer all pupils significant out of school hours learning activities and to encourage the participation of partners in mentoring, curriculum delivery, and work experience. (DfEE, 2000, p 9)

City academies must raise around £2 million from the private sector. Specialist schools initially had to raise £100,000, although this was subsequently reduced to £50,000 after it became clear that some schools were struggling to raise the required amount from the private sector. As with the CTCs, business sponsors are expected to help run schools and bring private sector values into their management. According to the DfEE,

> We know from ... [experience] that schools can benefit from involvement
> with business and other non-government partners. This partnership can
> bring a new focus and sharpness to the running of schools, to the great
> benefit of the children in their care. (DfEE, 2000, p 4)

Both the CBI and the EEF have responded positively to these proposals. The
EEF has even formed a consortium with other engineering interests to sponsor
three engineering specialist schools from 2002. The fact that specialist schools
can help to promote vocational skills in a wider range of areas, coupled with
the lower financial outlays required from companies, has generated a more
positive response from business than the CTC initiative. By September 2002,
34% of school children in the UK were being educated in 992 specialist schools,
including 18 business and enterprise schools, four engineering, 12 maths and
computing, 24 science colleges and 78 technology schools. The government's
official target is to have established 2,000 specialist schools by 2006 (*TES*,
2002), although David Miliband, the then Schools Minister, revealed in an
interview with *The Financial Times* in January 2003 that he predicts that a
"significant majority" will have specialist status by 2006/07 (Guha, 2003).

The Labour government also looked to business to provide innovative
solutions to run-down schools within Education Action Zones (EAZs).
Introduced from 1998, EAZs went further than any previous initiative in
incorporating business into the management of state education. Although
CTCs established the principle that businesses would be allowed to assist in
the management of schools independently of LEAs, the EAZs encouraged
businesses for the first time to lead partnerships that would take over the running
of groups of failing schools within a neighbourhood (Dickson et al, 2002, p
185). Indeed, the government went out of its way to encourage companies to
take the lead in establishing zones independently of local authorities (Dickson
et al, 2002, p 186). In addition to contributing at least £250,000 per annum
to running costs, it was hoped that business partners would provide additional
funding, expertise, technology, work experience and mentoring for children of
failing schools. The government contributed around £750,000 per annum.

The EAZs were important in preparing the ground for subsequent plans,
announced in 1999, to allow the wholesale take-over of schools by outside
bodies, including private companies. At the time of writing, two London
boroughs, Islington and Hackney, have been forced to transfer all or part of
their educational services to private firms, and many other councils, including
Bradford, Birmingham and Leeds, have called in private sector consultants to
help address the problems of failing schools (UNISON, 2001). The 2002
Education Act (part 5, section 70), meanwhile, requires that, where an LEA
seeks to set up a new secondary school it must invite proposals from interested
parties, including private firms.

The problem that both the government and BIAs such as the CBI have
found in trying to incorporate the private sector into education, however, is
that generating interest among companies to get involved in educational projects

has often been more difficult than expected, especially where there are no obvious or direct benefits to companies. Getting private firms involved in potentially profitable school take-overs or in more prestigious projects that provide free publicity for companies, especially when the outlay for companies is low, is relatively straightforward; but generating business interest in other forms of school linkages has often proved to be more difficult.

Despite the fact that by 1997/98 official estimates revealed that 47% of English secondary schools had more than three business representatives and almost 80% had at least one representative from business on their governing bodies (DfES, 1999), a number of studies have revealed that, at the level of the firm, there is often a great deal of reluctance to establish linkages with schools. While organised business, such as the CBI, may view partnerships as important to providing benefits for the whole business community, individual firms are sometimes harder to convince. Big business, with a longer-term outlook, can extract some benefits from 'soft marketing' and in capturing the consumers and workers of the future, but for many smaller firms there are relatively few obvious gains. Many surveys in the past have found reluctance on the part of small employers in particular to get involved with schools (Pike and Hillage, 1995). The reasons given for this reticence include the perception among companies that such linkages are relatively costly, not only in terms of the necessary staff time, but also because they bring relatively few rewards (IiE, 1995a; Pike and Hillage, 1995). The CBI, therefore, has found itself with the dual task of first persuading ministers to open up schools to business, and second, persuading employers to take up these opportunities:

> The business community must be encouraged to increase its involvement with educational organisations. Employers have a direct opportunity to influence the skills output of schools and colleges, improve the image and attractiveness of careers in the manufacturing and engineering sectors and encourage more pupils to study technical and scientific courses. (CBI, 1996, p 24)

Successive governments' attempts to attract more funding from companies have also proved to be relatively difficult. Firms were unwilling to invest anything like the total outlay required for the Conservative government's CTCs, for example, which meant that the government had to increase central funding and rely heavily on close business allies to raise around £2 million of the total costs of each CTC (Margrave, 1994). As Margrave (1994, p 65) points out, companies were reluctant to invest so heavily in one school for relatively limited returns when, "for an outlay of a couple of million pounds, a successful multinational could have a prestigious education programme that reached all schools in the country".

Labour has also found that generating even relatively modest contributions from business for its various initiatives has proven to be difficult in some instances. In the case of the EAZ, the results were mixed. Some EAZs did manage to attract interest and financing from large companies, including the likes of Shell (which chaired the Lambeth Zone), IBM, ICL, McDonalds, Tesco and Barclays Bank; but others struggled to generate any real interest or finance. Newcastle's EAZ, for example, was sponsored by Newcastle United Football Club, but did not have any major corporate involvement and struggled to raise the necessary private finance. Derek Wise, whose responsibility it was to raise corporate sponsorship for that EAZ, explained in an interview with *The Guardian*, that:

> I felt just like a third-world country going to a first-world country with a begging bowl, and coming away with nothing. I remember going to Boots. They were trying to be kind, but we were not on the same planet. They offered me a load of cardboard they had left over from their window displays. They said: "Here's some cardboard you can have", and they thought they were being incredibly helpful.... (Evans, 2002)

Even where companies have made donations to the various EAZs, many of them have taken the form of 'in-kind' contributions, including time spent on projects by business people. Another example from Newcastle included the contribution of a local branch of Waterstones which 'donated' a shop window for a limited time to be used to display children's essays. The reported 'value' of this corporate donation was £500 per week (Evans, 2002). In fact, according to the government's own figures, the average cash donations from business to the various EAZs amounted to less than £110,000 in 2001 (DES, 2001, p 23) and just 12 of the 73 EAZs launched between 1999 and 2001 had successfully raised the expected £250,000 per annum from business (Barnard et al, 2001, p 2).

Difficulties have also been experienced in raising the necessary contributions from business for the development of specialist schools. In order to provide a boost for the flagging project, the government announced in September 2002 that it would set up a Partnership Fund to assist those schools that were finding it difficult to reach the £50,000 contribution from business.

Another reason why business may have been reluctant to become involved in school initiatives is that it is often unclear, both to companies and schools, what possible role companies might play. Previous studies have found, for example, that business governors often do not feel that they represent the views of 'business' at all, and that the diversity of business opinion makes it difficult even to establish clearly what a 'business' view would be on many issues (IiE, 1995b, p 6). More recent research also found that companies contributed relatively little, in the way of innovative ideas and even economic and other resources, to the EAZ. Dickson et al (2002, p 195) suggest that:

> ... the nature and limited scale of private sector initiatives cast doubts on suggestions that businesses have the willingness, energy, creativity or know-how to radically transform the provision of education.

Despite this, the Labour government remains convinced that business can help to solve the current problems of education and, for that matter, other parts of the welfare state.

Towards a business-centred curriculum: While organised business has welcomed the moves towards establishing closer business–education links, the key reason for establishing such links in the first place was not to open the way for the private sector to take over the management of schools, but rather to exert greater control over the teaching within schools. In actual fact, the main advantage to developing closer links between business and schools for the CBI is that it offers the possibility of business helping to steer school curricula towards those skill areas needed by employers. For many years, it has pushed for more work-related learning through standardised assessments, target-led outcomes and a higher volume of testing in order to locate and tackle skill shortages and raise standards (*CBI News*, March 1981, November 1989). The CBI has also argued for the setting of national educational attainment targets (*CBI News*, November 1988, pp 124-5) and for a greater emphasis on vocational education and training in both compulsory and post compulsory education (*CBI News*, March 1981, April 1988, September 1988) in order to put the UK on "at least equal terms with [its] main competitors" (*CBI News*, 31 March 1989, p 3). Successive governments have responded by introducing a whole range of targets, 'benchmarks', and testing across the educational spectrum. The CBI played a direct role in the setting of these through its contributions to the work of the employer-dominated National Council for Vocational Qualifications (NCVQ; see discussion later in this chapter). This paved the way for General National Vocational Qualifications (GNVQs) and National Vocational Qualifications (NVQs), the content and assessment of which the CBI also helped to establish.

The integration of the NCVQ and the School Curriculum and Assessment Authority (SCAA) into the new Qualifications and Curriculum Authority (QCA) in 1997 was a further attempt to close the gap between academic and vocational qualifications. The objective of the QCA, according to Nick Tate, its chief executive in 1998, was to create a closer partnership between business and education and he appealed for greater input from business:

> Business needs to help us revise the national curriculum so that it meets the needs of a rapidly changing economy. Business needs to tell us what qualities it is looking for in the young people pursuing qualifications in schools and colleges. Above all, business needs to be the dominant voice in the development of vocational qualifications. (Tate, 1998)

In order to investigate how the involvement of business people and firms in schools could be increased still further, the Labour government commissioned *A review of enterprise and the economy in education* in 2001, which was carried out by Howard Davies, the former director-general of the CBI between 1993 and

1995. Davies (2002) recommended that learning about business, entrepreneurship and financial literacy be integrated into the school curriculum and that greater funding be given to enable the further expansion of school–business partnerships.

In response to the report, Gordon Brown pledged £75 million in the 2002 pre-Budget report over three years to promoting education about enterprise in secondary schools and colleges. Brown spelled out his vision of how such partnerships should develop in 2002:

> ... I want to see our business leaders as role models for our young, our teachers able to teach the value of enterprise, and a recognition in high as well as low unemployment communities that enterprise that is open to all holds the key to their regeneration. (Gordon Brown's speech to the CBI's annual conference)

In order to make the shift towards more vocational schooling a reality, the Labour government announced in 2002 that it would introduce more work-focused education for 14- to 19-year-olds. Under the proposals, school pupils from the age of 14 would be able to spend two thirds of their time on vocational or 'applied' learning in subjects ranging from business, engineering, manufacturing, health and social care and information and communications technology. The 14-19 Green Paper (DfES, 2002) begins by stressing the importance of addressing a problem frequently highlighted by business: poor attitudes towards work and employers. Indeed, the CBI's response to the Davies Review pointed out that: "We have an attitude shortage in this country, not a skills shortage" (CBI, 2001b, para 11). The Green Paper promised to go some way to tackling this:

> It is important that young people learn to know right from wrong; get along with their fellow students; work in teams; make a contribution to the school or college as a community; and develop positive attitudes to life and work. This is important not only for their own personal development, but also because employers increasingly emphasise not just academic qualifications, but skills and attitudes such as enterprise, innovation, teamwork, creativity and flexibility. (DfES, 2002, p 7)

It goes on to state that:

> ... new GCSEs in vocational subjects are to be available from September 2002 in some schools. We expect they will be far more widely available from September 2003. These new GCSEs will initially be available in Applied Art and Design; Applied Business; Engineering; Health and Social Care; Applied ICT; Leisure and Tourism; Manufacturing; and Applied Science.... The new Modern Apprenticeships are intended to meet high standards, endorsed by employers' organisations. (DfES, 2002, paras 3.29, 3.47)

It also argues that:

> ... it is essential for progression and for personal development that all young people should undertake some work-related learning. Such learning should be designed to develop pupils' employability and to help prepare them for working life. (DfES, 2002, para 3.13)

In order to achieve this, the Green Paper proposes to enable 14- to 19-year-olds to spend one or two days per week with a training provider, which could include colleges or employers. This would lead to greater pressure on schools and colleges to create

> ... new partnerships with employers to support the greater emphasis on work-related learning both within the institution and through work and community placements (DfES, 2002, para 3.33)

The proposals were warmly welcomed by employers, including the EEF, the British Chambers of Commerce and the CBI, as going some way to breaking down the barriers between vocational and academic qualifications (CBI, 2002c; CBI and CoC, 2002; EEF, 2003).

As a result of Conservative and Labour initiatives and reforms, schools policy is now much closer to the business agenda than it has been at any time in the past. Business has open to it many more opportunities to become involved in school management and to shape curricula and learning in schools. This has been in response both to the perceived needs, as well as the actual demands, of business against a backdrop of declining competitiveness in the UK. The CBI has been instrumental in pushing for change in certain areas, and has been directly involved in initiatives to help develop business links and more business-centred learning. In looking to business to provide answers to educational problems, however, the Labour government has gone further than business either desired or demanded. Although there have been concerted efforts made to promote closer education–business partnerships, both Conservative and Labour initiatives have struggled to generate sufficient interest from individual business people and firms.

Further and higher education

Further and higher education policy follows a broadly similar pattern to school policy, with successive governments since 1979 keen to increase the involvement of business in determining provision. The 1988 ERA established the former polytechnics as new universities which would be centrally funded and hence independent of their LEAs. At least half the members of the new university boards would have to be made up of industry or commerce members (Bastin, 1990, p 249). The 1992 Further and Higher Education Act established former further education colleges as corporations, again independent of LEAs, and stipulated that one third of the members of the corporation should be from business. As was the case in schools, therefore, legislation has helped to establish closer formal links between business and education.

The links between further education and business have become especially close since the early 1990s. Not only has business become more closely involved with institutional management, business has also been increasingly involved in further education curricula. The impact of business on the establishment of vocational qualifications within the sector has already been discussed above, but in addition to this some larger firms have even joined with colleges to help design tailor-made courses for their own local needs (Hoare, 2002).

Business links with higher education institutions also became more widespread and formalised in the 1980s and 1990s. Currently there are links based on research and development, consultancy services, student and staff placements and the direct corporate sponsorship of university posts and even entire departments. Moreover, the scale and variety of linkages has continued to expand rapidly in recent years (Howells et al, 1998).

Successive governments have played important roles in this expansion. The Council for Industry and Higher Education, established by the Conservative government in 1995, was designed to promote closer research links, especially in the areas of science and technology. Labour attempted to promote industry links still further by establishing the Higher Education Reach Out to Business and the Community (HEROBC) scheme in 1999, which was aimed at encouraging universities to submit joint funding bids with industry to the research councils. In 2001/02, HEROBC funding was worth £22 million. Research councils have also been instructed to ensure that research funding is geared towards the promotion of competitiveness and quality of life. Furthermore, the role of the Higher Education Funding Council for England (HEFCE) has been redefined so that it more closely meets the needs of business:

> An important part of HEFCE's strategy is to ensure that higher education is responsive to the needs of business and industry. HEFCE encourages partnerships between higher education institutions and industry, knowledge transfer, and employment skills. (DTI, 2001a)

Such initiatives have been generally welcomed by organised business, although splits exist on the question of the future of higher education. The CBI, for example, has vigorously campaigned for a major expansion in further and higher education since the early 1980s in order to meet the future demands of employers. It has also called for higher funding for both. In 1985 it wrote that:

> To remain competitive, business needs increasing numbers of well trained and educated graduates. Responding to the Government's green paper on Higher Education into the 1990s, the CBI expressed concern at the squeeze on higher education. While supporting the government's drive to increase efficiency, modernise management and achieve cost effectiveness in HE

[higher education], the CBI warned that teaching staff morale and resources were being undermined by the indefinite prospect of yearly cuts in resources, and ultimately the wealth creation process would suffer. (CBI, Annual Report, 1985, p 13)

The CBI campaigned heavily against Conservative spending cuts in higher education in 1986 and wrote to the education secretary complaining that cutbacks had "gone far enough", and that industry could not be expected to make up the shortfall for a much needed expansion in higher education (*CBI News*, 7 February, 1986, p 4).

Given this, the CBI welcomed the Labour government's commitment to the expansion of higher education student participation to half of all 18- to 30-year-olds, although it has remained remarkably quiet on the controversial issue of how to fund this expansion. The IoD, on the other hand, has taken a different view of the future training needs of employers, arguing that the UK requires an expansion of vocational rather than academic provision. The CBI and IoD are agreed that the common perceptions of vocational qualifications need to be improved so that they are viewed on a par with academic qualifications; but more recently, the IoD has gone further and argued that there needs to be a significant expansion in the numbers studying vocational qualifications and a reduction in those studying less 'useful' non-vocational degrees:

> ... one of the biggest problems for vocational training is, as we have already indicated, that far too many bright GCSE students are currently siphoned into HE (via A-levels) by the wrong-headed policy of encouraging 35% (target 50%) of students into HE, and away from vocational training. Of course, we are saying this from the business perspective – but it is written mindful of the many HE students who would be better advised to go into vocational training. As far as business is concerned the "parity of esteem" arguments are irrelevant – business is short of skills and they are all too frequently intermediate, practical skills. (IOD, 2002, p 2)

In actual fact, the Labour government acknowledged in 2003 that it would only be able to meet its 50% target were it to rely more heavily on vocational 'foundation degrees'. Margaret Hodge, higher education minister, stated in January 2003 that:

> ... most of the expansion of places will need to come from vocational degrees ... where education combines with businesses in the local and regional economy to devise two year courses which meet local skill shortages and business demands.... [We] are clear that if we can get the right engagement between the higher education providers and the employers, we can ensure an appropriate and relevant expansion in participation. (Margaret Hodge,

speech delivered at the Institute of Public Policy Research (IPPR) seminar 'Diverse Missions', 13 January 2003)

In response to the objections raised against the 50% participation rate by organisations such as the IoD, however, Hodge rhetorically asked:

> Do we need the extra graduates implied by the target? Yes we do. All our best understanding of what the demands of the labour market will be over the next decade confirms the need for more graduates. The Institute for Employment Research suggests that 80% of the new jobs that will be created in the next 10 years will require the skills and competences which go with higher education. The most recent CBI survey shows that employers expect a 50% increase in demand for graduates coupled with a 30% cut in the demand for people with low skills. (Margaret Hodge, speech delivered at the IPPR seminar 'Diverse Missions', 13 January 2003)

Labour's education policy to date has closely mirrored, or exceeded, the demands and expectations of business, especially those of the CBI.

Training

Employers have enjoyed extensive access to the training policy arena since the early 1970s. The Manpower Services Commission, established in 1973, formally integrated labour and employers into the national training executive, which was responsible for designing future training provision (King, 1993, p 220). As already outlined, however, the Conservative government of 1979 was wholly opposed to such corporatist arrangements. In the case of training, this really meant opposition to trades union involvement since employers increased their involvement and influence during the 1980s and 1990s. The setting up of the Training and Enterprise Councils in 1988 effectively shut labour out of this policy arena, but strengthened the hand of business significantly.

The creation of the TECs represented a major victory for employers. Central government and the CBI saw the development of TECs as important to guaranteeing a business–oriented approach to training. To ensure this, the government required that a majority of the members who sat on TEC boards were recruited from the private sector. Of a total of 15 or 16 directors, two thirds were to hold the office of chair or chief executive of a company, or be a senior 'operational manager' of the local branch of a large company. The remaining members were to be chief executives or their equivalents within relevant fields such as education, economic development, the voluntary or public sectors or trade unions (Graham, 1995, pp 276-7)[2]. The White Paper which launched the TECs outlined their roles and responsibilities as follows:

> The creation of TECs is a truly radical step. It will give leadership of the training system to employers, where it belongs. By increasing local employer

> responsibility for local training arrangements.... TECs will generate more
> private investment in training. As employers recognise the economic necessity
> to train and the returns available, they will be encouraged to make a larger
> investment in training. (Department of Employment, 1988, cited in Peck,
> 1991a, p 6)

According to Margaret Thatcher, the TECs would play "key local roles in the
achievement of national competitiveness" and would contribute to local
economies by

> ... developing competitive businesses capable of taking on and beating global
> competitors; developing and encouraging a world class workforce with the
> skills needed for successful businesses.... (cited in Graham, 1995, pp 272-3)

The CBI wanted the reforms to go further, arguing that training needed to be
employer-led, rather than provider-led, and determined by local business needs
and not by government or state training institutions (CBI, 1989a). In many
ways, employers were already determining the shape of training provision by
the late 1980s. By this time, the CBI had persuaded ministers of the need to
establish employer-centred learning through closer links between firms and
service providers, regularly upwardly revised educational targets, new vocational
qualifications and employment-led university expansion. The CBI was also
incorporated into the NCVQs (as detailed earlier in this chapter), which paved
the way for the introduction of NVQs and GNVQs in the late 1980s (CBI,
Annual Report, 1992, p 17). The NVQs were themselves established and
controlled by employer-dominated 'Industry Lead Bodies', which have since
been replaced, first by National Training Organisations in 1998, and then by
Sector Skills Councils in 2001. These organisations set out and coordinated
the necessary competences for vocational qualifications in their areas.

Non-business interests criticised the TECs for being dominated by elite and
short-term business interests rather than the needs of employees. The Labour
government responded to some of these criticisms by introducing the LSCs in
2000. The name change reflected the new responsibilities of the councils,
which included work-based training and further education. Like the former
TECs, the LSCs are driven by business needs, and they retain a significant role
for business, although the trades union and locally elected constituencies are
better represented. Despite this, concerns remain over the dominance of business
and former TEC members:

> Of 45 appointments to local LSCs, 17 went to people in executive posts on
> the soon-to-be-abolished TECs. Three went to people in TEC-related groups
> and two more posts are due to be filled.... At the head of the structure is
> the national learning and skills council, chaired by Bryan Sanderson, group
> managing director of BP Amoco. It will have a budget of £6 billion for 6
> million learners. (Crequer, 2000)

By 2003, of the 15 members of the LSCs national council, five were business representatives, including Digby Jones, director-general of the CBI, the chief executive of ATL Telecom, the former managing director of Coca Cola Great Britain, and a former partner of Anderson Consulting. The chair of the LSC is also the chair of BUPA and the former managing director of BP. The rest of the members are made up of various educationalists and government workers. The outgoing General Secretary of the TUC, John Monks, also sat on the board in 2003. As for the local LSC chairs and executives, the vast majority were occupied by senior business people (LSC, *Who's who, 2002/3*).

In taking over responsibility for all post-16 education and training (up to higher education level), the proposals for the LSCs also moved closer to an earlier CBI proposal in 1995, that urged the government to bring responsibility for all post-16 further education curriculum under one organisation (CBI, 1995). The Qualifications and Curriculum Authority in 1997 assumed responsibilities for all pre and post-16 curricula by taking over the duties of the NCVQ and the SCAA. Although the board structure of the QCA is less dominated by business than the NCVQ was, senior business executives still made up three of its eleven board members in 2003, including the Deputy Chair of BT and the Chair of Network Rail. Moreover, while employers may have lost some of their numerical strength on both the TEC bodies and the QCA, one the earliest moves by the QCA was to assure employers that it would continue to steer school and college curricula in their direction (as discussed earlier in this chapter).

Regarding the provision and delivery of training, the CBI has pushed successive governments into expanding vocational training and the adoption of ever-stricter qualification-based targets. The key concern of employers at the turn of the new century was the employability of young people and general skill shortages in the wider population. The CBI and Chambers of Commerce argued in a joint paper in 2001 that young people still lacked the right attitudes to work and the basic skills needed to contribute fully to the workplace (CBI and CoC, 2002). Governments have responded to such concerns by increasing the vocational relevance of education in a number of ways. The establishment of NVQs and GNVQs by the Conservative government were an important early move. More recently, the 14-19 Green Paper (discussed earlier in this chapter) proposed the setting up of Centres of Vocational Excellence (CoVEs) within existing further education colleges, with the intention of providing "high-quality specialist vocational training focused on meeting employers' needs" (DfES, 2002, p 66, fn 16). Labour has also attempted to expand vocational and post-compulsory training through initiatives such as the University for Industry and LearnDirect, both set up in 1998.

The move to establish training credits from 1990 also constituted an attempt to ensure that training provision would be better geared towards the needs of employees and employers. This policy was actually a long-established demand of the CBI, which argued that training credits would give greater freedom to individuals wishing to 'purchase' their own training from recognised establishments, including firms themselves. The overriding objective behind training credits for the CBI was to establish:

> A market for training so that individuals and employers are better able to influence the training on offer. Government should fund individual credits for all 16- to 18-year-olds to cover the cost of learning associated with courses leading to NVQ Level III or its academic equivalent. (*CBI News*, November 1989, p 16)

The Conservative government began piloting such schemes in 1990, although it was left to the Labour government to fully, if temporarily, introduce training credits in the guise of the ill-fated Individual Learning Accounts. Although these were quickly wound up amid allegations of widespread fraud committed by training providers, the government and the CBI remain committed to the idea of training credits in principle.

As was the case in education, government policy in the area of training has been systematically geared towards the needs of business. This is not surprising given the more direct reliance of employers on training provision, but the prioritising of business interests above labour interests was a break with pre-1979 attempts to incorporate both in the policy arena. Although trade unions have gained a stronger voice under New Labour, this is primarily because they came from a relative position of extreme weakness. Employers have retained much of their dominance in the LSCs, which raises bigger concerns than their dominance of the TECs given the LSC's expanded role in education and training. Taking all of these issues together, employers have an extremely powerful voice in post-16 education today.

Healthcare

The key aims of Conservative health policy over the 1980s and 1990s were to encourage an expansion in private provision, control expenditure and transform the culture of the NHS. The most important change came with the introduction of internal markets in 1989. The 1989 NHS Act introduced general practitioner (GP) fundholding and created health service trusts. The Act established two kinds of purchaser: the district health authorities (which were allocated budgets to purchase secondary care) and GP fundholders, who would purchase care on behalf of patients. The providers, hospital trusts, would compete with each other (and in some cases with those from the private or voluntary sectors) to offer services to the purchasers. Trusts were also granted some freedoms in relation to pay, skill mix and service delivery (Le Grand and Vizard, 1991, pp 78-9).

As in education and training, the Conservative government realised that radical change in the NHS would first require a transformation of culture and organisational structures. To this end, the Conservatives again looked to business for assistance. In order to bring the values of the private sector to the NHS, it recruited senior managers and other business representatives into the management structures of the NHS (Ashburner and Cairncross, 1993, pp 358-9). To pave the way for this, the government first removed local authority representation from the health boards with the introduction of the 1990 NHS and Community Care Act.

Labour has also looked to business for inspiration in tackling the problems within the health service. Health Action Zones, for example, were an attempt to establish innovative and integrated solutions to local health care needs in partnership with the voluntary and private sectors (Whitfield, 2001, pp 106-7). Their remit was to "bring together all those who contributed to the health of the local population to develop and implement a locally agreed strategy for improving the health of local people" (Department of Health, 1997, cited in Barnes and Sullivan, 2002, p 81). Although Vauxhall Motors, SmithKline Beecham, ASDA and various local chambers and CBI branches did get involved in some of the HAZs, business involvement has been more marginal than in the EAZ, and their role and contribution within them has been less well defined (Barnes and Sullivan, 2002, p 95). Even the large pharmaceutical and private health services, with the exception of SmithKline Beecham, have failed to get involved.

In fact, until recently, business has demonstrated very little interest in general health issues (aside from those companies with commercial interests in medicine). For example, unlike in education, the CBI did not call on employers to get involved in health trusts and did not produce a single policy statement of any significance between 1979 and 2000, despite the many heated public debates surrounding the NHS during that period. The CBI has devoted more attention to the NHS and to health services more generally in recent years, however, encouraged by two key factors. First, the CBI has become increasingly concerned about what it views as the 'indirect costs' being imposed on employers as a result of inefficiencies within the NHS. The CBI has complained that the failure of the NHS to treat its patients promptly has meant that employees spend longer out of work than necessary, resulting in higher costs to employers both in terms of financial support and in lost production. In addition, the CBI has argued that the lack of understanding among GPs of occupational health issues has meant that they are "either unable or unwilling to manage minor illnesses with a view to returning employees to work" (CBI, 2001a, p 3).

The conclusion reached by the CBI is that "publicly-funded healthcare in the UK is inefficient" (CBI, 2001a, p 1). The solution it offers is the increased incorporation of the private sector into the management, funding and delivery of health services. Tax incentives, it argues, should also be used to encourage employers to invest in occupational health. At the same time, private insurance should be promoted and charges for healthcare should be introduced.

This brings us to the second reason for increased CBI interest in the health service – the expansion of the opportunities for the private sector to get involved in, and profit from, the NHS. The PFI, for example, has created new opportunities for business to capitalise on public sector investment in the NHS.

The Conservative government determined that all hospital building plans from 1993 would have to first consider whether new investment could be made under PFI (Monbiot, 2000a, p 62). Under Labour, almost 90% of new hospital developments are being carried out under the PFI (Ruane, 2002, p 201).

The CBI also argued in 2002 for the greater use of the private sector in delivering healthcare, although by then the Labour government had already begun embarking on such schemes. In December 2002, Alan Milburn, then Secretary of State for Health, announced that private health companies will be able to bid, along with other NHS bodies, to run failing hospitals (James, 2002; Pollock, 2003). In the first such take-over, the *Good Hope* NHS hospital in Sutton Coldfield was taken over by SECTA in August 2003 (Shifrin, 2003a, 2003b). Around the same time, Milburn also invited the private sector to bid for contracts to run fast-track surgeries that are being set up by the government to help tackle waiting lists (Dean, 2003). The Labour government has also stepped up its efforts to shift the culture of the NHS closer to that of the private sector by proposing the establishment of foundation hospitals in 2003. In proposing foundation hospitals as semi-independent organisations, Alan Milburn acknowledged the influence of the IoD in the developing of the initiative. Under these controversial proposals which, at the time of writing, were yet to be passed by Parliament, greater competition would be encouraged between healthcare providers as semi-independent public 'companies'. Moreover, in a repeat of Conservative strategies to bring business people into the NHS in order to facilitate change, the Labour government, at the time of writing, is preparing the ground for foundation hospitals by trying to recruit senior private sector managers for key positions within NHS boards (Carvel, 2003).

To summarise, business interest in healthcare is low compared with some other areas of social policy, although it has increased in recent years as new openings have been provided for private sector inputs into the NHS. As in education, the government has increasingly looked to business to help provide solutions to problems of management and service delivery. The growing costs of providing good quality healthcare, coupled with the failings of the service to provide prompt treatment in non-emergency cases, has also alerted business to the financial and non-financial costs imposed on it by the NHS. The response of business has been to support and encourage the government's push for greater private sector involvement in the NHS in an attempt to reduce the role of the state in healthcare.

In many respects, therefore, policy developments in the NHS under New Labour have served business well. Attempts have been made to seek help from firms in order to tackle health inequalities; senior business people have been more closely integrated into the management structures of the NHS; private health firms have been provided with new opportunities to bid for health service contracts; and lucrative PFI deals have been awarded to a growing number of specialist private contractors.

Social security

Conservative social security policy was directed by two key objectives: to control expenditure, and to shift more of the responsibility for social protection onto individuals and the private sector. The spiralling social security budget, which grew by 109% between 1973/74 and 1995/96, was a major concern to a government keen to cut public spending. The Conservative government was also keen to introduce changes to benefits that it argued were negatively impacting on work incentives and competitiveness. To address this, the government attempted to reduce disincentives among firms to employ additional workers and disincentives among the unemployed to seek work (Timmins, 1996, p 283). To this end, benefits for 16- to 18-year-olds were abolished, taxes on employers were cut, and in-work benefits were extended.

A second important policy response was to attempt to reduce the cost of benefits by shifting responsibility for them onto employees and, in some cases, employers. Attempts have been made to increase the reliance on private cover in a number of areas, including mortgage protection, sickness and ill-health and retirement. Some of the costs of statutory sickness benefits and maternity pay, meanwhile, have been pushed onto employers. Successive governments have also endeavoured to increase occupational and private pensions.

Employers have responded by encouraging those proposals that would reduce costs or increase competitiveness and opposing those proposals that risked imposing higher costs onto firms. The biggest battles have been fought over changes in sickness benefits (Dean and Taylor-Gooby, 1990), the planned abolition of the state earnings related pension scheme (SERPS) (Dean and Taylor-Gooby, 1990; Taylor-Gooby and Lakeman, 1998, p 27), and the imposition of higher administrative burdens imposed by in-work benefits. Outside these key areas, organised business has contributed relatively little to the social security debate. This is surprising given the potential impact of social security on labour markets and the level of controversy surrounding key policy changes since 1979.

This is not to say that business has shown no interest in the general direction of social protection. Where it has commented, the CBI, like its international counterparts, has tended to focus on the role that social protection schemes can play in increasing flexibility in labour markets, reducing labour costs and increasing work incentives. However, it is not always easy to extract a clear notion of CBI thinking from its documents. Take, for example, the following discussion paper which began by stressing that

> ... we believe that a labour market ... does respond to supply and demand.... [I]t is perfectly possible to price oneself out of a job or indeed into one.... However, there are some – especially those with a large family or who are in receipt of rent or rate rebates – for whom the financial incentive to work at all is at best marginal and in some cases clearly negative. If this incentive were improved, their attitude to work might change as well. This disincentive

> exists because of ... lack of qualification ... income tax ... and social security
> provisions which are untaxed. (CBI, 1980a, p 23)

Although the overall tone of the document was in line with government thinking at the time, its conclusions did not follow those of the Conservative government. Not only did the paper resist calling for cuts in social security provision, it argued that such payments were necessary in order to reduce the inevitable pain caused by the necessary 'modernisation' of the economy'. The paper concluded that

> ... unemployment will continue to be a significant problem for some years ahead [and] the situation will need to be managed competently, sensibly and humanely in a comprehensive and as far as possible a non-partisan way. This will require specific help for areas of high and persistent unemployment and perhaps for particular groups where the incidence of unemployment is exceptionally high.... If unemployment were known to be temporary; if it were known to affect people equally whatever their occupation or wherever they lived; if the level of support for those out of work *did not necessarily imply a significant reduction in living standards*; and if perhaps above all, those out of work had non-work activities which gave enjoyment and purpose to their lives, then unemployment would no longer be a serious social problem although it would of course remain an economic one. (CBI, 1980a, p 40; emphasis added)

According to this view, unemployment benefits could be used as a way of assisting employers to shed labour. This is a rather idealised picture of unemployment, however, which is quite different to the negative views of welfare benefits that are more typical of business and CBI opinion. The CBI has generally been more supportive of state intervention geared at reducing disincentives to work, such as benefit cuts and wage subsidies. It has opposed the imposition of employer-administered in-work benefits, however, on the basis of the costs such schemes place on business, as the following statement illustrates with regard to the proposed introduction of Family Credit in 1986:

> The Government originally proposed that the new Family Credit ... should be administered by employers via the pay packet. The CBI strongly opposed this proposal as it would significantly add to the burden on business. Members also believe that the relationship between benefits and pay should not be confused by paying benefits in the pay packet. Last month the Government announced that Family Credit would now be payable by the DHSS directly to mothers, as is the case with FIS [Family Income Supplement]. (*CBI News*, 11 July 1986, p 3)

Similar views were expressed by business when Labour announced its plan to extend the number of in-work benefits from 1997 and, again, the government was eventually forced to agree to pay such benefits through the Inland Revenue after having initially favoured paying benefits through the wage packet. Following this change, the CBI warmly welcomed Labour's tax credits for families and the lower paid, which is not surprising given the potential for such benefits to reduce wage costs.

In other ways too, there is only a very narrow gap between the government and the CBI. The CBI, in common with international business (see Chapter Four of this book) and New Labour, argues that the affordability of all forms of social protection depends on levels of competitiveness and productivity within the economy. As the CBI puts it,

> The key to the dilemma on social protection lies in higher employment. A high employment level is the only feasible way to make EU social protection systems more sustainable, since that is how revenue is increased and payments to those in need are decreased. (CBI London Week in Brussels, address by Allan Larsson, director-general, *Employment Industrial Relations and Social Affairs*, 4 March 1998)

For the CBI, the solution to unemployment could be found in supply-side measures: increasing work incentives; ensuring that work pays by lowering taxation; increasing the availability of work by reducing non-wage labour costs; and increasing the availability of adequate and flexible training (CBI, 2000b).

Pensions have been the cause of more tensions between business and central government. Organised business, including the EEF and the CBI, for example, opposed the Conservative government's plan to abolish SERPS and introduce compulsory occupational and private pensions in 1985, for fear of the increased costs that would be imposed on business. The major sticking point for business was that the proposal would have meant that employers would have had to continue paying contributions for SERPS pensioners (which would be abolished in three years), but at the same time fund the alternative private pensions of current employees (CBI, 1994, pp 61-2). Business opposition was instrumental in the government's eventual about-turn on the issue, as Norman Fowler, minister responsible for the introduction of the proposals, made clear in his biography:

> I had against me almost the whole of the pensions industry.... Even more ominously, both the CBI and the influential Engineering Employers' Federation had moved against me. (Fowler, 1991, p 222)

In the end, the government announced that it would retain a modified SERPS for the foreseeable future, a victory for which the CBI took a great deal of credit:

> The Government originally wanted to abolish SERPS, but has bowed to pressure from the CBI and others and is now retaining it in modified form. ('Pensions switch will hit costs', *CBI News*, 2 May 1986, p 3)

The CBI's longer-term policy was less defensive of SERPS, provided that the transitory costs were met by individuals and not industry. This is clear from the CBI's response to the government's Special Inquiry into Pensions in 1982:

> ... against an uncertain economic future, it is important for the Government not to add further cost burdens to the state and occupational pension schemes, but rather to allow people more choice in the extent to which, and ways in which, they wished individually (and at their own expense) to top up their provision for retirement. (CBI evidence to the government's Special Inquiry into Pensions Provision, April 1984, p 7)

A gradual move towards voluntary occupational or private schemes was more acceptable to the CBI, as it removed the threat of additional costs on employers and allowed all interests to better prepare for change. The measures eventually introduced in the 1986 Social Security Act – to reduce SERPS from 25% to 20% of lifetime earnings (rather than the best 20 years) which would affect those retiring after 2001 – were accepted without protest by the CBI.

Regarding the basic pension, the CBI maintained its support throughout the period and expressed this most recently in its submission to the 2002 Pensions Review. Since the early 1980s, the CBI has pushed for a three-tier pension system, made up of state, occupational and private schemes, along similar lines to the proposed schemes pushed at the EU and global level by employers (see Chapter Three of this book). In 1982, the CBI argued that the state pension could be maintained for the foreseeable future, but that the three-tiered approach should be phased in over time. Labour's stakeholder pensions scheme, which the CBI praised as an important step in the right direction, follows this model.

In actual fact, there is very little dividing Labour and employers with regard to the future of pensions. This is especially true now that the government has announced plans to abolish compulsory retirement ages (Hall, 2003). The introduction of a flexible retirement age has been at the heart of the CBI's pensions policy since the early 1980s. In 1981, the CBI emphasised the importance of a flexible retirement age that would allow employees to retire early, thus helping employers to shed labour during this period of economic slump (CBI, 1981a, p 36). During the relative prosperity of 1988 and concerns about labour shortages, the organisation argued for a flexible retirement age which would allow employees to retire later (*CBI News*, 29 April 1988, p 4). Although this proposal failed to persuade the Conservative government, it was met with a more favourable response from the present Labour government, persuaded by an EU Directive outlawing age discrimination (Hall, 2003) and the views of advisors, such as the head of the government's Pensions Commission,

Adair Turner. Turner, who also happens to be the former director-general of the CBI, informed *The Observer* in April 2003 that people will have to work beyond the age of 65 if pensions are to survive in future (Jones, 2003; Morgan, 2003). The problem, however, is that the spirit of the EU Directive to defend the rights of workers does not necessarily coincide with the needs of employers. As soon as the government began making serious noises about the introduction of more flexibility around retirement, the CBI raised concerns about the risk of undermining the 'usual' retirement age for workers since this may expose employers to the charge that they are discriminating against workers if they do not give them the option to remain in work (CBI, 2003). In short, employers want the flexibility to shed or retain older workers without giving employees the right to continue to work beyond a certain age. It is not yet clear how the government will reconcile these difficulties.

Again, there is little to divide New Labour and business approaches to social security. Both insist that social security has to be made to fit better with the demands of contemporary labour markets. Unemployment benefits should be provided by the state with conditions that recipients actively seek work. For other benefits, the private sector should be relied upon wherever possible, although state support will remain important for the 'deserving poor'. In short, there has been an attempt to ensure that the key functions of social security are shifted further away from poverty alleviation and closer towards economic imperatives.

Social housing

While the Conservative government did attempt to introduce private sector involvement in the public sector through such schemes as the Housing Action Trusts and Tenants Choice (or 'pick a landlord' scheme) and CCT in the area of housing management (introduced in 1988), it was possible to control the extent and costs of public provision relatively simply without involving business in its transformation. The introduction of the 'Right to Buy' scheme, the reduction of housing subsidies to local authorities, and tighter controls over local authority borrowing and capital expenditure in order to virtually remove local authorities from future house building, were important mechanisms through which central government could control direct provision. Controlling housing benefit proved to be more difficult.

A central concern for organised business has been the impact of housing shortages on labour supply. Concerns over the impact of housing on labour mobility have led to a number of business initiatives and strategies. The CBI has expressed concerns especially about the impact of housing problems on geographical mobility, particularly from North to South (*CBI News*, 19 February-3 March 1988, pp 8-9). A lack of affordable accommodation in the South is identified as being a particular problem which has been exacerbated by the selling off of public housing. The CBI did not advocate a return to social housing to solve these problems, however, but argued that employers should engage in local initiatives, for example, providing land or capital to housing associations in exchange for nomination rights for employees, in order to increase access to housing where this was a particular problem:

> The CBI has made [it] clear that firms should not just look to government for solutions where problems impinge on business. Business must provide its own. In the housing field, businesses have been given the opportunity to do just that. (*CBI News*, 4-19 March 1988, pp 12-13)

The problem of housing and labour shortage has, if anything, grown more acute in the 2000s, particular in the South East. This has presented problems for both the public and private sectors. For this reason, the CBI has argued recently that significant reform of the housing market is required, including the expansion of affordable housing (CBI, 2002b). Despite the urgency of the problem, however, the CBI has failed to put forward solutions to the problems of social housing, preferring instead to call for greater relaxation of building controls in order to allow the private sector to build more housing to meet the demand for owner occupation.

In many ways, business views on the problems of the housing market, especially within social housing, are the most underdeveloped of all the major areas of social policy. None of the CBI's key policy outputs since the 1970s have attempted to develop a clear and coherent strategy on housing. This is surprising given the centrality of housing as both an important sector of the economy and an important determinant of labour costs and availability. Policy proposals, where they have been developed, have tended to focus on issues central to the owner-occupied sector, such as land development, planning and interest rates.

Conclusion: business and British social policy

Business has played a significant role in the development of UK social policy over the past 25 years or so. Successive governments have sought to steer the welfare state towards more business-centred provision that is thought to help increase competitiveness and productivity. Business has also been utilised by governments as an important ally in helping to bring social provision, and social spending in particular, under control. For its part, business has engaged in social policy debate and has influenced some key policy outcomes. However, its interest in, and influence on, social policy is variable. With regard to business interest in social policy, this varies according to the area of provision in question. The key predictor of level of interest is the extent to which social policies have an *immediate and direct* impact on businesses. Of particular concern is the extent to which social policy impacts on the simple costs of 'doing' business, including labour costs, and the supply and qualifications of workers.

For its part, the CBI has defended services that directly benefit business, such as infrastructure spending, and those that help to improve labour productivity, such as education and training. At the same time, the CBI has attacked those services that are generally unproductive and has argued for greater controls on 'unproductive' spending, for example, on the wages of public sector workers and certain local services. It has also pushed for greater business involvement in those areas of social policy that contribute towards productivity, especially those impacting on the skills of labour. While it has opposed spending on public sector wages, business has defended spending on purchases from the private sector, since they help to support business sales, including capital investments.

On the question of social security transfers, business opinion is less clear-cut. On the one hand, they assist the management of the unemployed, but on the other they push up labour costs and taxation, so we would expect business opinion to be divided and subject to change in this area.

In some key areas of social policy, especially on the big questions relating to the future of social policy, the CBI has been remarkably quiet since the 1970s. One explanation for this is that business tends to respond to initiatives and provision according to how far it impacts on its interests. Another is that there has been little need for the CBI and other parts of business to seek to influence social policy during this period since, in most ways and in most areas, social policy has been steered in a pro-business direction. Structural influences, reinforced by globalisation, as already discussed in the previous chapter, have promoted cuts in spending on unproductive services and expansion in productive services. Business has become involved only where its interests have been directly threatened. It has sought to make governments aware of the damaging impact of cuts in capital expenditure and has attempted to push policy towards business-friendly social provision that helps to promote profitability. Beyond this, it was enough to limit its campaigns to the major questions that were of key interest to most parts of business, such as tax reform and labour costs. Provided business could secure for itself cuts in general and corporate taxation and commitments to reduce spending in non-productive areas, it could limit its focus to its core interests.

In only a few instances has the CBI tried actively to push policy making in a completely new direction; in most cases it has tended to respond to an agenda set by central government. Because of the significance of structural pressures, most policies of the Conservative or Labour governments have been introduced because of the perceived or expressed needs of business, and with due caution paid to how the policy may impact on business.

Notes

[1] The former director-general of the CBI, Adair Turner (2001, p 265) explained in his memoirs that this figure was arrived at partly because of competitiveness and also because of the perceived need to "commit to some rule, however debatable the precise figure" for fear that otherwise "expenditure will tend to grow relentlessly".

[2] Early research on the composition of TEC boards indicated that 67% of their membership was drawn from the private sector (Plummer, 1994, p 20).

SIX

Business and local welfare services

Introduction

The preceding chapters of this book have detailed how business concerns have been promoted up the social policy agenda since the late 1970s. New opportunities have been presented to businesses and business people wanting to become more closely involved in a range of welfare services. Even where business has been reluctant to take up these opportunities, central government has gone out of its way to encourage greater private sector involvement in social policy. Service providers, meanwhile, have been forced to incorporate business people into their management structures and have regard to business preferences in their decision making. Nonetheless, business involvement in welfare services has been patchy. This chapter looks at the extent of business involvement in local provision, taking the city of Bristol as a case study.

Local government, business and social policy

Chapter Five detailed how local government has been systematically undermined by central government since the 1980s through a number of mechanisms which served to strengthen business interests locally and weaken elected officials (Valler et al, 2000, p 411). To begin with, central government exerted increasing controls over taxation and spending levels. This was partly in response to lobbying by organised business for lower levels of corporate taxation and spending at the local level, and was partly due to the Conservative government's desire to control overall levels of public expenditure. This resulted in the introduction of the 1984 Rates Act, which forced local authorities to consult with businesses about the setting of local taxation and the provision of local services.

This act also introduced rate capping, whereby central government placed a 'cap' on the amount of local taxation that could be levied by councils. The most important change came with the 1988 Local Government Finance Act, which introduced the Community Charge (Poll Tax) and the Uniform Business Rate (UBR). The Poll Tax imposed a flat rate tax on most adults in order to pay for local services. The UBR shifted the responsibility for the setting and collection of business rates to central government in response to the business criticism that, in setting business rates, local authorities often paid very little attention to business interests, which represented a tiny minority of the local electorate. This was especially a problem in very poor boroughs, within which many voters were exempt from making any contributions to local revenue under the precursor to Poll Tax, the local rates tax. According to Midwinter and Monaghan (1993, p 64) the fact that business was one of the biggest contributors to local revenues, but had a relatively weak voice locally, was one of the main reasons for the introduction of changes in local taxation.

However, by themselves, spending controls were ineffective at changing the culture of the welfare state, which was a key Conservative aim. Attention thus turned to attempts to directly tackle the power and autonomy of local authorities, and transformations in the role and responsibilities of local councils were introduced in a number of areas. In some services, a weak elected presence remained, but in others, local authority responsibility and involvement were removed altogether. By contrast, private sector involvement in welfare services was viewed as essential to the planned transformation in social policy, and business inputs were steadily increased in a range of services. In order to facilitate this, the Conservative government created a number of new access points for business.

Decentralisation meant greater autonomy from local authorities for many services, although central government and various quango bodies often gained greater powers and responsibilities for regulating service delivery. Within education, training and health, the Conservative government used new powers to insist on the involvement of business interests. A series of reforms gradually, but purposefully, squeezed elected representatives out of locally managed services and replaced them with business people – predominantly businessmen according to Peck and Tickell (1995a). At the same time, organised labour was squeezed out of key areas of decision making, such as training policy, in which it had previously played an instrumental role. In their place, the government installed sympathetic business people to help run services from strengthened management boards, which would allow them to carry through Conservative reforms on the ground (Whitfield, 2001, p 69). The introduction of CCT, introduced in 1980 for construction and extended to other services from 1988, and the establishment of the PFI in 1992, steadily cemented a new relationship between business and the state, forcing local authorities to open up services to the private sector. For example, CCT forced local authorities to contract out services to private sector providers, while PFI forced councils and other public sector bodies to consider allowing the private sector to build and manage major infrastructure projects in exchange for rental and service fees. Through this series of reforms, as a result, local authorities were gradually transformed from providers to enablers of services – facilitating provision through purchasing services from outside sources, including corporations.

The scope for business involvement in decision making has also been increased in other areas of local policy making, including taxation, spending and local economic development. Even where local authorities have retained some responsibilities for services, they have been forced to consult and work more closely with local partners, especially local business representatives. Successive governments have placed increasing faith in the private sector as the only interest capable of creating solutions to local social problems; less and less faith has been placed in the capacity of the public sector to bring about such solutions. As Deakin and Edwards (1993, p 1) put it,

> The idea that 'inner city problems' ... can be solved or even alleviated by targeting public resources into them ... is now defunct.... Clearly, only the private sector could produce the jobs and economic buoyancy that the inner cities lacked, and equally self-evident was the superior drive, energy and effectiveness of a private sector increasingly fired by the enterprise culture.

This new focus on private sector involvement in social policy went further than merely encouraging business interests to get involved in local services. From the 1990s, the inclusion of business in partnerships with local authorities and other key actors became increasingly essential to securing funding from central government in a number of different areas, from economic redevelopment to tackling social exclusion (Coulson, 1997, p 34; Coates et al, 2000).

Business has not just reacted to these changes, but has itself played an important role in their development. Organised business in particular has promoted business involvement in state services and local communities as a means of influencing provision and marketing companies through their 'good deeds' in the community:

> Firms are as interested in goals of steady growth and stability as in profit maximisation and risk. These interests lead to an interdependency with government intervention in the market, and to the gradual involvement of business in community affairs which have no apparent *direct* link with business profits. Yet, in essence, this involvement is often defended in terms of self-interest. (Moore and Richardson, 1987, p 6; emphasis in original)

Business in the Community (BiTC), an organisation that promotes corporate social responsibility by pointing to its mutual benefits for firms and citizens, argued in the mid-1990s that the crisis of the welfare state and the rise of the 'free enterprise culture' meant that business was especially well placed to step into the breach and make positive contributions to social provision (see page 163). This resulted in an epidemic of partnership fever, which, according to Peck and Tickell (1995b, pp 5-6), fostered:

> ... a dense web of interconnected agencies, lobby groups and committees. In virtually all of them the voice of business is especially strong, and it is invariably businessmen who occupy the most powerful positions.

A similar argument is put forward by Bassett (1996, p 539):

> There seems general agreement that before the 1980s the influence of business on local politics was on the whole more indirect and more limited.... This

situation has certainly changed in the UK over the past decade, with new business elites becoming increasingly involved in urban policy-making, often through the widening network of partnership organisations which are to be found in many urban areas.

It would appear that the very process of recruiting business voices into such partnerships has itself created a new momentum towards still further involvement of business in areas that have been, for several decades at least, the domain of the state. Business has been invited to take a more active role in local problem solving, and this has in turn given it new confidence to expand its role in local communities.

The net result has been an explosion of opportunities for business involvement in various forms of social provision. The voice of business has thus been increased in at least two ways: through direct representation, and through partnership working. The rest of this chapter documents local business involvement in social provision in Bristol.

The city of Bristol

Despite being described as England's 'Sunbelt City' in the mid-1980s (Boddy et al, 1986), Bristol suffered the highs and lows of other cities during the 1980s and 1990s. High concentrations of unemployment characterise some parts of the city (unemployment averaged 24% in some areas between 1981 and 1994; DiGaetano and Klemanski, 1993, pp 72-3; M. Stewart, 1995, p 13) and drug abuse and homelessness are ongoing problems. DiGaetano and Klemanski (1993) and M. Stewart (1995) also point to a history of high tensions and animosity between the historically Labour-dominated city council and the local business community as important to an understanding of the context of local politics in the city. In short, Bristol is a typical British city that has had its fair share of economic and social problems, as well as political tensions. It is not especially large or small, having a population of around 400,000, making it the eighth largest in England. In this respect, Bristol makes an ideal case study. If business is anywhere involved in social policy, we should find examples of it in Bristol.

The regional branch of the CBI

Bristol is the base of the South Western Regional Branch of the Confederation of British Industry (CBI). Its activities are shaped by its position as the regional branch of a more powerful national organisation. Historically, its involvement in local decision making has been in those areas that were unsuitably dealt with at the national level, including membership recruitment, regional development, local services and local taxation. Social policy did not feature heavily at all. The regional director of the CBI at the time explained that:

"We are interested in social policy if it affects businesses' bottom line. If it helps to improve efficiency, or if it damages competitiveness, then the CBI will get involved.... We are interested in [helping to develop] good environments for businesses." (interview with regional director of the CBI, 1997)

From this stemmed a general hands-off approach within the regional CBI towards most social policy issues. While the national body of the CBI has been keen to get local branches and individual members of the CBI more actively involved in local politics and local services (see Chapter Five of this book), particularly in the fields of education and training, this local branch did not pursue this policy, either by getting involved in welfare services itself[1], attempting to get its members involved, or by attempting to 'politicise' its membership. Since the regional branch of the CBI could do little to make significant changes to the bigger policy questions relating to local social policies, the most important of which are determined nationally, the local organisation was reluctant to devote resources to lobbying activities in this area. Moreover, despite the emphasis placed on business involvement in social provision by central government and the national CBI, the view of the regional branch was that it was increasingly difficult to get individual members involved in any activities which were not directly linked to the immediate returns of businesses. This included getting involved in local politics. The regional director of the CBI explained to me in 1997 that

"... the practice where businesses would second staff to serve as councillors or in similar capacities have long gone."

The regional director went on to suggest that, despite the general efforts of central government and national business organisations, business people are often reluctant to become closely involved with public policy issues because of the time and energies demanded of them and the time spent on insignificant issues concerning relatively small sums of money:

"They take a great deal of time deliberating on how they are going to spend £2.5 million pounds over the next, say, two years while business people are used to taking such decisions on a daily basis. They may have spent twice that amount that very day. I think that business people get very impatient and often give up membership quite quickly."

Partly because of this, the local CBI did not invest time and energy into trying to encourage or coordinate business involvement within local communities, nor did it have the necessary resources to keep track of such activities. This was despite the huge numbers of requests they regularly received from different public sector organisations for assistance in recruiting business people. The regional CBI generally viewed the local Chambers of Commerce as far better placed to undertake a more active social role in local communities, leaving the CBI to consider 'more important' questions, related primarily to economic issues.

The Bristol Chambers of Commerce and Initiative

Bristol's Chambers of Commerce merged with The Bristol Initiative (TBI) to form the Bristol Chambers of Commerce and Initiative (BCCI) in 1993. The chambers existed to represent Bristol's local trading interests; TBI, on the other hand, was unique to the city, being established by key 'elites' from business and elsewhere. It was geared towards the development of a range of urban regeneration and inner-city projects designed to improve the quality of life and trade within the city. Two main driving forces were behind its development. The first involved concerns over the increasing cuts in local authority spending and the effects this would have on local authority provision, and hence, local communities. In particular, local business interests were concerned about Bristol's infrastructure and the impact of visible poverty – including drug abuse, vandalism, crime and homelessness in the centre of Bristol – on local tourism and trade.

The second driving force behind TBI was the desire of key business and other non-business elites to gather forces capable of exerting greater influence on a city council that was perceived by the business community as "quite left wing and unreceptive to the needs of business" (personal communication with a senior representative of BCCI, October 1998). TBI was heavily influenced by, and echoed the views of, the national CBI's highly significant report entitled *Initiatives beyond charity*. Published in 1988, this report urged business people to become more actively involved within their localities in order to improve local trading and manufacturing environments. The Bristol Initiative provided a forum where the public and private sector could come together on a range of issues of concern to business and non-business interests alike. In bringing these interests together, business could not only help bring changes to local communities and, hence, improve the image of business within localities, it could also foster better relationships with key members of the council (Bassett, 1996).

Following the merger in 1993, the key members of the former TBI continued to exist as an elite group within the BCCI called the 'President's Group'. Its members were drawn from the most influential and high-ranking actors within the city, including the "Chief Executives of its major industries, the heads of education, the prime movers of the local authorities and of the church" (Rylance, 1995). These individuals had, what a senior member of the BCCI termed, "different interests from the majority of BCCI's members who are mainly small to medium-sized private companies" (Rylance, 1995). Since it incorporates non-business interests into the Chambers of Commerce, it also blurs the distinction between business and other 'elites'. The President's Group has succeeded in bringing together a network of well-connected individuals from different sectors. A representative of the BCCI explained in 1996 that:

"Unlike the situation even five years ago, there is now more cooperation [between the public and private sectors]. Recently there was a [social gathering] and most of the people there, from top positions in business, the council and the church, knew each other."

As well as providing a forum for local business and other elites to come together, the BCCI retained some of the grander hopes of TBI and aimed to have a positive impact on life within the city, primarily by helping to find solutions to some key social problems including crime, drug abuse and homelessness. To this end, it established a number of projects, including a Housing and Homelessness initiative and an Education and Training initiative. Each of these are considered in the relevant sections below.

The key differences in approach between the regional CBI and the BCCI were that the former viewed itself very much as a smaller appendage of its parent organisation, and its activities and outlook reflected this. The CBI identified much less with the city but instead focused on the region more broadly. The BCCI, on the other hand, had a strong local focus and identity. It also appeared to have greater confidence in itself as an organisation that was able to facilitate local change. It fostered many important business, public and political links locally, and felt that it could play an important role in bringing together this range of interests in order to tackle local problems, including social problems. In this way, paradoxically, its approach was closer to the national CBI's vision of local business citizenship than the CBI's regional branch.

Business and local social provision to 1997

The focus now turns to consider business involvement in various welfare services in Bristol during the mid-1990s. It is followed by a brief discussion of changes in Bristol following the election of the Labour Government in 1997.

Schools

The membership of the governing body of a medium- to large-sized LEA school (around 1,000 pupils) is typically made up of around six elected parent governors, six LEA governors, six co-opted governors, and three teacher governors. Business people are able to get involved in the running of schools by becoming parent or nominated LEA governors, but it is more usual for them to become co-opted governors, elected by the current governing body. As a result of Conservative reforms in the mid-1980s, schools had to have increasing "regard to the extent to which they and the other governors are members of the local business community" (cited in Thody, 1989, p 142). The fact that they can be represented in any form often makes it difficult to establish how many business people a school has on its board at any one time.

Six secondary schools were included in the sample for this part of the research. Between them, these schools had a total of 110 board members. Of these, 22 were business representatives, which included five senior business people (company directors and chairs of large firms), five middle ranking (senior managers of larger firms and directors of smaller firms), and ten junior business people (middle and lower ranking managers). Two of the senior business people were directors of smaller companies and the other three came from larger firms.

Regarding private sector funding and sponsorship, most schools did receive some financial support, although this tended to take the form of relatively small gifts of only a few hundred pounds. Where larger donations were given to schools they were for specific projects. Wessex Water, for example, gave £10,000 towards an Astroturf Project at one school in 1995, while British Telecom donated £3,300 worth of telecommunications equipment to another school during 1994/95.

Substantial funding was found only in the case of Bristol's City Technology College, John Cabot, where formal private-sector arrangements existed. John Cabot was established in September 1993 and had around 1,000 students at the end of the 1990s. Its mission statement reveals a strong business focus and promises to provide:

> ... not only the sound and broad educational foundation of the National Curriculum, but also a value-added emphasis on the practical, scientific, technological, mathematical and communication skills needed by manufacturing and service business. (John Cabot School, 1995/96 Prospectus)

The school's initial sponsors were Cable and Wireless PLC and the Wolfson Foundation, which between them contributed around £2.25 million of the £11 million total start-up costs of the school (Margrave, 1994, p 65). They also contributed additional monies of some £29,692 during 1995/96.

Regarding the governance of the school, both corporate sponsors appointed between them six of its seven trustees. Five members of its 11-member governing body were senior business people and three of these had connections with the sponsoring companies (in fact, both companies directly nominated one governor each).

Business links were also strong in a small but prestigious private school included within the investigation. Its governing body included two senior and well-connected business people, both of whom were members of the BCCI's President's Group with links to other welfare services: one the United Bristol Health Trust and the other, the council of the University of Bristol.

Further education colleges

Unlike LEA schools, which have only to consider the extent to which governors represent the local business community, colleges of further education since 1992 have had to ensure that at least one third of their governors are made up of business representatives. Business representatives made up over half of the total board members of the colleges investigated here. Further investigation of one college revealed that, of a total board membership of 15, six were business members, including, among them, a company director, a senior partner in a solicitors practice, the deputy chief executive of a television company, a senior manager and two middle managers. One of these, in addition to being a governor of the college, was connected to three other welfare service boards in Bristol: the Western Training and Enterprise Council (WESTEC), the University of Bristol and Bristol District Health Authority.

Universities

Previous research has revealed high levels of business involvement in the management of universities. Bastin's (1990) study, for example, found that 59% of independent board members within universities were drawn from private firms in the late 1980s. Over 85% of these were classified as chairs/chief executives/managing directors, and one third were from large companies (Bastin, 1990, p 250). The majority of university chairs also held senior positions in businesses (Bastin, 1990, pp 260-1). A similar spread of business board members was found in the two universities in Bristol.

The governing council of the University of Bristol consisted of 65 members in the late 1990s. A large proportion of these were nominated by outside agencies, including the city council and three county councils. Ten members were also nominated by the secretive and elitist Society of Merchant Venturers, a business-dominated 'club' that, according to Garret (1993), has "dominated Bristol's political, business and cultural life for centuries". It also has "enormous influence over bodies receiving public funds", according to the *Bristol Evening Post* (13 May 2003). Of its total membership, seven were members of BCCI's President's Group; four were members of the Avon Education Committee; three were represented on the board of United Bristol Health Trust; one on Weston Health Trust; one on Avon Health Authority; one sat simultaneously on the boards of Knightstone Housing Association and the Housing Corporation; two had seats on the BCCI's Employment, Education and Training Committee, and one sat on the board of Clifton College. In addition, eight were trustees of the Greater Bristol Foundation (GBF)[2], a charitable organisation which manages funds bequeathed by Bristol's wealthiest families. In terms of their business credentials, six members of the board held senior positions within Bristol companies (with one additional member being a retired director of a large brewing company), and four of these held more than one directorship or were the chairs of large firms. Hence, the University of Bristol not only managed to attract well-connected individuals to their board, but also very senior business people.

The governing body of the University of the West of England (UWE) was much smaller than that of the University of Bristol, having a total board membership of 25 members (13 independent, eight co-opted, plus the vice chancellor and three academic nominees), although it was no less dominated by business and other powerful interests. Its governing body included two representatives of business associations – the regional director of the CBI and the director of the Engineering Employers Federation (EEF); a proprietor of a small retail outlet; a partner within a chartered accountants firm; the director of a Bristol marketing company; and six directors of large national companies. Seven of the governors were also members of the President's Group, and two of those were trustees of the GBF. In addition, five of the governors were also members of other social policy boards. As well as having as a member the principal of Brunel College, the governing body also included a member of Avon Health Authority, a member of the United Bristol Health Trust, a member of WESTEC, and a member of Gloucestershire TEC.

Western Training and Enterprise Council (WESTEC)

As Chapter Five made clear, legislation was more prescriptive in relation to business representation on the now dismantled TEC boards than other services. Under statutory requirements, senior business people were given an in-built majority on their boards. The WESTEC board, as a result, consisted of 16 non-executive members, and one executive member, with only five members not having direct corporate connections although they were still extremely 'well connected' locally. They included the vice chancellor of UWE, Bristol's director of education, and the chief executive of the Bristol Development Corporation. The others held prominent positions within private companies: one was the partner of an accountancy firm, five were company directors, four were chairs or chief executives and one was a general manager. Six members of the board were also members of the BCCI's President's Group, and one of these sat on the CBI's National Council. In addition to the presence of the vice chancellor of the UWE, two of the board members held positions on other social policy boards, one being a non-executive director of Weston Health Trust, while another was both a governor of South Bristol College and of UWE.

The Employment, Education and Training Committee (EETC)

The BCCI's Employment, Education and Training Committee (EETC) was established in the mid-1990s as a partnership forum between the private sector, educational and training providers and local employment agencies. Its aim was to try to develop closer partnerships between these different interests. Its membership, which totalled around 39, included 13 senior representatives from private sector firms in addition to representatives of four local schools, two further education colleges, a local job centre, the CBI, both universities, the National Union of Teachers, and the local Education Business Partnership. The committee met regularly during 1995/96 and fed issues of concern to the President's Group of the BCCI, which, as already mentioned, included among its members, the leader of the council, the leader of the opposition, the chief executive of the council and the director of education. Once issues had been brought to the attention of the President's Group, the intention was for the BCCI to raise them with local senior politicians, MPs and members of the government. In this respect, therefore, the committee was really a talking shop and, although it provided important links between business, education and employment policy makers and service deliverers, and acted as a conduit for future educational initiatives (as detailed later in this chapter), nothing of substance emerged from the committee and it was disbanded in the late 1990s.

BCCI's Housing the Homeless Group (HHG)

The Housing the Homeless Group (HHG) was the second key project established by the BCCI. Set up in the late 1980s, the HHG's board included three managing directors and the director of housing from Bristol City Council. It also included representation from the voluntary sector and from local housing associations.

The name of the initiative is not particularly helpful in describing its aims, being neither a provider of homes for the homeless, nor a provider of services to help find housing for the homeless. The project had two main purposes:

* to help tackle social deprivation;
* to tackle the negative impact that homelessness and drug abuse were having on trade and tourism in certain parts of the city.

While it began life with much grander plans, however, the HHG subsequently evolved into a talking shop, providing a forum for public/private/voluntary sector exchange. The aim of the HHG, according to a senior member of the BCCI, evolved into one where the group would "trouble-shoot and help find solutions" to the problems of homelessness and drug abuse before handing over responsibility for them to other groups (primarily the public and voluntary sectors).

The initial plans of the HHG, to provide temporary accommodation in mobile homes, never got off the ground, and gave way to another proposal to provide luncheon vouchers for the homeless (although this also quickly folded). More successful was the HHG's involvement, during the mid-1990s, in a partnership with the local authority and several voluntary organisations, which helped to establish a local accommodation and training centre as well as a multi-agency centre for the homeless. The involvement of the BCCI in this partnership, as a key private sector interest, was instrumental in Bristol winning a £7 million Rough Sleepers grant from the government to help set up these initiatives. While the BCCI retains loose links to these projects, it no longer has formal ties to any of them.

Housing associations

Business involvement in housing associations (HAs) appeared, on the whole, to be more patchy than in other areas. The board membership of three of Bristol's largest housing associations was investigated. It is clear from this evidence that business involvement varies greatly from association to association. Priority housing association had just one relatively junior business member on its board. Bristol Churches' board included two retired business people (a former director, and a former bank manager). Knightstone had on its board a senior business person and an extremely well-connected member who was also a member of The Housing Corporation (which is responsible for funding housing associations) and of the University of Bristol council, as well as being married to a prominent and senior local business person. This unevenness reflects the lack of statutory controls over the board membership of housing associations.

Health

Although business did not have an especially high presence on health boards in Bristol, those that were represented tended to be relatively senior and well connected. Around 35% of the non-executive seats on the boards of the health trusts examined here were occupied by senior business people. The board of United Bristol Health Trust, for example, included the chair of a large television company, as well as the president of the BCCI. Of its seven non-executive members, four were members of the University of Bristol's council (including a pro-chancellor and the vice chancellor) and several others held chairs on other bodies including the BCCI's President's Group, the Merchant Venturers and the GBF.

Avon Health Authority also had two board members with clear business links: one was a company director and a member of WESTEC, UWE and South Bristol College; another held three company directorships and was a member of the University of Bristol council and BCCI's President's Group.

A similar pattern emerges within the other health trusts in Bristol. Frenchay Health Trust had two business representatives, including the director of a large car parts company who was also a member of one of Bristol's largest housing associations and was on the council of the University of Bristol. Phoenix NHS Trust board contained the retired commercial director of South Western Electricity Board (SWEB), the manager of a small business, and a member of the BCCI's President's Group. Weston Area Health Trust had just one company director on its board.

Although business interests did not form the majority members of health boards in Bristol, they were present in significant numbers, and tended to be more senior than business members in schools and better connected than the college members. Several are also connected to more than one social service, while others were well connected outside the social policy arena. Based on this evidence, it would appear that health trusts are moderately successful at attracting senior business personnel and other prominent individuals.

Review of the service boards

Table 6.1 presents a summary of the evidence collected in respect of the various services above. Around 29% of the total seats on welfare service boards were

Table 6.1: Business board membership of various services

Service	Number in sample	Total board members	Number	% of total	Number of business members and % of different ranking members as % of sub-totals						
					Senior		**Middle**		**Junior**		**Other/ not known**
					Number	As % of total business members	Number	As % of total business members	Number	As % of total business members	Number
LEA schools	6	110	22	20	5	22	5	22	10	54	2
CTC	1	11	5	45	5	100					
Private school	1	16	2	13	2	100					
Colleges of further education	3	47	26	55	4	15	8	31	8	31	6
Universities	2	90	20	22	15	75	4	20			1
TEC	1	17	12	71	11	92	1				
Health trusts	4	28 (non-executive)	10	35	7	70	2	20			1
Housing associations	3	26	5	19	2	40		20	1	20	1
Total	21	345	102	29.5	48	47	20	20	19	20	11

taken by business members, almost half of whom were senior business people. Business membership of the various boards made up between 13% and 71% of the total board membership. The TEC, college and CTC boards were the most business-dominated. Looking at business membership by status is also important since it gives an indication of which type of business interests are involved in welfare services. Having one or two powerful senior business people on welfare boards is more significant than several junior managers, some of whom may not have a strong business identity. A distinction here is made between senior (company directors and chief executives of large firms), middle ranking (senior managers of larger firms and directors of smaller firms) and junior business people (other middle and lower-ranking managers) although, as the last column shows, it was not possible to establish the status of each business board member. Where board members are retired, their previous post is used. This analysis illustrates that chief executives and directors are more likely to be found on the boards of the CTC, private school, TEC, universities and health trusts, and are less likely to sit on the boards of schools and colleges. This finding supports the work of others that suggests that senior business people are generally reluctant to become involved in schools. And this, despite the fact that governments and organised business have been even more eager to encourage business membership on school governing bodies than they have on other welfare service boards. This is also a surprising finding given the importance of education to future profitability and productivity. It also begs the question of why business people get involved in welfare services and what value, and values, business people bring to welfare services. These are important questions that go beyond the scope of this book, but more detailed analysis of the business membership of welfare service boards is revealing, as the following section illustrates.

Analysis of social policy networks

Among the business board members of the various services outlined above, some are especially prominent and influential within the city of Bristol. Many are connected, not only to one welfare service but to several, and are also members of other important business and 'elite' organisations. The following section employs social network analysis techniques[3] to reveal the extent of the connections between business board members, and how, through these members, some business organisations have a high presence within the social policy 'network' of services, even where no formal linkages exist.

The results of the analysis are presented in Table 6.2. The 32 board members identified here were significantly more active, and better connected than the others. Of the 32, four held elected office (one of these was also the director of a company) and five occupied senior positions within the public sector. The majority (22) were senior business people. In terms of their organisational linkages, 12 of the 32 sat on the board of WESTEC, ten on the University of Bristol's council, six were board members of the UWE, five sat on the boards of various health trusts, one sat on the board of a local further education

Table 6.2: Most active members of the social service network

Business actor	Member of BCCI's President's Group	Director/chair large company	Director/chair small/medium company	Elected office	WESTEC	Council of the University of Bristol	UWE	Dolphin Society (DS)/Society of Merchant Venturers (SMV)/Bristol Common Purpose (BCP)/(GBF)/St Stephens Ringers/Bristol Cyrenians	BCCI's HHG/EETC	Other social policy	Other relevant links
1	X		X	X	X						
2	X			X	X			GBF/BCP			
3						X		GBF/BCP		Board member – The Housing Corporation; Board of local housing association	Board of Bristol Development Corp; Local magistrate
4						X (Vice Chair)		GBF/DS/SMV		Board member – United Bristol Health Trust	
5	X	X					X	GBF/SMV/DS		Board member – South Bristol College	
6			X		X		X			Board member – Bristol District Health Authority board	
7	X				X			BCP/GBF			Board member – Bristol Development Corp

Table 6.2 cont.../

Table 6.2: contd.../

Business actor	Member of BCCI's President's Group	Director/chair large company	Director/chair small/medium company	Elected office	WESTEC	Council of Bristol University	UWE	Dolphin Society (DS)/Society of Merchant Venturers (SMV)/Bristol Common Purpose (BCP)/GBF/St Stephens Ringers/Bristol Cyrenians	BCCI's HHG/EETC	Other social policy	Other relevant links
8	X	X					X				Board member – Bristol Development Corp
9	X	X			X						Board member – Business in the Community
10	X	X							HHG		Board member – Regional CBI council
11	X	X					X				Regional director – EEF; Member of CBI's regional council
12	X	X (2 dir)				X				Board member – Bristol District Health Authority board	

Table 6.2 cont.../

Table 6.2: contd.../

Business actor	Member of BCCI's President's Group	Director/chair large company	Director/chair small/medium company	Elected office	WESTEC	Council of the University of Bristol	UWE	Dolphin Society (DS)/Society of Merchant Venturers (SMV)/Bristol Common Purpose (BCP)/GBF/St Stephens Ringers/Bristol Cyrenians	BCCI's HHG/EETC	Other social policy	Other relevant links
13	X								HHG (Founder)	Board member Phoenix NHS Trust	
14	X		X					GBF		Member of governing body of Clifton College	
15	X	X					X	GBF/SMV/SSR	HHG		
16		X (2)				X		GBF/SMV	HHG		
17	X			X				BCP			
18	X					X		GBF/BCP			
19	X	X						BC			
20	X	X			X						Member of CBI's regional council
21	X	X								Board member – United Bristol Health Trust; Member of governing body of Clifton College	

Table 6.2 cont.../

Table 6.2: contd.../

Business actor	Member of BCCI's President's Group	Director/chair large company	Director/chair small/medium company	Elected office	WESTEC	Council of the University of Bristol	UWE	Dolphin Society (DS)/Society of Merchant Venturers (SMV)/Bristol Common Purpose (BCP)/GBF/St Stephens Ringers/Bristol Cyrenians	BCCI's HHG/EETC	Other social policy	Other relevant links
22	X					X		BCP		Member – Avon Education Committee	
23	X						X		EETC	Principal – Brunel College of Art and Technology	
24	X (Founder member)	X (3)				X		SMV/GBF		Member of governing body of Clifton College	Member – Bristol Development Corp
25	X	X				X		GBF/SMV	HHG/EETC		
26	X			X		X		BCP/SMV/DS			
27		X (Former)				X		GBF/SMV			
28					X				EETC	Member – Western Education and Training Partnership	

Table 6.2 cont.../

Table 6.2: contd.../

Business actor	Member of BCCI's President's Group	Director/chair large company	Director/chair small/medium company	Elected office	WESTEC	Council of Bristol University	UWE	Dolphin Society (DS)/Society of Merchant Venturers (SMV)/Bristol Common Purpose (BCP)/GBF/St Stephens Ringers/Bristol Cyrenians	BCCI's HHG/EETC	Other social policy	Other relevant links
29	X	X			X						
30	X				X		X				
31	X	X			X						
32	X	X			X						

college and one on the board of a housing association. None of the 32 participated in local schools. Almost all had links to a business organisation (club or BIA) and the vast majority (25 in total) were members of the BCCI's President's Group.

By virtue of being better connected than other members of a particular board, such individuals may well have higher status – not to mention greater experience – than other board members. Indeed, their status is likely to have played a part in their election to different boards in the first place. It may also be the case that, where key members with similar interests and common board membership are present, this is likely to increase the potential for collusion, and the creation of a particular dominant set of (business) ideas within services.

Shifting the focus away from actors and towards organisations revealed that most welfare services in Bristol were linked to several elite organisations through at least one member. The BCCI was especially well connected. More significantly, elite organisations were often linked to welfare services through two or more members at a time.

Figure 6.1 illustrates those cases where at least two actors link two organisations. This reveals the President's Group of the BCCI as by far the most important non-social welfare organisation in terms of its links with Bristol's welfare services. The UWE is connected to the President's Group through seven actors and to the CBI through two actors. The University of Bristol is connected to the President's Group of the BCCI through three actors. The Merchant Venturers and the GBF are also important: eight and five actors respectively connect the GBF and the Merchant Venturers to the University of Bristol.

In linking directly the activities of business through the Chambers of Commerce and key elite players within Bristol, the BCCI has been important to the establishment of new routes of influence. It has served as a forum through which key individuals have been able to meet, and new service board members recruited. With such a presence in the largest welfare services, the BCCI has positioned itself expertly to propagate and disseminate business perspectives and approaches to welfare services. By bringing together elite interests from the public and private sectors, it has provided a number of opportunities for business to influence social policy (and other aspects of local politics) and many opportunities for formal and informal engagements between political, economic and social elites within the city. Through its well-connected membership, the President's Group continues to be assured that the most prominent business and non-business actors within Bristol will continue to be recruited to the organisation in future. The BCCI's engagement in highly visible social projects, publicised through the local newspaper (of which two of its board members are members of the President's Group), meanwhile, has provided a vehicle for those companies keen to publicise their good deeds within the community. The activities of the BCCI have also gone some way to improving the image of business more generally within the city.

These findings are important to the study of business and social policy for a

Figure 6.1: Bristol's social policy network (numbers refer to number of actors connecting organisations)

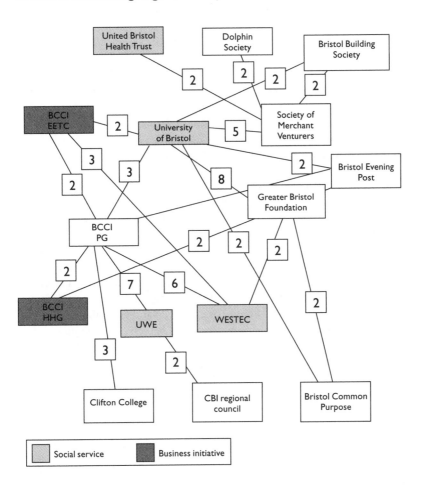

number of reasons. First, they suggest that, while some welfare services have found it difficult to recruit business members (as highlighted in Chapter Five), some business people are extremely active in social policy networks. The existence of extremely well-connected individuals within welfare services has undoubtedly been encouraged by the creation of competition between services for senior business representatives during the 1980s and 1990s.

Second, they suggest a bias towards certain services. The analysis so far has indicated a bias towards education and training services; this chapter reveals that larger services with the biggest budgets and highest standing in the community are preferred over smaller, 'less important' ones. For this reason, there is very little involvement among the 'well connected' within schools or colleges. Certain welfare services (the two universities in particular) provide key meeting places for a number of senior business people and it is possible that membership of these services is as much about the opportunities provided by membership to the individuals concerned as it is of benefit to the service, or even the benefits to business in a wider sense. Should this in fact be the case, it raises real questions about the value to the wider business community, the economy and to welfare services themselves of having business people involved.

Third, they suggest that, where local business elites exist, they are likely to be present on social service boards. The greater number of openings for business involvement in welfare services since the mid-1990s is likely to have increased the role of these elites or helped to establish new ones.

Developments since 1997

The changes introduced over the 1980s and 1990s have opened up new opportunities for business involvement in social policy, and business has clearly made good use of some of these openings, although business involvement in welfare services is still markedly uneven.

New Labour have built on the Conservative reforms, and while in some instances there have been attempts to create more transparency in appointments to public bodies, business has been further incorporated into the management and provision of welfare services since 1997. The most important development has been the extent to which Labour has embraced and built upon the notion of partnership. In fact, partnership working has become the defining idea of the post-1997 Labour government and a key part of the Third Way reforms (Powell and Glendinning, 2002).

Although Labour has stressed the importance of building partnerships with actors other than those connected with business and the private sector, these have been the main beneficiaries of partnership strategies. The expansion of the PFI (discussed in Chapter Five) is one example of how the private sector has become more deeply involved in the funding and management of infrastructure. Bristol was funding the £57 million cost of rebuilding four of its schools as well as the £95 million cost of new mental health facilities through PFI in 2003 (*Bristol Evening Post*, 11 February 2003). These projects will increase still further business inputs into welfare services in Bristol.

Several other important initiatives have been introduced in Bristol since 1997. Although the city did not develop a Health Action Zone (HAZ), it did develop three separate Education Action Zones (EAZs), with private sector support from two local arts centres, the *Bristol Evening Post*, AXA Sun Life (insurance company), Cap Gemini Ernst and Young (IT services and management consultancy), Computershare (financial services company) and Espresso (a provider of digital networks and curriculum materials to schools). Two trusts, the Medlock Trust and the Society for Merchant Venturers, between them pledged cash donations of around £100,000 between 2000 and 2003 for one of the zones.

Eight specialist schools have also been established with private sector funding in Bristol. Two specialise in sports, two in arts, one in languages and three in technology. Since all but one of them came into existence in 2002, it is too early to evaluate the full impact of the change on the management of the schools and the full extent of business involvement within them.

Bristol also opened its new City Academy school in September 2003. This academy specialises in sport and is being sponsored by a consortium led by Bristol City Football Club, which has donated £1.35 million, UWE, which has donated £45,000 and the BCCI, which has donated £200,000. As in other instances, these private interests will be expected to play an active role on the board of the school.

Regarding Bristol's City Technology College, Cable and Wireless was replaced as a main sponsor by Rolls Royce in 2001, although the school claims to maintain close contact with its former sponsor (John Cabot School, Report of the College Governors, 2002/03). The school also continues to get generous funding from business. In 2002 it received a donation of £6,000 from Rolls Royce and £37,495 from Research Machines plc (John Cabot School, Report of the College Governors, 2002/03).

WESTEC, Bristol's former TEC, was replaced in 2001 by a new Learning and Skills Council (LSC). It is currently chaired by the chief executive of the BCCI, who also occupies the position of High Sheriff of Bristol and chairs the West of England Strategic Partnership and the Western Partnership for Sustainable Development. Not surprisingly, he was also one of the key 32 most senior business people connected to welfare services identified in Table 6.2.

The links between business and the LSC also led to the development of another new initiative which sought to increase the skills of school leavers who are otherwise unlikely to attend further education. The Education Unlimited initiative was an idea developed by the BCCI and launched by the LSC in July 2003. It is intended to act as a 'virtual college' where students will visit various sites of training that are linked through the scheme. The chief executive of the BCCI explained, in an interview carried out in July 2003, that Education Unlimited was designed primarily to develop skills and foster better attitudes among the 15% of school leavers who currently do not attend college in Bristol.

Another recent and relevant development was the announcement in 2003 that Castlemore Securities, a land development company, has agreed to transfer 0.53 acres of land and donate £300,000 for a new school expansion in Bristol as part of a Section 106 agreement that will, in exchange, allow the company to develop a further 18 acres of land in the city for commercial and residential use ('Quay 2 dream now a reality', *Bristol Evening Post*, 15 May 2003). Under Section 106 of the 1990 Town and Country Planning Act, councils can make planning permission contingent on social investment undertakings by the private sector. Such investments were originally intended to cover primarily social housing, but now include a wide range of projects, from school buildings, parkland developments and road building.

Since these are all relatively new developments, it is impossible to say quite how they will impact on business involvement in social provision in future, although it is highly likely that Labour's plans will further strengthen elite networks in and around local services. The possibilities for business involvement in social policy have increased significantly under the Labour government. Quite how far business has been integrated within local services, and the actual impact of this on services since 1997 requires further investigation, but Labour has certainly increased the *potential* for greater business influence, not just on social policy, but on local politics more generally.

Labour's faith in business to come to the rescue of failing social policy, however, appears to be as misplaced in Bristol as in other cities. While some individual business people and companies may become more actively involved in social provision, many companies, in common with organised business, are ultimately much more concerned with issues that impact on local economic development rather than social development, and their concerns are shaped more by an overriding desire to improve profitability and productivity. Although the Labour government has gone out of its way to attract new sources of money and business 'expertise' into local services, they appear not to have fully considered how business would respond to such plans. If the views of the chief executive of the BCCI are representative, such endeavours have actually alienated senior business people rather than promoted enthusiasm for greater business involvement:

> "The Education Action Zone doesn't work here.... There's loads of money thrown at it, but it isn't in any context. Local businesses get dragged in, but they really can't see much of a change and they can't rest their hopes on a credible long-term plan. So they get disappointed...." (Interview with chief executive of the BCCI, July 2003)

When asked about what business brings to such initiatives and why he felt businesses often fail to bring innovation to projects, he explained that it was probably because services are primarily interested in their own ends:

> "... business is constantly asked to fork out because that's what they [schools and other public services] want in the end; they want resources.... We've had five or six schools come to us because they need match funding to become specialist schools, and when you [say] 'we haven't got the money, but how else can we help you' ... it starts off okay in theory but when you get to the crunch point it's money they want. And that's just too much. We do put a lot of money into the system but there's not a bottomless bucket."

This clearly illustrates some of the problems with Labour's proposal to look to the private sector for solutions in education. It again illustrates the ignominy of public services struggling to find private sector backing. It also suggests frustration on the part of business with such requests.

The BCCI's involvement in Bristol's new city academy, on the other hand, had clearer perceived benefits for the organisation, primarily because it was felt that the new academy could make a positive contribution to the Education Unlimited initiative.

This would suggest that, although Labour has clearly been able to attract sponsorship from some firms and business associations, its ability to further close the gap between business and welfare services in future will be hampered unless it provides additional incentives for business to become more directly involved. Reducing the costs of sponsorship, as it has done in those specialist schools that have struggled to raise the necessary funds (see Chapter Five), is likely to help, but the more one looks at the whole issue of business involvement, the less obvious the benefits of closing this gap appear to be – whether we are talking about welfare services or business interests. We will return to these issues in the conclusion of the book.

Conclusion: business and local social policy

Business has been given increasing opportunities since the late 1970s to help shape social policy within their localities. Central government has played the biggest role here in creating new openings for business involvement. The evidence presented here points to variable interest and involvement in services, with some parts of business responding more enthusiastically to these opportunities than others. Those areas in which business has become most intricately involved are not the ones in which central government has placed most emphasis on the importance of private sector engagement.

In Bristol, private sponsorship has been most significant in education and training services, but only where sponsorship is a formal requirement, as in the case of city technology colleges or the new city academies and specialist schools. This will change, of course, when the planned PFI projects get off the ground.

Direct business involvement in the management of welfare service boards has become one of the most important forms of business engagement in social policy at the local level. The investigation above reveals strong business representation on welfare service boards, although it also revealed that business engagement is variable between services. This variability can only partially be explained by statutory requirements and what we might assume to be the collective interests of business. Involvement was highest in the TEC, the universities, colleges and health trusts, but lower within schools. This is surprising given the importance of schooling to employers, and given the range of government and business initiatives aimed at developing business–school partnerships since the 1970s (as detailed in Chapter Five). A high level of business involvement within TECs is to be expected since they are subject to the tightest central government requirements, although involvement was also high in the University of Bristol, which was subject to the least formal controls.

This research also revealed that certain actors and organisations are especially well connected and play central roles within the 'social policy network' of Bristol. Despite the fact that some services have found it difficult to locate business people and firms that are prepared to give up the necessary time to become actively involved in their management, this research has located several 'elite' actors who play an extremely active role within local community life. The majority of these elite players are senior business people.

As for the institutions of business, BIAs and other elite clubs were found to be more important than private companies, although the establishment of specialist and academy schools and the development of action zones continue to increase company engagement with social policy at the local level. The regional CBI and the BCCI viewed their roles and interests differently. The CBI's activities were shaped by its position as the regional branch of a more powerful national organisation and it tended to direct its energies towards recruitment, member services and local lobbying on key issues of direct concern to local employers, rather than become engaged with local services and social projects. The CBI also appeared to have much less of a local city identity and focus than the BCCI. In this respect, the approach of the regional CBI was, paradoxically, at odds with the strategies for local engagement advocated by the national organisation, especially in the areas of education and training.

The BCCI responded more positively to the national CBI's call for more active corporate community involvement and, as a result, it had a much higher presence within Bristol's social policy network. The merging of TBI and Bristol's Chambers of Commerce enabled senior business people to co-opt local civic leaders and senior managers from public services onto its President's Group in an early business-led public–private partnership. This increased the voice of business locally in a whole range of areas.

The biggest determinant of the level of business engagement with social policy at the local level is not organised business, however, or even local councils, but central government. Central government has created competition for 'active', well-connected business people among service providers. Services that face pressure to develop closer business links and attract private finance will naturally prefer to attract business people with a good track record of dealing with public services from large companies that could mean higher monetary benefits and sponsorship deals. In this competition, schools compete with universities who compete with TECs and with health authorities, and business people generally choose to get involved in the most prestigious, largest organisations with the biggest budgets and greatest autonomy. The implications that flow from this for future social policy will be considered in greater detail in the concluding chapter.

Notes

[1] The regional director of the CBI subsequently became a member of Bristol's TEC.

[2] The GBF was established in 1985 by the Merchant Venturers. The GBF provides charitable support to a range of causes, from housing associations and disability organisations to adult literacy classes and community transport schemes.

[3] The names of all board members of Bristol's secondary schools, further education colleges, universities, TECs and housing associations were inputted into a database, alongside the membership lists of business organisations and business clubs. Scrutinising board membership lists and associated biographical notes and declarations of public interest also revealed important information about the associations of various business people. Although obtaining complete information about board members is always difficult, it was nonetheless possible to obtain relatively comprehensive information from a number of services and business organisations, including all secondary schools (13 in total), three further education colleges, two universities, nine housing associations, five health trusts, and Bristol's TEC in addition to important information from the BCCI and the CBI. After all of this information had been fed into the database, it was analysed using Ucinet IV (developed by Borgatti et al, 1992).

SEVEN

The social policies of corporations: occupational welfare and corporate social responsibility

Introduction

Previous chapters have focused primarily on business and state social policies. This chapter shifts the spotlight onto firms and corporate social policy, through which businesses are able to shape overall levels of social provision within societies. Occupational welfare and corporate community involvement – or to use a more commonly applied nomenclature, corporate social responsibility (CSR) – are of growing importance to governments and service providers keen to meet growing needs and tackle social problems within changing welfare environments. Central government has, as previous chapters have illustrated, tried to increase firm involvement in local services and encourage the expansion of occupational welfare as a way of shifting some of the pressure away from the state and onto employers. Firms have faced new demands for increasing levels of occupational provision and involvement in local partnerships with public services. Despite its growing importance, however, corporate social policy remains a relatively under-researched area. This chapter investigates corporate social policy in both its forms. First it presents an audit of occupational welfare before examining the development of the CSR strategies of some of the largest firms in the UK.

Occupational welfare

Occupational welfare represents an important element of the overall compensation paid to employees, and a significant part of employers' overall wage costs. Statutory social provision includes: national insurance (NI) contributions as well as the funding and provision of statutory benefits; approved occupational pensions (where companies have provided the option for workers to opt out of state supplementary pension schemes); sickness benefits; maternity leave; and redundancy pay. Non-statutory or voluntary provision makes up a lower proportion of total wage costs and includes: above-statutory occupational and private pension schemes; health insurance; various types of private insurance; educational and training programmes; and housing provision.

The extent of voluntary occupational welfare is determined by a number of factors. Workers often push for increased occupational provision as a top-up to wages and as a form of protection against various social risks (discussed later in this chapter). Firms may make such provisions in order to increase employee productivity, attract more highly skilled workers (Papadakis and Taylor-Gooby, 1987, p 106; Fitzgerald, 1988, pp 12-13; May and Brunsdon, 1994, pp 154-6) or to exert greater controls over labour (Papadakis and Taylor-Gooby, 1987, p 176). This has been important particularly in the past, where occupational pensions, for example, have been used as a tool both to prevent industrial action and to ease the shedding of older labour (Graebner, 1980; Quadagno, 1984, p 637). Good quality occupational welfare can also create a sense of loyalty and commitment to the company, reinforced through length-of-service requirements to certain forms of provision (Jones, 1983, p 64; Quadagno, 1984, p 637; de Swaan, 1988, p 171; Gordon, 1991, p 168; Russell, 1991, p 271).

Governments also help to determine the extent of occupational welfare. Statutory regulations clearly have the biggest impact by forcing employers to make provision for workers, but states can also help shape non-statutory occupational welfare through fiscal policy that makes it advantageous for companies to provide, and employees to accept, pay in the form of non-wage benefits rather than cash. Although many forms of non-wage benefits have been increasingly brought into the tax system, some benefits, including some forms of occupational welfare[1], are exempt from taxation and therefore represent better value than money wages for employees and employers.

Governments also have an incentive to encourage the expansion in occupational welfare since it may remove some of the burden from state welfare. As documented in previous chapters, governments since the 1980s in particular have looked to employers to take more responsibility for the management and funding of a variety of welfare benefits, from sickness benefits and maternity pay, to occupational pensions and in-work tax credits. Occupational welfare has also been viewed as important to reducing some of the costs of welfare as well as improving the balance between work and 'life', including family and caring responsibilities that fall, disproportionately, on women.

Despite the important position it continues to occupy, we know little more about occupational welfare today than when Titmuss (1958) outlined its importance in the 1950s. The gaps within the literature have been repeatedly pointed out:

> It is quite remarkable how little is known about 'fringe' benefits.... [V]ery little attention has focused on the non-wage benefits that are often a part of the 'reward package'. (Mann and Anstee, 1989, p 6)

> There is very little in the way of pre-existing policy research, no easily accessible data-bases or, indeed, even sample surveys of what employer care is being provided in Britain and by whom. The literature that exists comes from the field of human resource management or is provided by companies themselves. (May and Brunsdon, 1994, p 147)

The role of the firm in setting and delivering social policy has been a neglected subject in scholarly writings about private sector social policy. (Rein, 1996, p 27)

While some commentators have acknowledged the important contribution made by occupational welfare to total levels of welfare provision (Jones, 1983, p 64; De Swaan, 1988, p 171; Gordon, 1991, p 168; Russell, 1991, p 271), it is seldom discussed in anything like the detail it warrants in the academic literature. The reasons for this lack of attention relate, not only to its complexity, but also to a general lack of detailed knowledge about the nature and extent of occupational welfare. It also relates to confusion surrounding the concept of occupational welfare and what should be included within its rubric. Since Titmuss' (1958) influential examination of occupational social provision, definitions of occupational welfare have tended to focus on the full gamut of employee fringe benefits, which include goods and services as diverse as sports-club membership, subsidised canteens, travel expenses, company cars, uniforms and clothing allowances. May and Brunsdon (1994, p 147), for example, follow Murlis (1978) in defining occupational welfare as non-wage provision that "increases the well-being of employees at some cost to the employer". Bryson (1992, p 140) includes in her definition intangible benefits such as "contributions to general enjoyment and personal development".

Such wide-ranging definitions, however, go beyond any useful conception of social policy. Where the objective is to understand more about the organisation and operation of social policies, it is clearly unhelpful to view occupational pensions in the same way as employee uniforms, and health screening programmes in the same way as subsidised canteens. Rather, it is more useful to think of occupational welfare as that which eliminates or reduces social risks connected with the workplace. Just as welfare states were designed, in Beveridge's (1948) parlance, to slay the five giant social risks – ignorance, idleness, disease, squalor and want – occupational social policies can help to reduce their symptoms, if only for some workers, some of the time. Childcare provision and family-friendly policies may help reduce the risk of unemployment; occupational pensions and sickness benefits may help to tackle want; occupational training may help to reduce ignorance; employer-provided housing may help reduce squalor; and occupational healthcare may help to tackle disease and ill-health. Despite the fact that employment itself creates its own risks, and the fact that employers do not necessarily aim to reduce social risks when they make such provision, this is one way in which occupational provision can operate.

Settling on a clearer idea of what constitutes corporate welfare is only the first problem facing students of social policy. Two further, although not unrelated, problems also exist. First, data within the social policy field has thus far tended to provide only 'snapshots' of provision in narrow policy areas, rendering generalisation and/or further temporal analysis difficult. Contributions to specific areas of employer provision have been made in the area of housing policy (Forrest et al, 1991), occupational pensions (Mann, 1989), care services (May and Brunsdon, 1994) and a range of family-friendly policies (Callender et al, 1996; Forth et al, 1996; Cully et al, 1999; Dex and Smith, 2002). Green et al (1984, 1985) provide perhaps the most comprehensive contribution to the debate thus far, but their work is now rather dated. What is required, therefore, is an updated account of occupational welfare that brings together various indicators of the extent of provision.

A second problem is that the analysis and presentation of available data has revealed a great deal about general non-wage labour costs, but very little about the social policy dimensions of such costs (see, for example, the work by Murlis, 1978; Hart, 1984; Tachibanaki, 1989; Russell, 1991). This is a problem should the objective be to clearly distinguish social from other types of provision as discussed above. The reason for this lack of specific focus on social policy is that the best available data on non-wage costs are primarily designed to gauge overall employee compensation costs and hence tends to aggregate all forms of non-wage provision. Official data collected and presented by the EU as part of its quadrennial Labour Costs Survey, for example, has been primarily aimed at gauging the comparative labour costs within each of the EU member states. Although Martin Rein (1996) has made good use of this data to reveal a more accurate picture of the total contributions made by firms to overall levels of social provision within states, more recent data, especially the 2000 release, reveals much more about the true costs of the mandated and voluntary social provision of corporations. New analysis of the 2000 data is presented here alongside qualitative estimates of the extent of occupational welfare compiled from the Workplace Industrial Relations Surveys, the annual Labour Force and General Household Surveys and others.

An audit of occupational welfare

Non-wage labour costs, which include employer social security contributions, voluntary social contributions, vocational training costs and various other employee benefits, make up a significant proportion of total labour costs. As well as having a direct impact on total welfare provision, non-wage labour costs impact on the relative costs of employing workers. They are increasingly important in the context of globally (or regionally) competitive labour markets. In fact, UK labour costs are relatively low compared with its main competitors because of its lower than average non-wage costs (Table 7.1). Wages and salaries contributed around 82% in the UK in 2000, around 75% in Germany and less than 70% in France. That same year, employers' statutory social protection contributions made up around 8% of total wage costs in the UK compared with almost 16% in Germany and almost 20% in France. With respect to voluntary contributions (which include all benefits that fall within the statutory areas, but are made at a more generous level than is required by law, for example, supplementary maternity and sickness benefit schemes, supplementary unemployment insurance and private pensions), the UK is less

Table 7.1: Employer contributions to overall social protection receipts (1980-2000) and breakdown of wage costs (2000)

	Employer contributions as a % of overall social protection receipts (1980-2000)							Breakdown of wage costs (2000)			
	1980	1985	1989	1990	1995	1999	2000	Wages and salaries	Employers' statutory social protection contributions	Employers' voluntary imputed and social contributions (includes sickness and redundancy payments)	Other labour costs
Germany	41.5	41.2	40.9	42.2	40.2	37.0	36.9	75.4	15.7	6.8	2.1
France	55.5	52.2	52.1	50.4	47.4	46.4	45.9	68.1	19.9	7.7	4.3
Italy	60.0	52.5	52.4	52.6	50.3	43.3	43.2				
UK	33.4	29.6	28.4	27.9	25.4	28.0	30.2	81.5	8.4	7.0	3.1

Source: EC (2003b, p 3)

out of line, with British and German employers contributing around 7% of total wage and French employers contributing around 7.5%.

Contributions for social protection (which in this instance refers to all forms of intervention aimed at addressing risks or meeting needs in a defined list including: sickness and healthcare, disability, old age, family, unemployment, housing and poverty/social exclusion) also vary between countries. According to figures produced by Eurostat, French employers contributed around 46% of the total social protection costs in 2000, Italian employers 43.2% and German employers around 37%. The UK was one of the few countries where employers have borne an increasing proportion of social security costs since the mid-1990s, although at 30.2%, the burden is relatively low compared with its major competitors.

Shifting the focus to the UK, non-wage labour costs made up around 12% of total hourly labour costs in the early 1970s, increased to around 18% in 1981, fell back to around 14% in the mid-1990s and by 2000 had increased again to stand at around 18% (Labour Market Trends, 1996, table 5.7; UK Labour Costs Survey, 2000). Regarding contributions to social protection receipts, Figure 7.1 illustrates that employers' social protection contributions are worth almost 7% of GDP, with statutory provision equalling around 3.8% and voluntary provision worth around 3% of GDP. Employees contribute around 6% of GDP (through NI contributions) and central government contributes around 13% (obtained from general taxation receipts).

A more complete account of the total costs of occupational welfare is included in Table 7.2. This table is based on calculations from the UK's submission to the 2000 Labour Costs Survey. It highlights the costs and relative importance of varying forms of occupational welfare. According to this data, total employers' contributions to voluntary social provision (social protection costs plus training costs) are higher than the value of their contributions to statutory provision.

Figure 7.1: Social protection receipts as a percentage of GDP

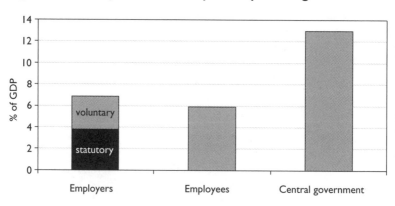

Source: Compiled from the UK's Labour Costs Survey submission for 2000 and EC (2003b)

Table 7.2: Occupational welfare provision (2000) as a percentage of total wage costs by sector and GDP

	Statutory social security contributions (NI contributions plus statutory sickness and maternity)	Above-statutory social security contributions	Direct payments in the event of sickness	Payments to employees leaving the enterprise	Vocational training costs (paid by employer)	Total above-statutory and other voluntary provision	Total occupational benefits (excluding statutory social security)
Mining, manufacturing and construction	8.3	6.3	0.5	1.6	2.7	11.1	19.4
Retail, hotels, restaurants and other personal services	8.6	6.5	0.5	0.7	2.3	10.0	18.6
Distribution, financial and property services (financial intermediation, real estate, renting and business activities)	7.7	5.8	0.5	0.5	2.4	9.2	16.9
Public sector (education, health and social work, other community, social and personal service activities)	9.5	3.5	0.9	0.3	0.4	5.1	14.6
All (% of overall wage costs)	8.4	5.6	0.6	0.8	2.0	9.0	17.4
All (% of GDP)	3.8	2.5	0.3	0.3	0.9	4	7.8

Source: Author's own calculations based on the UK's Labour Costs Survey submission for 2000 (downloaded from www.statistics.gov.uk/STATBASE/Product.asp?vlnk=10176, accessed April, 2003)

The most expensive single form of occupational welfare (after statutory social security) is above-statutory social security provision, followed by vocational training provision. The costs of above-statutory sickness and redundancy schemes are relatively low (although statutory sick pay is included within statutory social security and supplementary insurance schemes are included within the above-statutory social security category).

Table 7.2 reveals some disparities between the different sectors. The public sector records, surprisingly, the lowest vocational training costs of all sectors which probably reflects the higher pre-work qualifications of staff working within it. That this sector should also report much lower voluntary social security expenditure is probably explained by the lack of emphasis on private provision for employees and the greater importance placed on public sector occupational pensions, reflected in higher than average statutory social security contributions.

It is not surprising to see higher costs resulting from redundancies within the mining, manufacturing and construction sectors, given the level of job losses these sectors continue to experience. Indeed, high redundancy costs explain the fact that this sector has the highest total occupational welfare, as a percentage of wage costs, of all the sectors. Given the general lack of security within the retail, hotel and restaurant sector, it is surprising that this has relatively high occupational welfare costs compared with distribution and financial services sectors.

Now that general data on the costs of occupational welfare have been examined, it is useful to consider the extent of provision by welfare area.

Occupational pensions

The trend during the postwar period has been for the membership of occupational pensions to increase rapidly until the late 1960s, but with a subsequent levelling off and decline since the mid-1980s (Government Actuary, 1994, p 4). Table 7.3 illustrates that 59% of full-time employees were members of occupational pension schemes in 1975, rising to 65% in 1979 but falling to 56% by 2001. The trends are different for men and women and for the public and private sectors, however, as Table 7.4 illustrates. The number of men to women with occupational pensions in 2001 was 54% and 58% respectively, although the figure for part-time women falls to 33%. Even the apparent equality regarding occupational pension membership between men and women working full time also masks the fact that men are much more likely to have private pensions than women, and of course, employers also contribute to such pensions, especially for senior workers. Overall, 22% of men had private pensions in 2001 compared with 13% of women (*General Household Survey*, 2001, table 6.1). Table 7.5 also reveals sharp differences between the public and private sectors. Less than half (48%) of women working full time within the private sector had occupational pensions compared with 69% within the public sector. For women working part time, just 21% of those working in the private sector

Table 7.3: Changes in occupational provision (1975-2002)

Year	Membership of occupational pension scheme (% full-time employees covered)[a]	Housing rented with job or business[b]	Refunds of housing expenditure (% of employees)[c]	Vocational training costs (% of total wage costs)[d]	Employees participating in training (% in last four weeks)[e]	Employer contribution to off-the-job training costs (total costs)[f]	Redundancy costs (% of total wage costs)[g]	Employer-provided PMI (% of employees covered)[h]	Help with childcare (% of employers providing nursery or childcare subsidy)[i]
1975	59	3		1.9			0.4		3 (women, all sectors)
1979	65	3		2.0 (1980)			1.1 (1980)		
1985	61 (1983)	2		1.5	8.5 (1984)		2.4 (1986)		4 (women, all sectors 1988)
1990	61	1 (1991)		1.5	14.3	64.4	1.0	4.9	
1993	58	1		1.7 (1992)		69.4	2.3 (1992)	7.0	
1995	57	2	2		14.4 (1994)	67.6	1.2 (1994)	7.1	
1998	57	2	1	0.09 (1996)	15.6	67.4	1.35 (1996)	7.0; 8 (men=10%; women=4%)	*Men* Private sector 2, Public sector 6; *Women* Private sector 3, Public sector 9
2000	56 (2001)		1 (men, 2001)	2.0	14.3		0.8	7 (men=9%; women=4%)	4 (all workers, all sectors)

Notes: PMI = private medical insurance

a Calculations based on General Household Survey data (1995, table 5.3; 2001, table 6.3).

b General Household Survey (2001, table 4.1).

c Family Resources Surveys (1995/96-2001/02).

d Eurostat Rapid Reports (1991, p 2); Labour Costs Surveys (1996 and 2000) (own calculations).

e Education and Training Statistics for the UK (1994-98).

f Labour Force Survey (1985-96, Spring figures).

g Labour Market Trends, Feb (1996, table 5.7); Labour Costs Surveys (1996 and 2000) (own calculations).

h IRS Employment Trends (1995, no 578, p 14); London: Industrial Relations Services; Family Resources Survey (1998/1999-2001/2).

i Callender et al (1996, table 1.8); Cully et al (1999, table 7.3).

Table 7.4: Provision by occupational status

	Member of occupational pension scheme (full-time men) % (2001)[a]	Member of occupational pension scheme (full-time women) % (2001)[b]	Member of occupational pension scheme (part-time women) % (2001)[b]	Numbers with employer-paid PMI plans by occupation group % (1995)[c]	Housing (% workers renting with job or business)[d] (1992)	Employees receiving training (% of full-time employees) (1998)[e]	
						Any training in past year	Training of 5 days or more
Professional	69	73	62	7	4	79	26
Managers				9	3	77	27
Intermediate/non-manual	62	58	45	3	2	67	18
Semi-skilled/skilled				3	4	68	21
Unskilled	40	33	23		0	14	12
Total	54	58	33		1	62	21

Notes: PMI = private medical insurance
[a] General Household Survey (2001)
[b] General Household Survey (2001)
[c] Calculated from the General Household Survey (1995, tables 8.4, 8.5)
[d] General Housing Survey (1992)
[e] Cully et al (1999, table 7.4)

had occupational pensions compared with 43% of those working in the public sector. For men working full time the gaps were narrower but still significant: 78% of men in the public sector had occupational pensions compared with 50% within the private sector.

A number of other variables also impact on the shape and extent of occupational pensions. Regarding occupational status, around 40% of unskilled men and 33% of women working full time are members of occupational pension schemes (see Table 7.4). This compares with 69% of professional men and 73% of professional women with occupational pensions. Again, the likelihood of belonging to an occupational pension scheme falls sharply for part-time workers. Moreover, companies often have a number of different pension schemes in place which contribute more of the costs and provide more generous provision to higher status employees. According to government figures (Government Actuary, 1994, p 33), less than half the firms with schemes in place contribute the same amounts to the pensions of all employees. Industrial sector is also an important determining of the shape of pensions provision. Table 7.5 reveals that 73% of men and 80% of women working full time in the energy and mining industries are covered by occupational pension schemes, but just 17% of men working in agriculture and related industries are covered (the relatively small numbers of women working in this sector prevented an accurate estimate for female employees). The table also illustrates that larger firms are more likely to offer some form of occupational pension scheme than smaller firms.

Family-friendly provision

Figures on the number of employers who provide workplace childcare are reproduced in Table 7.3. These figures do not suggest that childcare has increased dramatically since 1979. Estimates of workplace childcare collected in 1979 and 1988 revealed that between 3% and 4% of women employees had access to childcare. More recent estimates, collected in the 1998 Workplace Industrial Relations Survey (WIRS) study, found that 3% of women working for the private sector, but 9% working for the public sector, had some form of nursery provision or childcare subsidy. This compared with figures of 6% and 9% respectively for men working within the private and public sectors (Cully et al, 1999). This meant that, overall, just 4% of all employees have access to workplace childcare provision in 1998, a surprisingly low figure given the emphasis that has been increasingly placed on family-friendly employment practices since the 1990s.

The disparities between different industries are also stark. Focusing purely on those companies with workplace nurseries reveals that 1% or less of companies within the distribution, hotel and engineering sectors provide workplace nurseries compared with 7% of employers within retail and other services.

Estimates of the number of employers who offer extra-statutory maternity benefits also vary greatly between the sectors. Forth et al (1996), using WIRS data, estimated that around 25% of public sector employers offered extra-

Table 7.5: Provision by sector

	Occupational pension scheme membership (men, full-time) % (2001)a	Occupational pension scheme membership (women, full-time) % (2001)a	Occupational pension scheme membership (women, part-time) % (2001)a	Number of companies with workplace nurseries (1996)b	Participation in job-related training (last four weeks) (2000)c	Never offered training % (2000)d	Extra-statutory maternity leave (% firms providing) (1996)e	Extra-statutory maternity pay (% firms providing) (1996)e
Energy and water supply	73	80			17.7	20.2		
Retail and other services	61	54	33	7	15.9	37.8	7	14
Transport and communications		54	30		11.3	35.2		
Banking, finance and insurance	53	54	30	2	16.8	29.4	8	11
Engineering	58	59	26		11.5	40.2		
Manufacturing	52	43	26		11.9	43.0		
Construction	36	54	16	–			3	4
Distribution, hotels and catering	36	35	15	1	12.8	42.0	3	5
Agriculture	17	–		9	8.2	52.4		
Public sector	78	69	43	2	23.6	18.3	25	30
Private	50	48	21	2			4	7
All sectors	55	57	30					
1,000+ employees	81	83						
100-999	67	69						
25-99	51	58						
Less than 25	32	35						

a General Household Survey (2001)
b Forth et al (1996, table 5.1)
c Statistics of Education (2000)
d Statistics of Education (2000)
e Forth et al (1996, table 3.3)

statutory maternity leave, and 30% offered extra-statutory maternity pay compared with equivalent figures of 4% and 7% for the private sector (Table 7.5). Within the private sector, the retail and financial sectors are most likely to provide extra-statutory maternity leave and pay.

Housing

Although housing provision for employees was very common during the late 19th and early 20th century, it has declined rapidly since then. Figures released in 1995 (reproduced in Table 7.3) estimate that around 2% of employees lived in employer-provided housing in the mid-1990s, compared with 3% in the mid-1970s. The figure today is so low it is not included in most surveys. Data from the Family Resources Survey (Table 7.3) reveals that the number of employees who received refunds of housing expenditure from employers was as low as 2% in 1995 and 1% in 1998. By socio-economic grouping, 4% of professionals and 4% of semi-skilled workers rented from their employer in the early 1990s, with no instances reported for unskilled workers.

Health insurance

Around 5% of employees received private medical insurance (PMI) from their employers in 1985, increasing to 7%-8% by the end of the 1990s (see Table 7.3). Data on PMI can be further broken down by sex: 9% of men compared with 4% of women were covered by such schemes in 2000. Like most other benefits, health insurance is targeted towards higher status employees. Seven per cent of professionals and 9% of managers received PMI in 1995 compared with 3% of semi-skilled workers (see Table 7.4). The number of unskilled workers covered by such skills was too insignificant to calculate.

Training

The proportion of employees participating in training (in the four weeks prior to being surveyed) increased from 8.5% in the mid-1980s to around 15% in 2000 (Table 7.3), although this does not say anything, of course, about the quality of the training received. Not even the whole costs of training are necessarily met by employers, especially when it takes place outside the company. Figures produced by the Labour Force Survey (reproduced in Table 7.3) on employer contributions to the costs of off-the-job training indicate that the share of employers' contribution remained relatively static at around 64% between 1985 and 1996 with additional costs being met by employees and the government.

Regarding job status and training, we can again locate differences between lower and upper-ranking employees. Table 7.4 reveals that professionals and managers are more than twice as likely to receive training lasting for five days or more as unskilled workers, and receive more training than all non-managers.

The gap between workers is also wide when we extend the focus to any training received in the past year. Broken down by sector, Table 7.5 reveals that public sector workers (which are listed separately from other private sector occupations in the table) receive more training, yet Table 7.2 revealed that spending on training within the public sector is relatively low compared with other sectors. These figures confirm that the public sector offers more training opportunities than the private sector, and that the utilities and finance industries offer the most training opportunities within private firms.

Summary of key trends in occupational welfare

Employers' contribute as much as 30% of the overall social protection costs received in the UK. This is less than in some other countries, due mainly to relatively low employers' statutory social security contributions, although payments towards extra-statutory and voluntary provision are more in line with those of France and Germany. Together these make a significant contribution to the protection of workers from various social risks. When we consider the whole range of benefits that are paid to workers, including sickness benefits, above-statutory maternity and sickness pay, pensions, redundancy payments and training costs, their overall value was equivalent to almost 7% of GDP in 2000.

The data also illustrates the extent to which occupational welfare is patchy and variable especially between the sexes and between classes. Men tend to do better out of occupational provision than women, as do higher status employees. There may be a relationship between these two variables of course. The data also revealed changing patterns of provision over time, although the figures did not suggest that this is having a dramatic impact on costs to employers. Rather, the evidence suggests that some forms of provision are highly variable (most obviously redundancy costs), some are declining (occupational pensions and housing provision) and some others have been relatively constant (private medical insurance, vocational training and childcare provision). Housing provision is needed by fewer workers and has almost disappeared entirely. Training needs have increased over time and state investment in training has certainly increased as a result. Occupational pensions have declined in importance since the 1970s, although the introduction of compulsory employer provision, in the form of occupational or stakeholder pensions, may reverse this decline. Private medical insurance, the most 'middle-class' occupational benefit, has remained reasonably stable over time.

The implications of these findings in understanding the extent to which business shapes social provision will be explored in the conclusion to this chapter. The chapter now turns to investigate the other aspect of a firm's social provision, corporate social responsibility.

Corporate social responsibility (CSR)

As the preceding chapters of this book have illustrated, there is growing interest among international governmental organisations, national governments, academics, voluntary organisations and business organisations, in the contribution of corporations to welfare through their actions as socially responsible 'citizens' or stakeholders. These various voices have sent out an appeal to corporations to behave more ethically, to respect the human rights of workers, to demonstrate a more responsible attitude towards the environment and to become more involved in social projects within their local communities. The OECD has established guidelines for multinationals; the EU (EC, 2001a) published its own Green Paper on Corporate Social Responsibility in 2001; and the UK established the first dedicated government minister for CSR in 2000. Business interests, for their part, have established their own organisations with the aim of promoting responsible corporate behaviour.

Like occupational welfare, CSR goes beyond social policy to include a vast range of corporate activities, from the positive treatment of workers to fundraising for good causes, and from ethical investment practices to involvement in state services. For our purposes, it is again more useful to examine those aspects of CSR that can help to alleviate or reduce social risks (as outlined with regard to occupational welfare earlier). The range of such activities is broad. The examples put forward in the UK's first report on CSR (DTI, 2001b) included corporate involvement in schools, participation in the New Deal programmes and involvement in EAZs, alongside environmental protection reporting and charitable giving. Companies have responded by shifting their own community involvement towards areas that have traditionally been occupied by the state. According to Business in the Community (BITC), an organisation devoted to promoting CSR and which is supported by many of the UK's largest companies, the 1990s brought new responsibilities for corporations:

> Traditionally, areas such as housing, education or health were seen as the responsibility of government. Businesses, if they made any contribution at all, tended to do little more than write cheques to needy charities. But with the rise of the free enterprise culture of the 1980s coinciding with the crisis of the modern welfare state and the fall of the communist one, there has been a growing conviction that such activities are also the preserve of business.... (BITC, Annual Report for 1995, p 3)

For corporations, CSR offers a way of promoting and establishing their brands, improving the physical and social environments in which they operate and attracting more highly skilled and productive employees. For governments, CSR offers new opportunities to attract funding for local services (see Chapter Six of this book) and promote positive corporate behaviour in the absence of regulatory controls which have been made difficult under globalisation as detailed in Chapters Three and Four. However, since CSR is entirely voluntary for the companies involved, it is left to governments to plead with corporations to carry out their business activities in a responsible manner and to persuade them to behave like good corporate 'citizens'. Indeed, business has welcomed CSR as a substitute for tighter regulations, which have been vehemently opposed at all levels (see Chapter Three). Although the OECD and the EU have toyed with the idea of introducing tighter international controls over corporate behaviour, the UK has been at pains to stress that it views CSR as voluntary. Its 2001 report into CSR stated that: "The Government is clear that CSR cannot be imposed through regulation" (DTI, 2001, p 30). Despite this, CSR does offer new opportunities for corporate engagement with social provision. The following sections examine the CSR strategies of 25 of the UK's largest companies, which have been randomly selected from the FTSE 100 index.

An audit of corporate social responsibility

Corporate social responsibility has become increasingly important since the 1990s to companies keen to demonstrate their ethical credentials. Today almost all the major corporations produce detailed statements on their CSR strategies and increasing numbers produce social and environmental reports alongside their annual financial statements. A visit to the websites of most major companies, especially those that sell direct to the public, reveals the lengths to which corporations now feel they must go in order to publicise their social endeavours. Locating the social projects in which corporations are involved, therefore, is relatively straightforward. The following analysis examines various indicators of corporate social policy, beginning with corporate charitable giving.

Corporate charitable giving in the UK has shown a steady increase in recent years, from a relatively low base. According to an investigation carried out by *The Guardian* and the *Directory of Social Change*, FTSE 100 companies gave 0.95% of pre-tax profits to good causes in 2002, compared with 0.4% in 2001 and 0.29% in 1995/96 (Armstrong, 2002). Just ten FTSE 100 companies gave 1% or more in 1996; by 2002 this had risen to 27%. Although corporate contributions appear to be increasing, however, the fluctuations can partly be explained by rising and falling profits and partly by changes in the calculations of what constitutes corporate giving. As this book has already alluded to, increased demands for finance and other business assistance from a number of different organisations have led to changes in the ways in which firms calculate the value of what they do. As the editorial of the *Corporate Citizen* journal made clear in 2001:

> You name it, companies are trying to put a monetary value on it. What this does, is make meaningful comparisons difficult. A 17 percent rise in 2000, in money terms an extra £50m, does not mean millions more pouring from the corporate coffers into good causes and charitable activities throughout the UK. (Corporate Citizen, 2001)

For these reasons, the figures presented here are broken down into cash and in-kind donations (Table 7.6). Together the cash and in-kind contributions of the 2001 FTSE 100 was equal to some £643 million (Armstrong, 2002). Reuters was the biggest FTSE 100 donor in 2001, giving £6.4 million in cash donations together with in-kind donations worth an estimated £13.7 million.

Although it is essential not to exaggerate the importance of corporate giving as protection against social risks, corporations can, through their donations, influence the capacity of the voluntary sector to contribute to social welfare and, increasingly, contribute to state provision in various areas. In this respect, corporate giving, in cash and in-kind, has grown in importance to social policy more generally in recent years.

For their part, companies do not necessarily make any distinction between, on the one hand, charitable work and various sponsorship deals in sports and the community, and on the other, corporate involvement in social policy initiatives including school sponsorship or the running of Action Zones.

There are also clear signs that companies are rationalising their community contributions in a way that is bringing them into closer contact with welfare services. Table 7.6 illustrates the range of projects the largest companies have been involved in between 2001-03. Some of those companies with the best developed CSR strategies appear to be shifting their priorities away from philanthropy and towards more outcome-based giving that has clearer benefits for the company. Successive governments and business charities, such as BITC, have encouraged such approaches in order to expand corporate involvement in welfare services. Marks & Spencer, for instance, revised their CSR strategy in 2001 to fit with the new priorities:

> Our new policy ... focuses on building sustainable partnerships with community organisations and being more proactive in developing community-based initiatives under three broad themes: health; education and learning; and safety.... Many of our business units focus on health and wellbeing including Foods and Beauty. It is important to us that we have a well-educated pool of young people from which our future employees will come. Our customers and employees want to live, work and shop in safe places. Together, these three areas work towards eliminating social exclusion. (Marks & Spencer, 2001, accessed via the Corporate Citizen website www.dsc.org.uk/corporatecitizen/aut01/corevalues.htm)

Such policies can involve corporations in areas that were previously entirely the domain of the state. What is immediately apparent from looking at these 25 companies is the great efforts that large companies expend in 'proving' they are 'socially responsible' despite the relatively low level of giving provided by some in practice. Each of the companies included in this part of the study had environmental and/or social statements, and most appeared to have well-developed CSR strategies and policies, although one of them, Anglo American, directed almost all of its CSR efforts outside the UK. Many, like Marks and

Table 7.6: CSR activities

Firm	Donations (2001)			Educational involvement (2001-03)						Other community involvement (2001-03)		
	Total community cash donations	In-kind donations	% profits	Action zone(s)	School links	Dedicated education liaison office	Curriculum materials	Work experiences/ exchanges	HE links	Community training	Poverty/ homelessness	Supports staff involvement
Anglo American	13,931,034	68,965	0.60									
Astrazeneca	13,100,000		0.47	X 2	X	X	X	X		X		X
BAA	1,500,000	1,250,000	0.51		X		X	X				X
BAE	1,123,047		1.60	X	X 3		X					
Barclays	24,814,000	4,104,093	1.00	X	X		X				X	
BAT	3,900,000		0.19						X			
BOC	945,000	55,000	0.97				X					X
BP	65,310,344		0.72		X	X	X	X				X
BT	8,725,285	3,800,359	1.02	X 3		X	X	X		X		X
Cadbury Schweppes	1,094,262	726,998	2.00	X 5	X		X	X		X	X	X
Centrica	4,026,849	595,539	0.76		X	X	X	X			X	
Corus	550,558		–		X			X				
Dixons	996,041	200,000	0.40	X	X	X	X	X	X	X		
Glaxo SmithKline	25,555,000	49,794,000	1.22		X	X	X	X				X
GUS	828,000		0.22		X	X	X	X				
HSBC	21,135,862		0.38	X	X		X	X				X
Lloyds	34,400,000	6,00,000	1.10		X			X				X

Table 7.6 cont.../

Table 7.6: contd.../

Firm	Donations (2001)			Educational involvement (2001-03)						Other community involvement (2001-03)		
	Total community cash donations	In-kind donations	% profits	Action Zone(s)	School links	Dedicated education liaison office	Curriculum materials	Work experiences/ exchanges	HE links	Community training	Poverty/ homelessness	Supports staff involvement
Marks & Spencer	6,005,000	1,065,000	1.30	X	X		X	X		X		X
Prudential	736,079	1,287,467	0.58		X		X					X
Reckitt Benckiser	689,655		0.14									
Reuters	6,400,000	13,700,000	12.70	X	X 2			X				X
Sainsbury	4,800,000	6,200,000	1.92		X		X	X			X	X
Shell	58,620,690		2.30	X	X	X	X	X	X			X
Sixcontinents	908,527	626,769	0.22		X			X		X	X	X
Unilever	8,826,854	832,156	3.40		X		X	X				X

Spencer, placed a great deal of emphasis on the importance of educational services to their overall CSR strategies. Similarly, BP stated that:

> Support for education has for many years been the highlight of our community programme. Today, our work with education authorities, the local Education Business Partnership and schools forms the basis of many highly successful ongoing activities, delivered through the efforts of our staff working with schools [and our] full-time Educational Coordinator. (BP, 2002 Environment/social case studies in Europe, www.bp.com/environ_social/case_studies/europe/index.asp)

The devotion of resources into educational policies is viewed as increasingly important to long-term profitability for some companies. School links reflect well on corporations and can promote a company or a brand in the eyes of children who are current as well as future consumers, not to mention employees. The fact that school–business links have been promoted heavily by government and organised business, as illustrated in previous chapters, is also likely to have had an impact on the policies of companies. The key reasons for corporate involvement in schools, therefore, centre on the possibilities for soft-marketing, improvements in educational performance and the development of skills among both current and future workers.

To meet these competing demands and concerns, many companies have developed curriculum materials that promote knowledge of the sector within which they trade as well as provide information about the company itself. Seventeen of the companies included here have produced such materials. Many, including BP, Corus, Shell and Cadbury Schweppes, have their own dedicated educational websites for disseminating the materials. BP explained the rationale for its involvement in its 1999 social performance report:

> For more than 30 years, BP Amoco, through the BP Educational Service, has supplied schools and colleges in the UK with material based on our business activities and covering topics of current interest and concern. Our aim is to help young people, teachers, parents and the community better understand our business and industry and, at the same time, help develop the knowledge and skills that young people will need for worthwhile careers. (BP, 1999, p 24)

There is a clear danger, however, in allowing corporations to promote their brands in this way. Both the Consumers Society and a committee of MPs have heavily criticised some companies for producing material which has, at times, resembled company 'propaganda' (see *TES*, 1998).

The majority of companies, 16 in all, also had explicit policies to promote staff involvement in community projects, including in schools. Some also gave staff time off to participate in school governance; BAA, for example, gave staff up to six days leave to participate as school governors. BP stated that it actively supported around 500 employees who were governors, and Lloyds that it gave paid leave to over 1,000 employees who were members of school governing bodies in 2001.

These school-focused policies were underpinned by a number of specific company strategies to develop closer links with schools. Of the companies examined here, 19 made explicit mention of the importance of developing such links. Seven, including Astrazeneca, BOC, BP, CORUS, GlaxoSmithKline, GUS and Shell, employed dedicated education liaison officers. BP had even developed its own comprehensive Link Scheme which supported over 200 schools in 2001/02, and involved up to 500 staff in various aspects of the project:

> Currently there are 234 schools enrolled in the scheme, formally supported by equal numbers of BP Link Officers and Link Teachers. Because the Scheme encourages the occasional involvement of other employees, we estimate that about 500 BP people in total are in some way participating [in] activities [which] include IT and literacy projects for 5- to 11-year-olds, work experience and teacher secondments at our sites, art competitions, management training for teachers, technology and environmental challenges, mentoring for disaffected youngsters, and activities to encourage business understanding for all ages. (BP, 2000, p 30)

Unilever also claimed to have well-established links with around 200 schools and colleges (www.unilever.co.uk/community/education.html). The explicit reasons for developing such links varied between companies, but they generally stressed the positive impact they had on employees. For example, GUS 'adopted' six local schools in order to "provide schools with a link to the commercial world" and to develop the skills of employees by forcing them to make "use of their skills in a very different environment" (GUS, 2002, p 5). For Reuters, the involvement of their employees in schools was one of the most important reasons for its own educational projects. One such project involved staff directly in the classroom:

> Reuters Foundation have 'adopted' five secondary schools around the world – one in each region – with the aim of encouraging Reuters employees to get involved in their local communities.... The Foundation has provided each school with the necessary equipment to set up a state of the art computer room. In addition, Reuters staff maintain a close relationship with the school through activities such as running lunchtime IT sessions and teacher mentoring. (Undated, www.foundation.reuters.com/Educational/ adopt_school.htm, accessed June 2003)

This issue of teacher mentoring was also a priority for many of the other companies. Corus and HSBC both offered training to teachers in management and leadership skills. Student placements were also offered by most of the companies here. BP and HSBC claimed to provide around 1,500 work placements each per year. Both teacher mentoring and student placements offer ways of generating interest among teachers and students in a particular firm or industry and allow companies to communicate their needs to schools and potential future employees.

The establishment of EAZs and specialist schools was also well supported among the companies looked at here. Ten of the companies supported 20 different EAZs between them. Barclays Bank, BAA, British Aerospace (BAE), British Telecom, Cadbury Schweppes, Dixons, HSBC, Marks and Spencer, Reuters and Shell all sponsored EAZs. One company, Dixons, sponsored a city technology college and several others were sponsoring the development of new specialist schools in 2002. The specialist school initiative was welcomed by BAE as important to fostering skills and an industrial interest among children, and the company encouraged the development of engineering schools as a way of promoting the industry and encouraging children into engineering as a career:

> As Specialist Schools … they will be able to focus their newly acquired extra resources to develop the subjects they are specialising in. Students will have a first-hand experience of modern engineering and will be able to make a fully informed career choice. (BAE, 2003)

HSBC also strongly endorsed the specialist schools initiative and gave financial support to help establish a language college in Liverpool in 2001.

Although further and higher education did not feature as heavily in the CSR policies of firms, several of the companies highlighted their support to universities. Perhaps because it would be barred from school involvement, British American Tobacco focused its attentions on higher education. It pledged a total of £3.8 million in 2000/01 to Nottingham University to establish the Centre for Corporate Responsibility. This was dwarfed by BP's £25 million endowment to Cambridge University in 2001 which, at the time, was one of the biggest university donations in history (Simms, 2003). Some of the money was used to establish a BP Chair at the centre. Shell also provided funding to Nottingham University to pay for six new technicians at the Centre for Pavement Engineering and Dixons established a Chair at Edinburgh University in 2000/01.

Although most of the social policy-related initiatives of firms tended to be in education services, several of the companies looked at here also had policies that were geared towards tackling poverty. Some were extremely ambitious. Allied Zurich explained in its CSR material that "Zurich UK's Community Trust has also made a commitment to end child poverty" (www.zurich.com/about_zurich/community_involvement_uk.jhtml, accessed April 2003). Most were less ambitious, tending to consist of small-scale contributions to local charities. Barclays, Cadbury Schweppes and Sixcontinents provided donations to support the work of charities working with the homeless and Sainsbury's provided a valuable service, alongside other large supermarket chains, by regularly donating nearly expired food items to hostels.

Of the other projects and initiatives these 25 companies were involved in, only two could properly be described as having some social policy function. The first was GlaxoSmithKline's involvement in Luton's Health Action Zone (HAZ) and its donation of some £500,000 towards the cost of a new children's hospital in Wales. The other was Shell's donation of £100,000 towards the cost of accommodation and play areas for families with sick children within the Royal Aberdeen Children's Hospital.

Summary of key trends in CSR

This section has examined how elements of corporate behaviour that are included under the CSR umbrella can affect social policy. Changes in the policies of government and corporations themselves have brought CSR more into the sphere of state welfare, especially in the area of education. Corporations, meanwhile, have shifted their focus towards more self-interested activities, which has meant a far greater focus on projects that both promote a positive corporate image and potentially contribute towards future productivity and profits. Closer involvement in schools fulfils both criteria. The fact that central government has created more openings for corporate involvement in schools has further fuelled this.

Although many companies have shifted their focus towards parts of the welfare state, however, there is no clear evidence that companies are willing to increase net investments in social projects. Overall levels of charitable giving, not to mention the stated policies of companies, illustrate a different focus rather than a willingness to provide more community resources. This leads to the possibility that charities could, in future, actually lose out to corporate involvement in social policy. Moreover, the fact that companies appear to view their involvement in social policy in much the same way as their other charitable projects, hardly bodes well for a government keen to encourage innovative and long-term solutions to the problems encountered within state welfare. Such donations, whether of time or resources, are, like other forms of charity, unpredictable, patchy and highly dependent on continued profits as well as the good will of managers. They are certainly not the safest foundation for stable social programmes and policies.

Conclusion

This chapter has attempted to gauge the social policy contributions of firms by conducting an audit of occupational welfare and CSR. While a lack of consistent and comprehensive data presents some difficulties, the foregoing analysis has been able to draw on raw and previously published data to more carefully and thoroughly examine these important aspects of corporate social policy. It has sought to separate the social policy elements of non-wage benefits and CSR to reveal the important contributions that both can make to overall levels of welfare in societies. It has also detailed how corporate social policies have changed in response to shifts in state social policy. Successive governments have pushed corporations to take more of a role in the management and delivery of social welfare, both within the workplace and local communities.

Preceding chapters in this book have illustrated how governments since the 1980s have sought to shift some of the responsibilities for the management and funding of social protection onto employers. Firms have responded by making adjustments to occupational welfare and their community involvement. Regarding occupational welfare, there has been a reduction in certain areas, especially in housing provision and occupational pensions, but other areas, such as childcare provision, training and health insurance, have remained stable or have increased slightly. This is a rational response by employers faced with increasing costs and falling demand for occupational pensions, and declining needs for employee housing brought about by increases in owner occupation, mobility afforded by the motor car and better public transport systems when compared with the end of the 19th century, when employer-provided housing was commonplace. Falling unemployment and the need to attract skilled labour into key occupations has encouraged some employers to expand childcare facilities in order to enable them to attract skilled women back to work. Companies have also made adjustments to their approach to community projects. They have sought to steer their involvement towards those projects that bring clear returns for companies as well as recipients. The biggest transformation has been the increased emphasis on schools, which bring opportunities for companies in terms of soft-marketing and the ability to influence future employees and consumers.

There are clear dangers in this strategy. Greater emphasis on occupational welfare and CSR will inevitably mean increased uncertainty for employees and welfare partners. Occupational welfare is often patchy and may reinforce gender and class inequalities, not to mention other forms of inequality. It is not provided equally to men and women, nor to lower status workers. The devaluation of occupational pensions with the winding up of final salary schemes (where pensions are based on a proportion of an employee's wages at retirement) and their replacement by money purchase schemes (where the value of pension depends on the annuity purchased with the contributions previously made) has made occupational pensions less attractive, although since 2001, employers have had to provide access to either occupational or stakeholder pensions. Recent high profile cases of employees losing rights to their pensions when companies go bankrupt has also reinforced the insecurity of occupational welfare even when there is some statutory element to it, as there is in the case of pensions. Voluntary provision, of course, is just that, and is entirely dependent on the good will and profits of employers.

To place more emphasis on corporate involvement in social policy risks exposing welfare services to some of this uncertainty and to the relatively narrow interests of corporations. The fact that companies have been at pains to stress the financial rewards of closer engagement in schools raises some concern. Should the returns not be forthcoming, then either corporations are likely to disengage from schools, or they will have to be given greater incentives to remain involved. This is not likely to be a problem in the short term, but if the dependence of welfare services on corporate involvement continues to rise, disruptions in company contributions in future could leave schools and other services without the necessary funding or support they have grown to depend on.

Note

[1] The rules governing the taxation of non-wage benefits are complex and depend on current rates of pay. Those benefits which were exempt from tax for most taxpayers in 2001 included: employer contributions to pension schemes, medical screening, workplace nurseries, employer-provided accommodation, retraining expenses, work-related training and welfare counselling (see Inland Revenue, 2001).

EIGHT

Conclusion: corporate power and social policy in global context

This book set out to investigate the importance of business to contemporary developments in social policy. Business influence, it has argued, has increased at all levels since the 1980s. At the international level, big business has lobbied for the establishment of welfare states that underpin competitiveness and productivity. International governmental organisations (IGOs) such as the World Bank, regional blocs such as the EU, and national governments, have responded favourably to these arguments. Globalisation has acted as a reminder to governments of the importance of policies that assist businesses if they are to be successful in attracting new investment in future. This message has been reinforced by the international activities of business, which has organised more freely and with more coherence under globalisation. Within the UK, central government policies and the activities of organised business have meant that, since the 1980s, the voice of business has grown progressively stronger at the national and local levels. Business today helps to shape social policy debate, manages welfare services, and is more likely to be involved in the direct delivery of social provision than in the past. A summary of the key developments of forms of influence are mapped out in Table 8.1. These developments are discussed under five summary statements, followed by a discussion of their implications for present and future social policy.

1. Globalisation has increased corporate structural power and this, in turn, has had an impact on the capacity of the UK to formulate and deliver social policy

Structural power has been fuelled by the processes of globalisation, especially since the late 1970s. Most importantly, the mobility of business has increased. States have dealt with this in different ways, but liberal states, such as the UK, have attempted to capture free-floating capital by competing on 'lowest common denominator' grounds through relatively inexpensive, lightly regulated labour, coupled with low corporate taxation. The UK has tended to go down this route by choice, although past policy decisions and historically low levels of indigenous investment have reinforced structural constraints which include relatively high dependence on mobile capital. In addition, the relative power of labour has fallen due to the introduction of lighter regulations, higher levels of unemployment and a declining trade union movement over the period.

Table 8.1: Business influence on selected social policies

| | Structural factors | | Agency factors | | |
| | | | Nature of involvement | | |
		Political pressure	Informal/voluntary provision	Semi-formal linkages	Formal partnerships
Education and training	Greater emphasis placed by government on the role of education and training in fostering competitiveness. Shifting emphasis towards vocational education	Pressure from business organisations to create education and training services geared more towards the needs of business. Greater number of linkages between business and educational institutions	One-off sponsorship deals. Production of curriculum materials. Work placements for students/teachers. Workplace training	Membership of school, college, university, TEC and LSC boards. Sponsorship of college courses. Sponsorship of university departments. Provision of training under New Deal schemes	Direct funding of schools (eg CTCs, specialist schools or city academies). Private sector management of day-to-day running of individual schools or groups of schools (eg within EAZs). Company management of PFI-financed buildings
Health		Increased emphasis on private health insurance and provision. Increased investment in healthcare in order to speed the recovery of employees	Private health insurance provided for some workers	Membership of health service boards. Involvement in HAZs	Company management of PFI hospitals
Social security	Emphasis on social security that does not undermine competitiveness	Increased emphasis on competitiveness and tackling disincentives to work. Increased role of private insurance. Minimum state pension supported by private scheme. Benefits provided with work conditions	Above-statutory sickness benefits and occupational pensions provided for some workers	Provision of employment under New Deal schemes	Company management of PFI-built offices

Some globalisation theorists have argued that states are both able to resist growing corporate power and that, in many instances, states themselves increase corporate power through their own policies. This is a powerful argument and one that has a great deal of validity. However, two further pressures, seldom discussed in sufficient detail in the literature, operate to steer policies towards those which favour business. The first is that international governmental organisations, themselves faced with pressure from well-organised international business, are forcing states to open up their markets to foreign competitors and encouraging states to reduce public expenditure, taxation and regulations on labour, as well as contract out welfare services. Their influence has been felt especially by 'developing' countries eager to secure finance from organisations such as the World Bank, but IGOs, alongside international business itself, play an important role in shaping approaches to business and social policy within all nation states. International and regional agreements around trade and social conditions also reinforce the interconnectivity of nation states and the need to ensure that their own businesses remain internationally competitive, not just because of the impact that declining competitiveness can have on nations, but also because they need to create more favourable production regimes in order to encourage further investment and dissuade capital flight in future.

Second, structural power acts as a bar to the reversal of previous concessions made to business. If a state uses low taxation or low levels of social spending in order to attract mobile capital into a country, it would be extremely difficult for future governments to go back on those agreements since it would risk damaging present and future levels of investment. The key point here is that the ways in which governments respond to corporate pressures help to mould political and economic environments which, in turn, has an impact on present and future policies. Political and economic environments can be altered, of course, but any change in direction takes time. To reverse 18 years of Conservative social policy, the Labour government would have had to first pursue policies which would transform the UK economy so that a different compromise could be reached with business; where employers would agree to higher rates of taxation and tighter labour market regulations in exchange for policies to create a more highly skilled and productive workforce. This would also have to be undertaken in ways that did not undermine present rates of growth. In the event, Labour's Third Way facilitated a business-centred approach to economic and political decision making, including social provision, while providing minimal concessions to its core support. It represented an acceptance by the Labour Party that old-style social democracy was incompatible with modern global economies, since it risked undermining a structurally powerful and more mobile business sector than had been faced by the party the last time Labour were in power. Thus, the Third Way was itself a response by the British Left to globalisation. The Labour government accepted that it would not be able to provide welfare without first securing the support of business on the one hand, and ensuring that social policy did not threaten to undermine economic growth on the other. In light of this, Labour built upon the policies of the previous Conservative government by steering social provision towards those forms which, it was felt, would compliment and underpin business activities.

The actual impact of structure on social policies has been greater in some areas than others. Changes to education and training policy have been introduced with the aim of more closely meeting the human capital requirements of employers, including the promotion of vocationally relevant skill sets within schools and the post-compulsory sector. Changes in social security have similarly been introduced with the aim of increasing employability and work incentives and reducing labour costs. In these areas government has often responded as much to the *perceived* needs of business as its *voice*. However, it is more difficult to trace structural influences in the area of healthcare. If structural influences have played a part in the shaping of policy in this area it has been due to constraints over general spending. Structural power is therefore variable, not just over time, but also from policy area to policy area.

2. Globalisation has increased both the capacity and reasons for business to organise internationally

As a result of political globalisation, international business has become better organised and more influential since the 1980s, and has played an increasingly important role within IGOs, including, most importantly, the EU. Since its options for exit, and therefore structural power, are diminished at the international and regional levels, including within the EU, business has had to rely much more on agency in order to influence policy outcomes. The result of more successful lobbying has been that the gap between business views and international and regional governmental bodies has narrowed in recent years. International business has helped to establish a consensus around social policy that has shifted the policy agenda towards a more pro-business one. This is true for the more neo-liberal World Bank and IMF and the more social democratic EU. Each has pushed states towards productive social provision in which the private sector plays a more prominent role. Policies to control the negative aspects of corporate activities have been proposed, but after strong lobbying from business, the outcome has mainly taken the form of voluntary codes of behaviour. The EU and other IGOs have, for the most part, only been able to make direct appeals to international business to become more socially and environmentally responsible. The result has been the emergence of a new paradox: social provision has been made more necessary by globalisation but less possible by the rise of an increasingly powerful business sector.

The emergence of a more coherent business view on social policy at the international level is likely to counter the lack of coherence that often exists among national and local business interests. Encouraged by the developing international business view on social policy, national business interests will be able to promote clearer perspectives that have the backing of a powerful international lobby. The evidence from the UK certainly suggests that international business opinion is having a greater impact on the work and views of national bodies.

3. Nationally organised business has become increasingly important to the shaping of social policy debate and delivery

Since the 1980s successive governments have sought to steer social policy towards that which favours business primarily, although not entirely, in response to structural pressures. As far as agency is concerned, business has had mixed fortunes in terms of its access to policy arenas. Organised business was initially excluded from the national policy arena during the early 1980s. The CBI was actually consulted less after the election of the Conservatives in 1979 than it had been under the previous Labour administration. The Thatcher government preferred, instead, to deal with the more ideologically sympathetic Institute of Directors (IoD). The early effect of this was that the relative costs to the CBI of exercising its voice at the national level were increased and this forced the organisation to examine ways of how it might more effectively concentrate its resources on influencing government. One of its solutions was to place greater emphasis on mechanisms of business influence that were relatively inexpensive. It sought to improve its lobbying techniques through producing clear and concise policy statements and more concerted efforts to communicate the views of business direct to the general public. It also placed greater emphasis on the role of individual business members and its regional branches in exerting direct pressure on local government and local services. This coincided with central government efforts to ensure that local councils and service providers integrated business representatives within decision-making structures. While the Conservative government sought initially to keep a lid on business agency at the national level, it increased the number of openings at the local level; thus business inputs into service provision were more highly valued than its inputs into policy making. Although the national voice of business diminished during the early 1980s, it increased at the local level over the same period.

This is not to say that the CBI lost all influence at the national level during this time. It was able to win important concessions in a number of areas, including pensions and the direction of education policy. However, there is little doubt that the influence of the CBI did wane during the early 1980s, a point that reinforces the important role played by states in determining corporate agency power in particular. This changed again with the fall of Thatcher and the rise of Major as leader of the Conservative Party, an event that effectively re-consigned the IoD to obscurity and reconfirmed the CBI as the major voice of business. Under Labour, the voice of the CBI has been strengthened still further. Against the backdrop of increasing structural power, business agency at the national and local levels has become more salient. As a result, business was in a far stronger position at the beginning of the 21st century than it had been in decades.

Like its predecessors, Labour has used business as both a *justification for change* and as a *tool for facilitating change*. Labour has also added to the ways in which business can become more closely involved in the provision of welfare services. Companies have been asked to variously fund, manage and take over state services in several areas, including healthcare and education. Meanwhile, tax credits have been extended and employer-administered stakeholder pensions have been introduced.

Even with variable access to government, the CBI has played an important role in shaping social policy debate and direction as well as steering the policies of locally organised business interests and individual firms. Throughout, the CBI, along with other business interests, has sought to defend services that directly benefit business (such as infrastructure spending) and help improve labour productivity (such as education and training). At the same time, the CBI has attacked unproductive spending on services that contribute little to business, including high spending on public sector wages.

More generally, the CBI has attempted to push social policy in a more pro-business direction by arguing for:

- social provision funded through taxation on labour rather than business;
- increased emphasis on vocational skills within education;
- increased participation in post-compulsory education and training;
- the establishment of tighter educational targets;
- increased involvement of firms in key services;
- increased emphasis on contracted-out services;
- increased benefit targeting to the deserving poor;
- increased emphasis on private insurance.

This does not mean that business has devised clear strategies on each of these areas in advance of government. For the most part, the CBI appears to devote most of its energies to responding to government initiatives and only rarely does it try to set the political agenda itself. In fact, on the big questions relating to the future of social policy, the CBI tends to be remarkably quiet. One explanation for this is that business tends to respond to initiatives and provision according to their potential impact. Another is that there has been little need for the CBI and other parts of business to seek to influence social policy during this period since, in most ways and in most areas, social policy has been steered in a pro-business direction by central government. Structural influences, reinforced by globalisation, have promoted cuts in spending on unproductive services (especially generous social security which were thought to be undermining work incentives) and an expansion in productive services (especially education and training) without business having to place direct pressure on governments. Business has tended to become involved where it has needed to make governments aware of the negative impact that some cuts were having on companies, or where it wanted to develop the policy specifics, for example, shaping the detail of education and training policy. Beyond this, it was enough to limit its campaigns to the major questions that were of key interest to most parts of business, such as tax reform and labour costs. Provided business could secure for itself cuts in general and corporate taxation, alongside government commitments to reduce spending in non-productive areas, it could limit its focus to these key issues.

More recently, however, the CBI appears to be giving more consideration to the 'bigger questions' concerning social policy. The fact that it now works much more closely with international business organisations, including UNICE at the European level, has facilitated a clearer, more coherent and far-reaching approach to social policy that is remarkably close to the outputs of internationally organised business. The more that business is able to come together at various levels to define its interests, the more difficult governments will find it to resist responding positively to its demands.

4. Local business organisations and individual firms play an increasingly important role in the delivery of social provision

Business inputs into social provision increased at the local level over the period. Successive governments have boosted business involvement in local services and reduced the inputs of locally elected representatives. Business has been viewed as an ally by both Conservative and Labour governments against what have been perceived to be poorly managed local services. From the early 1980s, business campaigned heavily against high levels of local spending and taxation, especially business rates levied on local firms, and the Conservative government used these arguments in order to justify tighter controls over local authority taxation and service provision. Moreover, as part of this strategy, and in order to address a concern among the business community that local services did not cater well for their needs, the Conservatives began a series of reforms that were aimed at installing business people into the management structures of local services at the same time as trying to locate greater sources of private funding for them. There has been an increasing emphasis on business as local citizens, and business leaders as valuable, even essential, partners in social provision alongside other public and voluntary sector bodies. Companies have also been asked by central government to shoulder a greater responsibility for social provision through occupational welfare and corporate community involvement. Firms have also assumed greater control and responsibility for previously state-administered benefits in the areas of sickness and maternity benefits, various tax credits and pensions.

Business representation on the service boards investigated for this study was found to be relatively high (at around 27%), although business interest in welfare services is uneven; involvement tends to be higher in education and training services and the size and status of the service is also important. The size of business donations to services also varies according to service area and service type. Within Bristol there was greater interest among senior business people in health trusts and universities than in schools, despite concerted efforts on the part of Conservative and Labour governments since the late 1970s to generate business interest and involvement in schools.

Some business actors are especially well connected and particularly active within social policy networks. The increased number of openings to social and other public policy arenas has allowed elite business networks to develop and flourish. Organised business has also played a role here through the establishment of business-dominated elite 'clubs' to which senior decision makers within welfare services are invited. The President's Group of Bristol's Chambers of Commerce and Initiative (BCCI) was an example of this (see Chapter Five). Such developments increase the informal exchange between the public and private sectors, and facilitate the recruitment of senior business people to positions of power and responsibility. Perhaps more importantly, they also help to establish a pro-business consensus. Despite the emergence of well-connected and 'super-active' business members of social policy networks, however, some services have struggled to achieve the rapid increase in business members required by central government. The result has been increased competition between service providers for 'active', well-connected business people. In this environment, schools compete with health trusts and universities compete with LSCs. Notwithstanding stipulations laid down by government, welfare service providers understandably prefer to recruit business people with a good range of skills and experience who have demonstrated some enthusiasm for working in similar areas and who may bring some financial reward. Senior business people with an interest in getting involved in welfare services have a range to choose from, and it is no surprise that they should choose to get involved in the largest, most generously funded and most important ones.

Against this backdrop, larger companies have reduced their donations to general charitable causes and have instead developed more focused giving that has increased their involvement in welfare services that bring clear and direct returns for them. The clearest indication of this has been a much greater emphasis on developing closer partnerships with schools in recent years. In contrast to the involvement of individual business people wishing to become involved in prestigious services, firms are more interested in the immediate and long-term returns for the company, and involvement in schools brings such rewards in the form of soft-marketing opportunities and the ability to influence and shape the views and attitudes of present and future consumers and employees.

Regarding occupational welfare, the evidence relating to the extent of provision is mixed. While central government has attempted to increase the role and responsibilities of corporations for the administration and funding of social protection schemes, levels of occupational welfare did not rise significantly over the period. In actual fact, there was a reduction in some employer-provided benefits, especially in occupational housing provision and occupational pensions. Other benefits have increased, most markedly childcare provision, especially as employers have realised that encouraging women back to work after childbirth can result in lower costs and greater productivity. Lower levels of unemployment and tighter equal opportunities legislation have also undoubtedly played a part here; the option of replacing women workers who take time out of the workplace has been removed, and the extension of workplace provision to part-time workers, many of whom are women, has meant that employers have been forced to examine ways of recouping some of their investment by encouraging women to return to work. Help with childcare costs and nursery provision fulfils this requirement.

What is clear is that voluntary provision is not a suitable replacement for guaranteed state provision. Employers' social policy is very often based on voluntarism and this undermines rights to services and creates divisions among recipients. Neither is provision within the workplace based on need or equity criteria; rather, it is based on firm size, sector, gender and employment status.

5. Business interest in and views on social policy are variable

Successive governments have pushed social policy towards business–centred welfare, primarily in response to structural factors, the expressed views of business and the desire to exert greater control over state services. The problem with this strategy is that it is not always clear what business wants and needs. Moreover, businesses, in the form of individual firms, have at times been reluctant to get involved in welfare services. Where firms have become involved, they have done so selectively.

An important determinant of both the interest and subsequent response of business to social policy is its potential impact on labour markets, profits and competitiveness. Social policies that impact positively or negatively on business will activate business interest, and are more likely to trigger a decision to act, although this in turn will depend on the anticipated consequences of acting, or not acting, including: the likelihood of success, the relative costs of action and the likely benefits of acting. This book has illustrated a tendency among business to respond to the social policies of central government rather than develop and promote its own coherent agenda, although the development of greater coherence among international business interests may reduce this by providing national business interests with clearer and wider agendas that they can then attempt to 'sell' to governments. The key determinant of business interest and policy direction at the national level is the extent to which social policies impact on labour markets and the costs of doing business. Since not all social policy has any real or immediate impact on these, business is not uniformly interested in social provision.

Simply put, business requires a suitably educated and trained workforce which is productive but relatively inexpensive. It also requires access to markets. Business has therefore pushed for general reductions in the 'unproductive' state, including taxation and spending on social protection and healthcare, and an expansion in the 'productive' state, most clearly education and training services. Only minimalist welfare states, designed to provide temporary or basic protection when markets fail and when the private sector cannot provide assistance, are thought by business to be compatible with contemporary global capitalism. Questions relating to the quality of the services received tend to be neglected by business, and questions of equity hardly figure at all. The only area where the quality of service has to be guaranteed and the benefits of the service maximised is education. Moreover, only in education does business view the role of the private sector as a 'partner' rather than manager and/or direct provider. Generous funding for education and training is therefore promoted; privatisation and spending cuts, in contrast, continue to be advocated for most other parts of the welfare state. Purchases from the private sector and greater investment in infrastructure, including road and rail networks, are also advocated. Business is not, however, prepared to see higher taxes levied on firms to pay for such investments. Whether at the local or national level, business has fought for a reduction in corporate taxation.

Generally speaking, it is possible to conclude that there is no single, clear, coherent and constant view of social policy by business. While business appears to have established a more coherent view in recent years, and while there appears to be some consensus at present within particular policy areas, it is still difficult to move beyond general business views to establish what the position of business is on the specifics. This is because, at the level of specificity, business opinion varies. Although the CBI has put forward some business solutions to social policy problems – for example, more generally it has tended either to point to problems while leaving solutions to government, or has shown little interest in social policy until government has decided to reform provision in some way – only very recently has something resembling a business strategy on social policy emerged. Whether this continues to develop into a coherent and comprehensive strategy remains to be seen.

The implications for contemporary and future social policy

As a result of the foregoing arguments, business influence on social policy is more extensive today than it has ever been in the past. Business interests have been prioritised in social policy debates and they have helped both to determine the shape of social policy and define its parameters. Governments since the early 1980s have viewed business involvement in social policy as increasingly crucial to the continuing existence and development of social provision. This presents several key reasons for concern.

First, governments' attempts to steer social policy towards business serve to strengthen further an already powerful lobby. Business is already able to shape social provision without acting at all since governments are bound to consider its impact on future competitiveness, productivity and profitability. Increasing the voice of business in social policy means that future provision is less and less likely to reflect the concerns and needs of labour unless trade unions and other representatives of labour become more closely integrated into social policy. There are also signs that such moves are creating new opportunities for the establishment of local business elites which strengthens the relative position of business still further at the local level. Again, this does not bode well for the future of social policy.

Second, the desire of successive governments to prioritise business needs in social policy is problematic since, as has been demonstrated, business does not have constant and easily definable needs. In fact, business needs change over time and depend on their environments. Although there appears to be a current international business consensus on social policy, there is no telling how long this consensus will last, and how far it extends to widely varying welfare regimes. The current consensus fits well with the views of British business, but it does not necessarily fit well with the views of Swedish or German employers. To establish whether this is the case requires further research; but since business can be highly profitable in different welfare regimes, it would be inaccurate to conclude that all businesses *need* the same trading conditions to make profits. Hence, although the UK has prioritised what it perceives to be the needs of British business since 1979, these needs are themselves created. To be clear, those businesses that are heavily dependent on cheap labour *need* low regulations and low taxation; those that are dependent on skilled labour *need* high levels of investment in education and training and can tolerate higher regulations on labour.

Third, and related to the previous point, the ways in which business views social policy is also variable over time. Therefore, Leftist governments need to make every effort to convince business of the efficiency gains that could be had from the provision of welfare rather than respond to what they think business wants and needs. Business views are much more malleable than is often assumed. Business has clearly become convinced of the relative advantages of education and training but remains unconvinced about those stemming from state social protection and health schemes. But it is possible to make a convincing case even for seemingly unproductive welfare. Business arguments could be made for their retention or abolition – on the one hand they may assist the management of unemployed people and create more balanced consumption patterns, but on the other they may push up labour costs and taxation – so we would expect business opinion to be divided and subject to change in this area.

Fourth, while successive governments and organised business have pushed for greater business involvement in welfare services, there is little evidence to suggest that firms and business people share their enthusiasm for such involvement. While some large companies have demonstrated an interest in getting more closely involved in some areas, this has not been even and has not extended to providing the level of funding envisaged by governments. Business has been asked to take an increasing lead in resolving social problems, yet its response has been less than enthusiastic at times. The relentless increase in government demands for ever greater business involvement in services may be leading to partnership fatigue for many businesses and business people (J.S. Davies, 2002, p 175). The indications from this study are not that business is uninterested in greater involvement, but that levels of interest depend on the potential rewards to involvement that may be derived by individual business people or firms. Thus, government attempts to inject the values of the private sector into welfare services, as if business people all hold the same values and bring them to the services in which they participate, must itself be questioned in terms of its likely success.

Fifth, business involvement in social provision degrades the notion of 'public goods'. Social policy is built on the principle that the private sector will fail to provide services efficiently, equitably, or even at all in some key areas, including education, healthcare and social protection. In these areas, the state is necessary to provide essential services, in an uncorrupted form, and based on need rather than ability to pay. Incorporating the private sector into these areas undermines this principle. Business only gets involved in social provision if it gets something in return, such as soft-marketing opportunities or the ability to shape the attitudes and consumption habits of future workers or consumers. The present Labour government does not see anything wrong in this, yet incorporating the private sector into the welfare state risks undermining the strength of public services by steering them towards the more narrow and changeable views of business.

There is a further risk here. Placing business interests centre-stage is leading many services to re-examine how they might gear their outputs towards business. Nowhere has this been more true than in the case of education. Schools, colleges and universities have responded to government pressures to devise new ways of gearing educational services to local businesses; yet, as this study has shown, business views are multifaceted and variable. Perceptions of what constitutes the business view, therefore, will inevitably veer towards the kinds of stereotypes or taken-for-granted views that often prevail but which are not always accurate reflections of what is, or what could be. The fact is that it is extremely difficult for services to deliver exactly what business needs since, beyond some broad and very basic needs, not even business can be relied upon to always know what is in its interest.

Sixth, although the private sector appears to represent something of a panacea to various social problems for the present Labour government, there is relatively little evidence to suggest that business involvement brings radical solutions and improvements to services. In fact, the involvement of business may bring more benefits to individual business people and firms than to the services in which they become involved. Despite this, new investments into welfare continue to come with conditions that increased spending is informed by the inputs of business, whether in the form of board membership and management inputs, or the direct supply of services.

Seventh, greater emphasis on occupational welfare and CSR along the lines advocated by governments will inevitably mean increased uncertainty for employees and welfare providers. Occupational welfare is often patchy and can reinforce inequalities. It is not provided equally to men and women, nor to lower status workers (not to mention any other groups that are disadvantaged within employment markets). High profile devaluations and losses in occupational pensions entitlements have further highlighted the insecurity that often accompanies occupational welfare, even where there is some form of statutory 'guarantee'. Voluntary provision, of course, is entirely dependent on the good will and profits of employers. Placing greater emphasis on corporate involvement in social policy risks exposing welfare services to similar uncertainty and risks exposing them to the relatively narrow interests of corporations. If financial returns from corporate investment in services are not forthcoming, either corporations will disengage from services such as schools, or they will have to be given greater incentives to remain involved in future.

The ramifications of all this for the future of social policy are uncertain. Much depends on the direction of government policy over the next few years. Governments have helped to increase business power and steer social policy towards the business agenda; and now they need to counter it. The EU does offer an opportunity to do this, but the present trend is for devolution and opposition to top-down provision. It is likely that the Labour government will continue to muddy the gap between public and private and that business will continue to steer social policy towards its broad interests. The ultimate danger is that these policies will serve to increase still further the power and influence of business, resulting in further moves towards business-centred welfare. The paradox is that the continuation of this process will gradually undermine other aspects of welfare provision on which workers, and ultimately employers, depend. To be successful, economies require an educated, amenable, healthy workforce with sufficient spending power to maintain demand for some of the goods and services produced by business. The present business-centred welfare state, with its emphasis on education and private provision, and spending and taxation cuts, will only fulfil some of these requirements. A relatively strong state is therefore required which will defend social provision and protect business from itself. The present Labour government, however, seems unable or unwilling to fulfil such a role. Under these conditions the outlook for the welfare state is far from rosy. Increased corporate power under globalisation is undermining social policy in the UK.

References

Addison, P. (1977) *The road to 1945: British politics and the Second World War*, London: Quartet Books.

Alber, J. and Standing, G. (2000) 'Social dumping, catch-up, or convergence? Europe in a comparative global context', *Journal of European Social Policy*, vol 10, no 2, pp 99-119.

Allen, M. and Martin, R. (1999) 'New teachers for a new century?', *Education and Social Justice*, vol 1, no 2.

Annan, K. (1997) 'Secretary-general, in address to world economic forum, stresses strengthened partnership between United Nations and private sector', Press Release SG/SM/6153, Paris: UN.

Armstrong, M. (2002) *The giving list*, London: *The Guardian*, in association with the Directory of Social Change.

Ashburner, L. and Cairncross, L. (1993) 'Membership of the "new style" health authorities: continuity or change?', *Public Administration*, vol 71, pp 357-75.

BAE (2003) *BAE Systems sponsors specialist schools for engineering*, Hampshire: BAE Systems.

Balanya, B., Doherty, A., Hoedeman, O., Ma'anit, A. and Wesselius, E. (2000) *Europe Inc.: Regional and global restructuring and the rise of corporate power*, London: Pluto Press.

Baldwin, P. (1990) *The politics of social solidarity: Class bases of the European welfare state 1875-1975*, Cambridge: Cambridge University Press.

Barnard, N., Mansell, W. and Slater, J. (2001) 'Private firms for bid for failing schools', *Times Educational Supplement*, 29 June.

Barnes, M. and Sullivan, H. (2002) 'Building capacity for collaboration in English Health Action Zones', in C. Glendinning, M. Powell and K. Rummery (eds) *Partnerships, New Labour and the governance of welfare*, Bristol: The Policy Press, pp 81-96.

Bassett, K. (1996) 'Partnerships, business elites and urban politics: new forms of governance in an English city?', *Urban Studies*, vol 33, no 3, pp 539-55.

Bastin, N.A. (1990) 'The composition of governing bodies of higher education corporations', *Higher Education Quarterly*, vol 44, no 3, pp 245-63.

Bayliss, K. and Hall, D. (2001) *A PSIRU response to the World Bank's private sector development strategy: Issues and options*, Greenwich: Public Services International Research Unit (PSIRU).

Bayliss, K. and Hall, D. (2002) *Another PSIRU critique of another version of the World Bank private sector development strategy*, Greenwich: PSIRU.

Beishon, S. (1995) 'Homelessness and company giving', *Policy Studies*, vol 16, pp 49-57.

Beveridge, W. (1948) *Social insurance and allied services*, Cmnd 6404, London: HMSO.

BIAC (Business and Industry Advisory Committee) (1996) *Discussion paper by A. Sommer: Productivity to the rescue of social protection*, Paris: BIAC.

BIAC (1997) *Addressing the social impact of globalisation: Promoting the benefits of change*, Submission to the OECD Liaison Committee with International Non-Governmental Organisations, Paris: BIAC.

BIAC (1998a) *Business-government forum on health insurance for the modern welfare state: what division of labour for social and private insurance*, A report on a meeting of industry and healthcare experts held by the BIAC to the OECD Paris, 6-7 May, Paris: BIAC.

BIAC (1998b) Meeting of the Employment, Labour and Social Affairs Committee at Ministerial Level on Social Policy, 23-24 June, Paris: BIAC.

BIAC (1998c) *BIAC views on lifelong learning* (based on comments made by members of the BIAC Expert Group on Education at the OECD Seminar on Lifelong Learning, 18 November 1998), Paris: BIAC.

BIAC (1999) *A business review of tax competition*, Paris: BIAC.

BIAC (2000) 'BIAC statement', made to the International Conference on Jobs, Helsinki, 27-28 January, Paris: BIAC.

BIAC (2001) *Innovation and global sustainable growth*, Presented to the BIAC Consultation with OECD ministers, Paris, 16 May, Paris: BIAC.

BIAC (2002a) *Employment and learning challenges for the 21st century*, Paris: BIAC.

BIAC (2002b) *OECD and the sustainability of the market economy: Jobs strategy, regulatory reform, growth, sustainable development. What next?*, BIAC statement to the OECD council meeting at ministerial level.

BITC (Business in the Community) (1996) *Annual report*, London: BITC.

Block, F. (1990) 'Political choice and the multiple "logics" of capital', in S. Zukin and P. DiMaggio (eds) *Structures of capital*, Cambridge: Cambridge University Press.

Boddy, M., Lovering, J. and Bassett, K. (1986) *Sunbelt City? A case study of economic change in Britain's growth corridor*, Oxford: Clarendon Press.

Bond, S. and Chennells, L. (2000) *Corporate income taxes and investment: A comparative study*, London, Institute for Fiscal Studies.

Bond, S. and Jenkinson, T. (1996) 'The assessment: investment performance and policy', *Oxford Review of Economic Policy*, vol 12, no 2, pp 1-29.

Bonnett, K. (1985) 'Corporatism and industrial policy', in A. Cawson (ed) *Organised interests and the state: Studies in meso corporatism*, London: Sage Publications.

Borgatti, S.P., Everett, M.B. and Freeman, L.C. (1992) *Ucinet iV* (Version X), software, Columbia: Analytic Technologies.

Boswell, J. and Peters, J. (1997) *Capitalism in contention: Business leaders and political economy in modern Britain*, Cambridge: Cambridge University Press.

BP (1999) *BP Amoco Alive social performance report*, London: BP Amoco.

BP (2000) *BP Amoco Alive: social performance*, London: BP Amoco.

Bretschger, L. and Hettich, F. (2000) 'Globalisation, capital mobility and tax competition: theory and evidence from OECD countries', unpublished, http://cidei.eco.uniroma1.it/~degit5/papers/bretschger.pdf.

Brown, K. (2000) 'CBI chief's valediction is upbeat about euro: industry could cope with the single currency at an exchange rate of DM2.85, Sir Clive Thompson tells Kevin Brown', *Financial Times*, 10 July.

Bryson, L. (1992) *Welfare and the state: Who benefits?*, London: Macmillan.

Callender, C., Millward, N., Lissenburgh, S. and Forth, J. (1996) *Maternity rights and benefits in Britain, 1996*, London: HMSO/DSS.

Carley, M (2001) *Industrial relations in the EU, Japan and USA, 2000*, Ireland: European Foundation for the Improvement of Living and Working Conditions, www.eiro.eurofound.ie/2001/11/feature/TN0111148f.html.

Carvel, J. (2003) 'Headhunt for NHS boardrooms', *The Guardian*, 3 March.

Castles, F.G. (1986) 'Social expenditure and the political Right: a methodological note', *European Journal of Political Research*, vol 14, pp 669-80.

Castles, F.G. (1989) 'Explaining public education expenditure in OECD nations', *European Journal of Political Research*, vol 17, pp 431-48.

Castles, F.G., Widmaier, U. and Wildenmann, R. (1989) 'The political economy of the people's welfare: an initial presentation', *European Journal of Political Research*, vol 17, pp 361-5.

Cawson, A. (1985) 'Introduction: varieties of corporatism: the importance of the meso-level of interest intermediation', in A. Cawson (ed) *Organised interests and the state*, London: Sage Publications.

CBI (Confederation of British Industry) (1977) *Understanding British industry*, London: CBI.

CBI (1980a) *Jobs – facing the future: A CBI staff discussion document*, London: CBI.

CBI (1980b) *A businessman's guide to local authority finance and expenditure*, London: CBI.

CBI (1981a) *The will to win: Britain must mean business: a discussion document*, London: CBI.

CBI (1981b) 'Stop these spiralling rates', *CBI News*, 30 January, p 5, London: CBI.

CBI (1986a) 'Chancellor's £1bn spending boost welcomed', *CBI News*, 21 November, p 14, London: CBI.

CBI (1986b) 'Learning the hard way', *CBI News*, 7 February, p 4, London: CBI.

CBI (1986c) 'Social Security Bill victory', *CBI News*, 11 July, p 3, London: CBI.

CBI (1988a) 'Companies and the housing market' (part 1 of a two-part feature), *CBI News*, 19 February, pp 8-9, London: CBI.

CBI (1988b) 'Coping with the housing market' (part 2 of a two-part feature), *CBI News*, 4 March, pp 12-13, London: CBI.

CBI (1988c) 'Look to LENS to help local employer needs', *CBI News*, 29 April, London: CBI.

CBI (1988d) *Initiatives beyond charity*, London: CBI.

CBI (1989a) *Training and Enterprise Councils*, London: CBI.

CBI (1989b) 'TECs vital – but only part of answer', *CBI News*, 31 March, p 3, London: CBI.

CBI (1989c) 'Vocational education and training, *CBI News*, November, p 16, London: CBI.

CBI (1994) *A view from the top: Senior executives' attitudes to pension provision*, London: CBI.

CBI (1995) *A skills passport: A vision for our future*, London: CBI.

CBI (1996) *Fulfilling our potential: The business agenda for the South West*, Bristol: CBI.

CBI (2000a) *Business manifesto*, London: CBI.

CBI (2000b) *Europe brief: Europe at work, A CBI statement on social policy in Europe*, London: CBI.

CBI (2001a) *Business and healthcare for the 21st century*, London: CBI.

CBI (2001b) *CBI response to the Howard Davies review of enterprise and the economy in education*, London: CBI.

CBI (2002a) *Submission on budget proposals, 2002*, London: CBI.

CBI (2002b) *Response to Spending Review*, London: CBI.

CBI (2002c) *The CBI response to the government's green paper '14-19: Extending opportunities, raising standards'*, London: Human Resources Directorate, CBI.

CBI (2003) 'CBI opposes government move to scrap retirement age', Press release, 31 October. London: CBI.

CBI and CoC (Chambers of Commerce) (2002) *Learning and Skills Councils: Meeting the needs of business*, London: CBI and CoC.

CEO (Corporate Europe Observatory) (2001) 'High time for UN to break partnership with the ICC', www.xs4all.nl/~ceo/un/icc/html.

Cerny, P. (1997) 'Paradoxes of the competition state: the dynamics of political globalization', *Government and Opposition*, vol 32, no 2, pp 251-74.

Clawson, D., Neustradtl, A. and Bearden, J. (1986) 'The logic of business unity: corporate contributions to the 1980 congressional elections', *American Sociological Review*, vol 51, pp 797-811.

Coates, A., Farnsworth, K. and Zulauf, M. (2000) *Social exclusion and inclusion: Partnerships for neighbourhood regeneration in London*, Occasional Paper, London: South Bank University.

Coates, D. (1984) 'The political power of capital', in D. Coates (ed) *The context of British politics*, London: Huchinson.

Coen, D. (1997) 'The European business lobby', *Business Strategy Review*, vol 8, no 4, pp 17-25.

Coen, D. (1998) 'The evolution of the large firm as a political actor in the European Union', *Journal of European Public Policy*, vol 18, no 1, pp 75-100.

Cohen, N. (2002) 'National parks, state schools and hospitals, laws against pollution: all could be under threat from the World Trade Organisation', *New Statesman*, vol 15, p 735.

Coppel, J. and Durand, M. (1999) *Trends in market openness*, Economic Department Working Papers No. 221, Paris: OECD.

Corporate Citizen (2001) *Editor's comment*, Autumn, London: Corporate Citizen.

Coulson, A. (1997) 'Business partnerships and regional government', *Policy & Politics*, vol 25, no 1, pp 31-9.

Crequer, N. (2000) 'Business "TEC-over" of skills councils', *Times Educational Supplement*, 22 September.

Crouch, C. and Streeck, W. (eds) (1997) *Political economy of modern capitalism: Mapping convergence and diversity*, London: Sage Publications.

Cully, M., Woodland, S., O'Reilly, A. and Dix, G. (1999) *Britain at work: As depicted by the 1998 Workplace Employee Relations Survey*, London: Routledge.

Dahl, R. (1961) *Who governs? Democracy and power in an American city*, New Haven, CT: Yale University Press.

Davies, H. (2002) *A review of enterprise and the economy in education*, London: The Stationery Office.

Davies, J.S. (2002) 'Regeneration partnerships under New Labour: a case of creeping centralisation', in C. Glendinning, M. Powell and K. Rummery (eds) *Partnerships, New Labour and the governance of welfare*, Bristol: The Policy Press, pp 167-82.

Davis, J. and Bishop, C. (1989-99) 'The MAI: multilateralism from above', *Race & Class*, vol 40, no 2/3, pp 159-70.

de Swaan, A. (1988) *In care of the state: Health care, education and welfare in Europe and the USA in the modern era*, Cambridge: Polity Press.

Deacon, B. (1997) *Global social policy*, London: Sage Publications.

Deacon, B. (2000) 'Socially responsible globalization: the challenge for social security: social security in the global village', Paper presented to the International Social Security Association (ISSA) conference, Helsinki, 25-27 September.

Deakin, N. and Edwards, J. (1993) *The enterprise culture and the inner city*, London: Routledge.

Dean, H. and Taylor-Gooby, P. (1990) 'Statutory Sick Pay and the control of sickness absence', *Journal of Social Policy*, vol 19, no 1, pp 47-67.

Dean, M. (2003) 'New Prescription for Hospitals', *The Guardian*, 8 January.

Derber, C. (2002) *People before profit: The new globalization in an age of terror, big money and economic crisis*, New York, NY: St Martin's Press.

DES (Department for Education and Skills) (2001) *Education Action Zones: Annual Report*, London: DES.

Desai, R. (1994) 'Second-hand dealers in ideas: think-tanks and Thatcherite hegemony', *New Left Review*, vol 203, January/February, pp 27-64.

Devereux, M.P., Griffith, R. and Klemn, A. (2001) 'Have taxes on mobile capital declined?', *Economic Policy*, vol 35.

Devereux, M.P., Lockwood, B. and Redoano, M. (2002) *Do countries compete over corporate tax rates?*, Centre for the Study of Globalisation and Regionalisation Working Paper No. 97/02, Warwick: University of Warwick.

Dex, S. and Smith, C. (2002) *The nature and pattern of family-friendly employment policies in Britain*, Bristol/York: The Policy Press/Joseph Rowntree Foundation.

DfEE (2000) *City academies: Schools to make a difference: A prospectus for sponsors and other parties*, London: DfEE.

DfES (1999) *Survey of school–business links in England 1997/8*, London: The Stationery Office.

DfES (2000) *14-19: Extending opportunities, raising standards*, London: The Stationery Office.

Dickson, M., Gewirtz, S., Halpin, D., Power, S. and Whitty, G. (2002) 'Education Action Zones', in C. Glendinning, M. Powell, and K. Rummery (eds) *Partnerships, New Labour and the governance of welfare*, Bristol: The Policy Press, pp 183-98.

DiGaetano, A. and Klemanski, J.S. (1993) 'Urban regimes in comparative perspective: the politics of urban development in Britain', *Urban Affairs Quarterly*, vol 29, pp 54-84.

DoE (Department of Education) (1994) *School governors: A guide to the law*, London: DoE.

Domhoff, G.W. (1967) *Who rules America?*, New Jersey, NJ: Prentice Hall.

Domhoff, G.W. (1978) *Who really rules: New Haven and community power re-examined*, New Brunswick, NJ: Transaction Books.

Domhoff, G.W. (1987) 'Corporate-liberal theory and the Social Security Act: a chapter in the sociology of knowledge', *Politics and Society*, vol 15, no 3, pp 297-332.

Doogan, K. (1996) 'Labour mobility and the changing housing market', *Urban Studies*, vol 33, no 2, pp 199-222.

DTI (Department of Trade and Industry) (2001a) *Higher education funding councils and the Department for Employment and Learning in Northern Ireland*, Office of Science and Technology, London: DTI.

DTI (2001b) *Business and society: Developing corporate responsibility in the UK*, London: DTI.

EC (European Commission) (1997) *Towards tax co-ordination in the European Union: A package to tackle harmful tax competition*, Communication from the European Commission COM(97) 495 Final, Luxembourg: EC.

EC (2001a) *Promoting a European framework for corporate social responsibility*, Luxembourg: Office for Official Publications of the European Communities.

EC (2001b) *European social statistics: Labour costs 1988-99*, Luxembourg: EC.

EC (2003a) *Labour costs survey 2000: Member states*, Brussels: European Communities.

EC (2003b) *Social protection expenditure and receipts*, Luxembourg: EC.

European Council (2000) *Presidency conclusions, Lisbon European Council 23-24 March*, DOC/00/8, Lisbon.

EEF (Engineering Employers Federation) (2003) *Skills strategy is important step on road to upping vocational game but more funding is needed for apprenticeships*, London: EEF.

Ellis-Jones, M. and Hardstaff, P. (2002) *Serving (up) the nation: A guide to the UK's commitments under the WTO General Agreement on Trade in Services*, London: World Development Movement.

ERT (European Round Table) (1994) *Education for Europeans: Towards the learning society*, Brussels: ERT of Industrialists.

ERT (1998) *Job creation and competitiveness through innovation*, Brussels: ERT of Industrialists.

ERT (2000) *European pensions: An appeal for reform*, Brussels: ERT of Industrialists.

ERT (2001a) *Actions for competitiveness through the knowledge economy in Europe*, Background working paper of the ERT Knowledge Economy Task Force in preparation for the ERT message to the Stockholm European Council, March, Brussels: ERT of Industrialists.

ERT (2001b) *ERT position on corporate social responsibility and response to Commission Green Paper 'Promoting a European framework for corporate social responsibility'*, Brussels: ERT of Industrialists.

ERT (2002) 'The Maastricht inheritance', Speech delivered by Morris Tabaksblat (Chairman Reed Elsevier), 5 February, at the European Connection Conference – Decennial Celebration Maastricht Treaty, Brussels: ERT.

Esping-Andersen, G. (1990) *The three worlds of welfare capitalism*, Cambridge: Polity Press.

Esping-Andersen, G., Friedland, R. and Wright, E.O. (1976) 'Modes of class struggle and the capitalist state', *Kapitalistate: working papers on the capitalist state*, vol 4-5, pp 186-220.

Eurostat (1991) *Rapid reports: population and social conditions*.

Eurostat (1995) *Rapid reports: population and social conditions*.

Eurostat (1996a) *Social protection expenditure and receipts 1980-1994*.

Eurostat (1996b) *Labour costs: principal results, 1992*.

Evans, R. (2002) 'Twilight for the Zones: why has the government quietly abandoned its Education Action Zones after five years?', *The Observer*, 3 December.

Farnsworth, K. (1998) 'Minding the business interest: the CBI and social policy, 1980-1996', *Policy Studies*, vol 19, no 1, pp 19-38.

Farnsworth, K. (2003) 'Anti globalisation, anti capitalism and the democratic state', in G. Taylor and M. Todd (eds) *Democracy and protest*, London: Merlin Press.

Farnsworth, K. and Gough, I. (2000) 'The enhanced structural power of capital: a review and assessment', in I. Gough (ed) *Global capital, human needs and social policies*, London: Macmillan, pp 77-104.

Fawcett, H. and Papadopoulos, T. (1997) 'Social exclusion, social citizenship and decommodification: an evaluation of the adequacy of support for the unemployed in the European Union', *West European Politics*, vol 20, no 3, pp 1-30.

Fisher, J. (1994) 'Why do companies make donations to political parties', *Political Studies*, xlii, pp 690-9.

Fitzgerald, R. (1988) *British labour management and industrial welfare, 1846-1939*, London: Croom Helm.

Flora, P. and Alber, J. (1981) 'Modernization, democratization and the development of welfare states in Western Europe', in P. Flora and A.J. Heidenheimer (eds) *The development of welfare states in Europe and America*, London: Transaction Books, pp 37-80.

Forrest, R., Murie, A., Doogan, K. and Burton, P. (1991) *Employers and housing costs*, Bristol: SAUS, University of Bristol.

Forth, J., Lissenburgh, S., Callender, C. and Millward, N. (1996) *Family friendly working arrangements in Britain*, London: HMSO.

Fowler, N. (1991) *Ministers decide*, London: Chapman.

Fraser, D. (1984) *The evolution of the British welfare state* (2nd edn), London: Macmillan.

Gamble, A. (1990) *Britain in decline: Economic policy, political strategy and the British state*, London: Macmillan.

Garret, J. (1993) 'The merchants of power', Unpublished paper obtained from Bristol Common Purpose.

Garrett, G. (1998) *Partisan politics in the global economy*, Cambridge: Cambridge University Press.

General Household Survey (1995) London: HMSO.

Genschel, P. (2002) 'Globalization, tax competition and the state, *Politics and Society*, vol 30, no 2, pp 245-75.

George, V. (1996) 'Elite opinion of retirement pensions', *International Social Security Review*, vol 49, no 4, pp 53-69.

George, V. (1998) 'Political ideology, globalisation and welfare states in Europe', *Journal of Social Policy*, vol 27, no 1, pp 17-36.

George, V. and Taylor-Gooby, P. (1996) *European welfare policy: Squaring the welfare circle*, London: Macmillan.

George, V. and Wilding, P. (2002) *Globalization and human welfare*, London: Palgrave.

George, V., Taylor-Gooby, P. and Bonoli, M.G. (1995) 'Squaring the welfare circle in Europe, European welfare futures: the views of key influentials on the short-term development of welfare policy in six European countries', Unpublished working paper, Canterbury: University of Kent.

Giddens, A. (1979) *Central problems in social theory: Action structure and contradiction in social analysis*, London: Macmillan.

Giddens, A. (1998) *The third way: The renewal of social democracy*, Cambridge: Polity Press.

Gill, S.R. and Law, D. (1989) 'Global hegemony and the structural power of capital', *International Studies Quarterly*, vol 33, pp 475-99.

Gordon, C. (1991) 'New deal, old deck: business and the origins of social security, 1920-1935', *Politics and Society*, vol 19, no 2, pp 165-207.

Gore, C. and Kurray, K. (1990) 'A management model for industrial involvement in the educational process', *Educational Management and Administration*, vol 18, no 4, pp 49-53.

Gough, I. (1979) *The political economy of the welfare state*, London: Macmillan.

Government Actuary (1994) *Occupational pension schemes, 1991*, London: HMSO.

Graebner, W. (1980) *A history of retirement: The meaning and function of an American institution*, New York, NY: Yale University Press.

Graham, A. (1995) 'The accountability of Training and Enterprise Councils', *Parliamentary Affairs*, vol 48, no 2, pp 271-83.

Grant, W. (1993) *Business and politics in Britain*, London: Macmillan.

Grant, W. and Marsh, D. (1977) *The CBI*, London: Hodder & Stoughton.

Green, F., Hadjimatheou, G. and Smail, R. (1984) *Unequal fringes: Fringe benefits in the United Kingdom*, London: Bedford Square Press.

Green, F., Hadjimatheou, G. and Smail, R. (1985) 'Fringe benefits distribution in Britain', *British Journal of Industrial Relations*, vol 23, no 2, pp 261-80.

Green Cowles, M. (1995) 'Setting the agenda for a new Europe: the ERT and EC 1992', *Journal of Common Market Studies*, vol 33, no 4, pp 501-26.

Griffin, L.J., Devine, J.A. and Wallace, M. (1983) 'On the economic and political determinants of welfare spending in the post-World War II era', *Politics and Society*, vol 12, no 3, pp 331-72.

Grimshaw, D., Vincent, S. and Willmott, H. (2002) 'Going privately: partnership and outsourcing in UK public services', *Public Administration*, vol 80, no 3, pp 475-502.

Guha, K. (2003) 'Ministers speed up move to specialist education', *Financial Times*, 4 January, p 3.

GUS (2002) *Corporate social responsibility report*, London: GUS, www.investis.com/gus/storage/pdf/CSR_02.pdf.

Hacker, J.S. and Pierson, P. (2002) 'Business power and social policy: employers and the formation of the American welfare state', *Politics and Society*, vol 30, no 2, pp 277-325.

Hall, S. (2003) 'Retirement move raises work until 70 fear', *The Guardian*, 3 July.

Hammer, R. and Owens, J. (2001) *Promoting tax competition*, Paris: BIAC.

Harris, J. (1997) *William Beveridge: A biography*, Oxford: Clarendon Press.

Hart, R. (1984) *The economics of non-wage labour costs*, London: George Allen and Unwin.

Hay, C. (1999) *The political economy of New Labour*, Manchester: Manchester University Press.

Hay, C. and Watson, M. (1999) 'Globalisation: "sceptical" notes on the 1999 Reith Lectures', *Political Quarterly*, vol 70, pp 418-25, October-December.

Hay, J.R. (1978a) *The development of the British welfare state 1880-1975*, London: Edward Arnold.

Hay, J.R. (1978b) 'Employers' attitudes to social policy and the concept of social control 1890-1929', in P. Thane (ed) *The origins of British social policy*, New Jersey, NJ: Rowman and Littlefield.

Hay, J.R. (1977) 'Employers and social policy in Britain: the evolution of welfare legislation, 1905-14', *Social History*, vol 2, pp 435-55.

Held, D., McGrew, A., Goldblatt, D. and Perraton, J. (1999) *Global transformations: Politics, economics and culture*, Cambridge: Polity Press.

Hirschman, A.O. (1970) *Exit, voice and loyalty: Responses to decline in firms, organisations and states*, Cambridge, MA: Harvard University Press.

Hirst, P. and Thompson, G. (1996) *Globalisation in question: The international economy and the possibilities of governance*, Cambridge: Polity Press.

HMSO (1982) *Corporation tax*, Green Paper, Cmnd 8456, London: HMSO.

Hoare, S. (2002) The full whack, *The Guardian*, 3 December.

Holton, R.J. (1998) *Globalization and the nation-state*, London: Macmillan.

Holzmann, R. (2000) 'The World Bank approach to pensions reform', *International Social Security Review*, vol 53, no 1, pp 11-34.

Howells, J., Nedeva, M. and Georghiou, L. (1998) *Industry–academic links in the UK*, Ref 98/70 (December), London: Higher Education Funding Council for England.

Huber, E., Ragin, C. and Stephens, J.D. (1993) 'Social democracy, Christian democracy, constitutional structure, and the welfare state', *American Journal of Sociology*, vol 99, no 3, pp 711-49.

Hutton, W. (1998) 'Kinder capitalists in Armani specs', *The Observer*, 1 February.

ICC (International Chambers of Commerce) (1998) *Business and the global economy*, ICC statement on behalf of world business to heads of state and government attending the Birmingham Summit, New York, NY: ICC, www.iccwbo.org/home/trade_investment/bge_english.asp.

ICC (2000) 'Harmful tax competition', Letter dated 10 May 2000 from the Chair of the ICC Commission on Taxation to the Chair of the UN Ad Hoc Group of Experts on International Cooperation in Tax Matters, Commission on Taxation, 10 May, New York, NY: ICC.

ICC (2002) 'Business in society: making a positive and responsible contribution', available at www.iccwbo.org/home/news_archives/2002/businsocdoc.asp.

IDS (Income Data Services) (1993) *IDS Quarterly 66*, April.

IiE (Industry in Education) (1995a) *All their tomorrows: The business of governing*, London: IiE.

IiE (1995b) *Towards employability: Assessing the gap between young people's qualities and employers' recruitment needs*, London: IiE.

Inland Revenue (2001) *Expenses and benefits: A tax guide (480)*, London: The Stationery Office.

IoD (Institute of Directors) (2002) *Education and training: A business blueprint for reform*, London: IoD.

James, A. (2002) 'Private firms could run NHS hospitals', *The Guardian*, 19 December.

Jenkins, J.C. and Brents, G.B. (1989) 'Social protest, hegemonic competition, and social reform: a political struggle interpretation of the origins of the American welfare state', *American Sociological Review*, vol 54, December, pp 891-909.

Jones, H. (1983) 'Employers' welfare schemes and industrial relations in inter-war Britain', *Business History*, vol 25, no 1, pp 61-75.

Jones, R. (2002) 'Plan to beat pension crisis by scrapping retirement at 65', *The Guardian*, 16 December.

Jordan, G. (1991) *The commercial lobbyists: Politics for profit in Britain*, Aberdeen: Aberdeen University Press.

Kabeer, N. (2002) *Globalisation, labour standards and women's rights: Dilemmas of collective action in an interdependent world*, Sussex: IDS and Globalisation and Poverty Programme, www.gapresearch.org.

King, D.S. (1993) 'The Conservatives and training policy, 1979-1992: from a tripartite to a neoliberal regime', *Political Studies*, vol 2, June, pp 214-35.

Korpi, W. (1983) *The democratic class struggle*, London: Routledge and Kegan Paul.

Korten, D. (1997) 'The United Nations and the corporate agenda', www.globalpolicy.org/reform/korten.htm, accessed April 2003.

Korten, D.C. (1995) *When corporations rule the world*, London: Earthscan.

KPMG (2003) 'KPMG's 2003 global corporate tax rate survey: Emerging trends pinpointed', London: KPMG, www.kpmg.co.uk/kpmg/uk/press/

Labour Market Trends (1996) London: The Stationery Office.

Le Grand, J. and Vizard, P. (1991) 'The National Health Service: crisis, change or continuity', in H. Glennerster and J. Hills (eds) *The state of welfare: The economics of social spending*, Oxford: Oxford University Press.

Leys, C. (1989) *Capital and labour*, London: Verso.

Lindblom, C.E. (1977) *Politics and markets*, New York, NY: Basic Books.

Lukes, S. (1977) *Essays in social theory*, London: Macmillan Press.

Madely, J. (1999) *Big business, poor peoples: The impact of transnational corporations on the world's poor*, London: Zed Books.

Mann, K. and Anstee, J. (1989) *Growing fringes: Hypothesis on the development of occupational welfare*, Leeds: Armley Publications.

Mann, M. (1993) *The sources of social power, 3 vols, Vol II: The rise of classes and nation-states, 1760-1914*, Cambridge: Cambridge University Press.

Mares, I. (2001) 'Firms and the welfare state', in P.A. Hall and D. Soskice (eds) *Varieties of capitalism: The institutional foundations of comparative advantage*, Oxford: Oxford University Press, pp 184-212.

Margrave, R. (1994) 'A study in the politics of business/education partnerships: the British city technology college programme', *The Journal of Education Finance*, vol 19, no 4, pp 65-9.

Marsh, D. and Locksley, G. (1983a) 'Capital in Britain: its structural power and influence over policy', *West European Politics*, no 6, pp 3-13.

Marsh, D. and Locksley, G. (1983b) 'Capital: the neglected face of power?', in D. Marsh (ed) *Pressure politics: Interest groups in Britain*, London: Junction Books.

Marshall, D.D. (1996) 'Understanding late-twentieth-century capitalism: reassessing the globalization theme', *Government and Opposition*, vol 31, pp 193-215.

Marshall, T.H. (1950) *Citizenship and social class*, Cambridge: Cambridge University Press.

Martin, C.J. (1989) 'Business influence and state power: the case of US corporate tax policy, *Politics and Society*, vol 17, no 2, pp 189-223.

Martin, C.J. (2000) *Stuck in neutral: Business and the politics of human capital investment policy*, Princeton, NJ: Princeton University Press.

Martin, H.P. and Schumann, H. (1997) *The global trap: Globalization and the assault on democracy and prosperity*, London: Zed Books.

May, M. and Brunsdon, E. (1994) 'Workplace care in the mixed economy of welfare', in R. Page and J. Baldock (eds) *Social Policy Review 6*, Canterbury: Social Policy Association, pp 146-69.

May, T. (1984) 'The businessman's burden: rates and the CBI, *Politics*, vol 4, no 1.

Melling, J. (1991) 'Industrial capitalism and the welfare of the state: the role of employers in the comparative development of welfare states: a review of recent research', *Sociology*, vol 25, no 2, pp 219-39.

Midwinter, A. and Monaghan, C. (1993) *From rates to the Poll Tax*, Edinburgh: Edinburgh University Press.

Miliband, R. (1969) *The state in capitalist society*, London: Quartet Books.

Mintz, B. and Schwartz, M. (1990) 'Capital flows and the process of financial hegemony', in S. Zukin and P. DiMaggio (eds) *Structures of capital: The social organisations of the economy*, Cambridge: Cambridge University Press, pp 203-26.

Mishra, R. (1998) 'Beyond the nation state: social policy in an age of globalization', *Social Policy and Administration*, vol 32, no 5, pp 481-500.

Mishra, R. (1999) *Globalization and the welfare state*, Cheltenham: Edward Elgar.

Monbiot, G. (1999) 'Beating the agro-industrial complex', *The Guardian*, 22 July.

Monbiot, G. (2000a) *The captive state: The corporate takeover of Britain*, London: Macmillan.

Monbiot, G. (2000b) 'The United Nations is Trying to Regain its Credibility by Fawning to Big Business', *The Guardian*, 31 August.

Moore, C. and Richardson, J.J. (1987) 'Business and society in Britain: the politics and practice of corporate responsibility', Strathclyde Papers on Government and Politics, Glasgow: University of Strathclyde.

Morgan, O. (2003) 'Work On, Says Pensions Tzar', *The Observer*, 6 April.

Murlis, H. (1978) *Employee benefits: A survey of practice in 400 companies*, London: British Institute of Management.

Navarro, V. (1978) *Class struggle, the state and medicine: An historical analysis of the medical sector in Great Britain*, Oxford: Martin Robertson.

Navarro, V. (1989) 'Why some countries have national health insurance, others have national health services and the United States has neither', *International Journal of Health Services*, vol 19, no 3, pp 383-404.

Neighbour, J. (2002) 'Transfer pricing: keeping it at arms length', *OECD Observer*, 21 April.

Niskanen, W.A. (1971) *Bureaucracy and representative government*, Aldine, NY: Atherton.

North, D.R. (1990) *Institutions, institutional change, and economic performance*, Cambridge: Cambridge University Press.

O'Connor, J. (1973) *The fiscal crisis of the state*, New York, NY: St Martins Press.

OECD (Organisation for Economic Co-operation and Development) (1994) *Jobs study: Facts, analysis, strategies*, Paris: OECD.

OECD (1997a) *Beyond 2000: The new social policy agenda*, Note by the Secretary-General, Paris: OECD.

OECD (1997b) *Harmful tax competition: An emerging global issue*, Paris: OECD.

OECD (1999) *A caring world: A new social policy agenda*, Paris: OECD.

OECD (2000) *Towards global tax co-operation*, Report to the 2000 Ministerial Council Meeting and recommendations by the Committee on Fiscal Affairs Progress in identifying and eliminating harmful tax practices, Paris: OECD.

OECD (2001) *Revenue statistics 1965-2000*, Paris: OECD.

Offe, C. (ed) (1984) *Contradictions of the welfare state*, London: Hutchinson.

Offe, C. and Ronge,V. (1982) 'Theses on the theory of the state', in A. Giddens and D. Held (eds) *Classes, power and conflict*, Basingstoke: Macmillan, pp 249-56.

Offe, C. and Wiesenthal, H. (1980) 'Two logics of collective action: theoretical notes on social class and organisational form', in M. Zeitlin (ed) *Political power and social theory*, Greenwich, CT: JAI Press.

Ollila, E. (2003) 'Health-related public–private partnerships and the United Nations', in B.O.E.K.K. and S.P. Deacon (eds) *Global social governance: Themes and prospects*, Helsinki: STAKES, The National Research and Development Centre for Welfare and Health, Globalisation and Social Policy Programme.

Osler, D. (2002) *Labour Party PLC*, Edinburgh: Mainstream Publishing Limited.

Palast, G. (2001a) 'GATS got his tongue', *The Observer*, 15 April.

Palast, G. (2001) 'The WTO's hidden agenda', *The Observer*, 9 November.

Papadakis, E. and Taylor-Gooby, P. (1987) *The private provision of public welfare: State, market and community*, Sussex: Wheatsheaf.

Peck, J. (1991a) 'Letting the market decide (with public money): Training and Enterprise Councils and the future of labour market programmes', *Critical Social Policy*, 31, pp 4-17.

Peck, J. (1991b) 'The politics of training in Britain: contradictions in the TEC initiative', *Capital and Class*, vol 44, Summer, pp 23-34.

Peck, J. and Tickell, A. (1995a) 'Business goes local: dissecting the 'business agenda' in Manchester', *International Journal of Urban and Regional Research*, vol 19, no 1, pp 55-78.

Peck, J. and Tickell, A. (1995b) *The return of Manchester men: Men's words and men's deeds in the remaking of the local state*, Manchester: University of Manchester.

Peden, G.C. (1985) *British economic and social policy: Lloyd George to Marge*, London: Philip Allan.

Pfaller, A., Gough, I. and Therborn, G. (1991) *Can the welfare state compete?: A comparative study of five advanced capitalist countries*, London: Macmillan.

Pierson, C. (1996) *The modern state*, London: Routledge.

Pierson, P. (1994) *Dismantling the welfare state*, Cambridge: Cambridge University Press.

Pierson, P. (1995) *The scope and nature of business power: Employers and the American welfare state, 1900-1935*.

Pierson, P. (1996) 'The new politics of the welfare state', *World Politics*, vol 48, no 2, pp 143-79.

Pike, G. and Hillage, J. (1995) *Education and business links in Avon – Final report*, Sussex: Institute for Employment Studies, University of Sussex.

Piven, F.F. and Cloward, R.A. (1971) *Regulating the poor: The functions of public welfare*, New York, NY: Pantheon Books.

Piven, F.F. and Cloward, R.A. (1979) *Poor people's movements*, New York, NY: Pantheon.

Plummer, J. (1994) *The governance gap: Quangos and accountability*, London: Joseph Rowntree Foundation and LGC Communications.

Pollock, A. (2003) 'Foundation Hospitals will Kill the NHS', *The Guardian*, 7 May.

Pollock, A., Shaoul, J., Rowland, D. and Player, S. (2001) *Public services and the private sector: A response to the IPPR*, London: Catalyst.

Pontusson, J. (1995) 'From comparative public policy to political economy', *Comparative Political Studies*, vol 28, no 1, pp 117-47.

Poulantzas, N. (1973) 'The problem of the capitalist state', in J. Urry and J. Wakeford (eds) *Power in Britain*, London: Heinemann Educational Books, pp 291-305.

Powell, M. and Glendinning, C. (2002) 'Introduction', in C. Glendinning, M. Powell and K. Rummery (eds) *Partnerships, New Labour and the governance of welfare*, Bristol: The Policy Press, pp 1-14.

Price, D., Pollock, A.M. and Shaoul, J. (1999) 'How the World Trade Organisation is shaping domestic policies in health care', *The Lancet*, vol 354, pp 1889-92.

Przeworski, A. and Wallerstein, M. (1988) 'Structural dependence of the state on capital', *American Political Science Review*, vol 82, no 1, pp 11-29.

Quadagno, J.S. (1984) 'Welfare capitalism and the Social Security Act of 1935', *American Sociological Review*, vol 49, pp 632-47.

Quinn, D.P. and Inclan, C. (1997) 'The origins of financial openness: a study of current and capital account liberalisation', *American Journal of Political Science*, vol 41, no 3, pp 771-813.

Red-Star Research (2003) 'Donors and sponsors', www.red-star-research.org.uk/subframe3.html.

Rein, M. (1996) 'Is America exceptional? The role of occupational welfare in the United States and the European Community', in M. Shalev (ed) *The privatisation of social policy*, London: Macmillan Press, pp 27-43.

Retallack, S. (1997) 'The WTO's record so far', *The Ecologist*, vol 27, no 4, p 136.

Rhodes, M. (2000) 'Restructuring the British welfare state: between domestic constraints and global imperatives', in F.W. Scharpf and V.A. Schmidt (eds) *Welfare and work in the open economy*, Oxford: Oxford University Press.

Richardson, K. (2000) *Big business and the European agenda*, SEI Working Paper no. 35, Brighton: Sussex European Institute.

Richter, J. (2001) *Holding corporations accountable: Corporate conduct, international codes and citizen action*, London: Zed Books.

Rodgers, T. (1991) 'Employers' organisations, unemployment and social politics in Britain during the inter-war period', in S.W. Tolliday (ed) *Government and business*, Cheltenham: Edward Elgar.

Ruane, S. (2002) 'Public–private partnerships: the case of PFI', in C. Glendinning, M. Powell and K. Rummery (eds) *Partnerships, New Labour and the governance of welfare*, Bristol: The Policy Press, pp 199-211.

Russell, A. (1991) *The growth of occupational welfare in Britain*, Aldershot: Avebury.

Rylance, P. (1995) 'The President's Group of the Bristol Chamber of Commerce and Initiative', unpublished.

Scott, J. (1985) 'The British upper class', in D. Coates, G. Johnston and R. Bush (eds) *A socialist anatomy of Britain*, Cambridge: Polity Press.

Scott, J. (1991a) *Social network analysis: A handbook*, London: Sage Publications.

Scott, J. (1991b) *Who rules Britain*, Oxford: Polity Press.

Scott, J. and Griff, C. (1984) *Directors of industry*, Cambridge: Polity Press.

Shalev, M. (1983) 'Class politics and western welfare state', in S.E. Spiro and E. Yuchtman-Yaar (eds) *Evaluating the welfare state: Social and political perspectives*, London: Academic Press, pp 27-50.

Shifrin, T. (2003) 'Out on a limb', *The Guardian*, 4 June.

Simms, A. (2003) *Degrees of capture: Universities, the oil industry and climate change*, London: New Economics Foundation.

Singh, K. (2000) *The globalisation of finance: A citizen's guide*, London: Zed Books.

Sklair, L. (2001) *The transnational capitalist class*, Oxford: Blackwell Publishers.

Skocpol, T. (1979) *States and social revolutions*, Cambridge: Cambridge University Press.

Skocpol, T. (1985) 'Bringing the state back in: current research', in P.B. Evans, D. Reuschemeyer and T. Skocpol (eds) *Bringing the state back in*, Cambridge: Cambridge University Press.

Sommer, A. (1996) *BIAC discussion paper: Productivity to the rescue of social protection*, Paris: BIAC.

Stewart, J. (1995) 'Appointed boards and local government', *Parliamentary Affairs*, vol 48, no 2, pp 226-41.

Stiglitz, J. (2002) *Globalization and its discontents*, London: Norton House.

Strange, S. (1988) *States and markets*, 2nd edition, London: Pinter.

Strange, S. (1996) *The retreat of the state: The diffusion of power in the world economy*, Cambridge: Cambridge University Press.

Stryker, R. (1998) 'Globalization and the welfare state', *International Journal of Sociology and Social Policy*, vol 18, nos 2/3/4, pp 1-49.

Swank, D. (1992) 'Politics and the structural dependence of the state in democratic capitalist nations', *American Political Science Review*, vol 86, no 1, pp 38-54.

Swank, D. (2002) *Global capital, political institutions and policy change in developed welfare states*, Cambridge: Cambridge University Press.

Swank, D. and Steinmo, S. (2002) 'The new political economy of taxation in advanced capitalist democracies', *American Journal of Political Science*, vol 46, no 3, pp 642-55.

Swenson, P. (2002) *Capitalists against markets: The making of labor markets and the welfare states in the United States and Sweden*, Oxford: Oxford University Press.

Tachibanaki, T. (1989) *Non-wage labour costs: Their rationales and the economic effects*, London: London School of Economics and Political Science.

Tate, N. (1998) 'Business, say what you want', *Times Educational Supplement*, 26 June.

Taylor-Gooby, P. (1996) 'The sustainability of European welfare states in the face of international competition: the view from business', unpublished.

Taylor-Gooby, P. (1997) 'European welfare futures: the views of key influentials in six European countries on likely developments in social policy', *Social Policy and Administration*, vol 31, no 1, pp 1-19.

Taylor-Gooby, P. and Lakeman, S. (1998) 'Back to the future: statutory sick pay, citizenship and social class', *Journal of Social Policy*, no 17, pp 23-39.

Taylor-Gooby, P. and Lawson, R. (1993) *Markets and managers: New issues in the delivery of welfare*, Milton Keynes: Open University Press.

TES (*The Times Educational Supplement*) (1998) 'Editorial: fears as business moves into school', 4 December.

TES (2002) 'You Can all be Special Blair Tells Schools', 29 November.

TES (2003) 'Firm Foots Part of Bill for Failure of Southwark Privatisation', 11 July.

Tesner, S. (2000) *The United Nations and business: A partnership recovered*, London: Macmillan.

Testault, J.-L. (2003) 'Eastern Europe in a race to cut the corporate tax burden', *EU Business*, 27 January.

Thelen, K. and Steinmo, S. (1992) 'Historical institutionalism in comparative politics', in S. Steinmo, K. Thelen and F. Longstreth (eds) *Structuring politics: Historical institutionalism in comparative analysis*, Cambridge: Cambridge University Press.

Therborn, G. (1984) 'Classes and state: welfare state developments, 1881-1981', *Studies in Political Economy*, vol 13, Spring, pp 7-42.

Therborn, G. (1986) 'Karl Marx returning: the welfare state and neo-Marxist, corporatist and statist theories', *International Political Science Review*, vol 7, no 2, pp 131-64.

Thody, A. (1989) 'Who are the governors?', *Educational Management and Administration*, vol 17, pp 139-46.

Timmins, N. (1996) *The five giants: A biography of the welfare state*, London: Fontanna Press.

Titmuss, R.M. (1958) *Essays on 'the welfare state'*, London: Unwin Books.

Turner, A. (2001) *Just capital: The liberal economy*, London: Macmillan.

UEAPME (European Association of Craft, Small and Medium Sized Enterprises) (2000) *Contribution to the Lisbon Summit 'Employment, Economic Reforms and Social Cohesion', 23-24 March*, Brussels: UEAPME.

UEAPME (2002a) *UEAPME supports European Commission's tax strategy*, Brussels: UEAPME.

UEAPME (2002b) *Contribution to the European debate on social protection and pensions*, Brussels: UNICE.

UNCTAD (2002) *World investment report*, New York, NY: UN Conference on Trade and Development.

UNICE (Union of Industrial and Employers' Confederation of Europe) (1999a) *Releasing Europe's employment potential: Companies' views on European social policy beyond 2000*, Brussels: UNICE.

UNICE (1999b) *Proposal for guidelines for member states employment policies 2000 and draft recommendations to member states: UNICE position paper, 5 November*, Brussels: UNICE.

UNICE (2000a) *Commission communication on the social policy agenda: UNICE comments*, Brussels: Union of Industrial and Employers Confederations of Europe.

UNICE (2000b) *Contribution to the definition of a new agenda for social policy*, S/5/2000/PPSAP.doc, 5 June, Brussels: Union of Industrial and Employers Confederations of Europe

UNICE (2000c) *For education and training policies which foster competitiveness and employment: UNICE's seven priorities*, Brussels: UNICE.

UNICE (2001a) *Strategy paper on the sustainability of pensions*, Brussels: UNICE.

UNICE (2001b) *Executive summary of position of UNICE with regard to EU proposals on CSR, S/42/PP-CSR-Final-EN*, Brussels: UNICE.

UNICE (2002) *UNICE position paper on the future EU cooperation in the field of education and training: Executive summary*, Brussels: UNICE.

UNISON (2001) *Private sector involvement increases*, UNISON Report ED/29/01, UNISON.

Useem, M. (1990) 'Business and politics in the United States and the United Kingdom', in S. Zukin and P. DiMaggio (eds) *Structures of capital: The social organisations of the economy*, Cambridge: Cambridge University Press, pp 263-92.

Utting, P. (2000) 'Partnerships for development or privatization of the multilateral system?', Paper presented at a seminar organised by the North–South Coalition in Oslo, Norway, 8 December, www.corpwatch.org/campaigns/PCD.jsp?articleid=616.

Vaisanen, I. (1992) 'Conflict and consensus in social policy development: a comparative study of social insurance in 18 OECD countries 1930-1985', *European Journal of Political Research*, vol 22, pp 307-27.

Valler, D., Wood, A. and North, P. (2000) 'Local governance and local business interests: a critical review', *Progress in Human Geography*, vol 24, no 3, pp 409-28.

Vogel, D. (1989) *Fluctuating fortunes: The political power of business in America*, New York, NY: Basic Books.

Vogel, D. (1996) *Kindred strangers: The uneasy relationship between politics and business in America*, Princeton, NJ: Princeton University Press.

Wade, R.H. (2002) 'US hegemony and the World Bank: the fight over people and ideas', *Review of International Political Economy*, vol 9, no 2, pp 215-43.

Ward, H. (1987) 'Structural power – a contradiction in terms?', *Political Studies*, vol 35, pp 593-610.

Whitfield, D. (2001a) *Public services or corporate welfare: Rethinking the nation state in the global economy*, London: Pluto Press.

Whitfield, D. (2001b) 'The State with a Hole in It?', *Red Pepper*, May.

Wilding, P. (1997) 'Globalization, regionalism and social policy', *Social Policy and Administration*, vol 31, no 4, pp 410-28.

Wilensky, W. (1975) *The welfare state and equality: Structural and ideological roots of public expenditure*, Berkeley, CA: University of California Press.

Winters, J.A. (1996) *Power in motion: Capital mobility and the Indonesian state*, Ithaca, New York, NY: Cornell University Press.

Woods, N. and Narlikar, A. (2001) 'Governance and the limits of accountability: the WTO, the IMF and the World Bank', *International Social Science Journal*, vol 170, pp 569-83, November.

World Economic Forum (2002) *Global competitiveness report, 2001-02*, Geneva: World Economic Forum.

WTO (World Trade Organisation) (2003) 'The General Agreement on Trade in Services (GATS): Objectives, coverage and disciplines', available at www.wto.org/english/tratop_e/serv_e/gatsqa_e.htm, accessed 01/01/03.

Yeates, N. (1999) 'Social politics and policy in an era of globalisation: critical reflections', *Social Policy and Administration*, vol 33, no 4, pp 372-93.

Yeates, N. (2001) *Globalisation and social policy*, London: Sage Publications.

Index

Also available from The Policy Press

The ethics of welfare
Human rights, dependency and responsibility
Edited by Hartley Dean
Paperback £25.00 ($37.50)
ISBN 1 86134 562 3
Hardback £50.00 ($75.00)
ISBN 1 86134 558 5
234 x 156mm 224 pages tbc March 2004

Promoting welfare?
Government information policy and social citizenship
Penny Leonard
Paperback £23.99 ($39.95)
ISBN 1 86134 487 2
Hardback £50.00 ($75.00)
ISBN 1 86134 488 0
234 x 156mm 176 pages October 2003

Comparing social policies
Exploring new perspectives in Britain and Japan
Edited by Misa Izuhara
Paperback £18.99 ($29.50)
ISBN 1 86134 366 3
234 x 156mm 272 pages February 2003

The welfare we want?
The British challenge for American reform
Edited by Robert Walker and Michael Wiseman
Paperback £18.99 ($29.95)
ISBN 1 86134 407 4
Hardback £50.00 ($59.95)
ISBN 1 86134 408 2
234 x 156mm 208 pages May 2003

Europe's new state of welfare
Unemployment, employment policies and citizenship
Edited by Jørgen Goul Andersen, Jochen Clasen, Wim van Oorschot and Knut Halvorsen
Paperback £23.99 ($35.00)
ISBN 1 86134 437 6
234 x 156mm 308 pages
November 2002

To order further copies of these publications or any other Policy Press titles please contact:

In the UK and Europe:
Marston Book Services, PO Box 269, Abingdon,
Oxon, OX14 4YN, UK
Tel: +44 (0)1235 465500, Fax: +44 (0)1235 465556,
Email: direct.orders@marston.co.uk
In the USA and Canada:
ISBS, 920 NE 58th Street, Suite 300, Portland,
OR 97213-3786, USA
Tel: +1 800 944 6190 (toll free), Fax: +1 503 280 8832,
Email: info@isbs.com
In Australia and New Zealand:
DA Information Services, 648 Whitehorse Road,
Mitcham, Victoria 3132, Australia
Tel: +61 (3) 9210 7777, Fax: +61 (3) 9210 7788,
E-mail: service@dadirect.com.au

Further information about all of our titles can be found on our website:

www.policypress.org.uk